VICTOR HERBERT

American Music-Master

Books by

CLAIRE LEE PURDY

VICTOR HERBERT
American Music-Master

STORMY VICTORY
The Story of Tchaikovsky

SONG OF THE NORTH
The Story of Edvard Grieg

HE HEARD AMERICA SING
The Story of Stephen Foster

Co-author of

MY BROTHER WAS MOZART

Victor Herbert

VICTOR HERBERT

American Music-Master

By CLAIRE LEE PURDY

Illustrated By EVERETT SHINN

Music Drawings By RUDOLF W. KOHL

JULIAN MESSNER, INC. ***NEW YORK***

PUBLISHED BY JULIAN MESSNER, INC.
8 WEST 40TH STREET, NEW YORK

PRINTED IN THE UNITED STATES OF AMERICA
By Montauk Book Manufacturing Co., Inc., New York

Contents

VICTOR HERBERT

American Music-Master

Castles in Spain

1897. The Diamond Jubilee, celebrating the sixtieth year of Queen Victoria's reign over the British Empire, was held in this year. In the United States, William McKinley was President. Nearly everyone was humming, whistling, or singing Paul Dresser's *On the Banks of the Wabash*. The Curies in Paris were about to announce their discovery of radium. The Gold Rush to the Klondike was on. Fashionable girls and women in New York hurried to matinée performances of *Tess of the D'Urbervilles* (with the incomparable Minnie Maddern Fiske in the title rôle). Styles of the moment featured the Pompadour hair dress, skirts of enormous width sweeping the streets, and tight-fitting sleeves with puffed tops.

BACKSTAGE, the air was electric with excitement. In the dressing rooms, soloists gave the final touches to their make-up and tested their vocal chords with soft *mi-mi-mi's*. Anxious members of the chorus strolled about the wings, trying to feel at ease in their bizarre and colorful costumes. All were nervously aware of the expectant audience beyond the footlights.

The audience shared to some extent the tension of the players; for that unique moment had arrived, that partly pleasant, partly painful moment just before the opening of the curtain on a first performance of a musical play.

They were a well-fed, well-dressed crowd of first-nighters assembled on that evening of March 16 to enjoy Victor Herbert's new comic opera *The Serenade*. The elaborate chandeliers at the Knickerbocker Theatre (Broadway at Thirty-Eighth) shed pleasant light on a glittering "dress circle," where bejeweled women were gowned in the modish Pompadour sateens and silks of Vandyke red, Venetian heliotrope, and lotus blue, and the men were in the correct black and white of evening attire. This was the "gay nineties."

A pleasant murmur of animated conversation was accompanied by the rustling of programs. Tucked in among the advertisements extolling the after-theater lobster of the Hofbrau Haus, the Cadillac, and the Casino, and the crêpes-suzette at Maxine's was the announcement that the evening's entertainment would be presented by the most popular operetta troupe of the day, the "Famous Original Bostonians."

The house lights dimmed. The musicians in the orchestra pit ceased tuning their strings and testing their reeds. The audience hushed its lively conversation. A spotlight from the proscenium focused on the center aisle at the rear of the theater, and everyone turned to view the handsome man smiling and bowing to right and left as he walked briskly forward in the moving circle of the limelight.

"Who is he?" whispered a young thing with velvet bows in her dark hair.

"My dear! That is Victor Herbert!" she was told pityingly by her escort. "The composer of tonight's operetta. He frequently conducts, the first night."

"Handsome, isn't he?" breathed a fidgety little woman who was chaperon for a bevy of giggling schoolgirls.

"He's Irish, I'm told," one of the girls whispered back.

"Look! There's his wife!" Several pairs of opera glasses were focused on the statuesque blond woman sitting motionless in the shadows of a lower box.

"They say she has a glorious voice . . . sang at the Metropolitan ten or eleven years ago . . . German opera, you know. . . . Retired very soon after her début. . . ." Thus the gossips buzzed.

"Sh-h-h!" The up-to-the-last-second talkers were fiercely subdued by art's devotees.

One of the critics in the third row leaned over and whispered to his neighbor. "*There* is the only Broadway composer for the comic-opera stage who writes his own orchestrations. He catches the popular ear, all right, but he's no one-finger melodist from Tin-Pan Alley. Herbert knows his business as a composer!"

Victor Herbert rapped smartly for the orchestra's attention. With the crisp professional touch of men who make music their trade, the musicians swung into the march rhythm of the overture to *The Serenade.*

As the music moved gayly from four-four time to six-eight, to two-four, then to the waltz rhythm of three-four, back to six-eight, and finally to a brilliant three-eight tempo, it was by turns stirring, lively and robust, romantic, full of devilment and youthful joy. The well-tailored man with the dark hair and intelligent brown eyes conducted with deft, sure, meaningful gestures. The musicians found his style sympathetic and glanced up confidently to catch the signals of his baton.

Thunderous applause greeted the orchestra and conductor as the last note of the overture sounded mirthfully in the auditorium. A brief acknowledgment from the conductor-composer, and the curtain rose.

The stage presented an attractive, romantic scene—a huge old castle in Spain. There were high windows with iron grilles beyond the deep embrasures, and crimson draperies against the white walls. Tall-backed Spanish chairs, studded with huge brass nails, were drawn up at three sides of a heavy oak table. Carved chests flanked the wide fireplace where a log fire roared. An iron kettle bubbled on its crane, and wild ducks spitted above the flames dripped fat.

Sitting around the oak table was as picturesque a crew of cutthroats as ever gathered for mischief in the Spanish mountains. Boots of fine-grained leather, rakish hats or bright bandannas, capes thrown carelessly over one shoulder—thus they were costumed as they lounged at their ease.

Suddenly the loungers came to life. The wine tankards were filled, and the lusty group made the rafters shake with the opening chorus of Act I:

> "In attitudes alert! Hist! Hush!
> With keen and piercing eyes,
> Our breath we bate, and grimly wait,
> The trav'ler to surprise. Hist!"

Soaring tenors and rich basses held the theater audience entranced as the words of the song revealed that these men were a band of brigands—the "Royal Madrid Brigandage Association." They were making their headquarters in an old Spanish castle situated in a wild spot in the mountains. Near by was another old castle, said to be haunted by the restless spirit of a murdered knight, done to death by a treacherous host of long ago. The haunted castle belonged to the Duke of Santa Cruz, who occupied his remote estate only at rare intervals.

The brigands sang boastfully that they cared not a snap of the fingers for the government and its laws. They proclaimed proudly that the brave Romero, their captain, was feared far and wide in the land. A rousing toast to smiling

Romero, standing apart from his men as he listened to the singing, and the chorus concluded with a mock-serious whispering:

"Hist! Hush!"

Pleased with the tribute of his bandit comrades, Romero struck a dashing attitude, one booted foot on his chair, his hands resting lovingly on his short musket, a horseman's firearm called a carbine. In a rumbling bass he sang the *Song of the Carbine.*

"*I* am the law," his song declared. "I—not the government. And how do I enforce my decrees? Why, with my trusty carbine! Here's a friend that always answers at your call. Pif! Paf!" Romero pointed the carbine at one of his men, who dodged in pretended terror.

> "Argue with it if you can, sirs, when it speaks.
> Pif! Paf!"

Romero fired the musket at the roof beams, and the brigand chorus joined him in laughter, making the great hall echo with the wild sound. Then with a good will, Romero added his lusty bass to the rousing chorus.

Victor Herbert's audience was won completely. At the close of this colorful scene, there was applause which did not entirely subside until the stage was set for the second scene and the curtains parted to reveal a dark mountain road approaching the haunted castle of Santa Cruz.

First to appear on the road was a group of serving girls and a small company of armed men. The girls were servants of the Duke of Santa Cruz and his ward, Dolores, who were on their way from Madrid to occupy the Duke's estate in the mountains. The armed men were the Duke's bodyguard. Somehow, the nobleman and his ward had become separated from their company and had fallen behind. As for the guard, they did not look as if they would have been much protection anyway. They came tiptoeing along the road with the ridiculous song

> "Peering left, and peering right;
> We admit we're in a fright,
> And much inclined to mutiny."

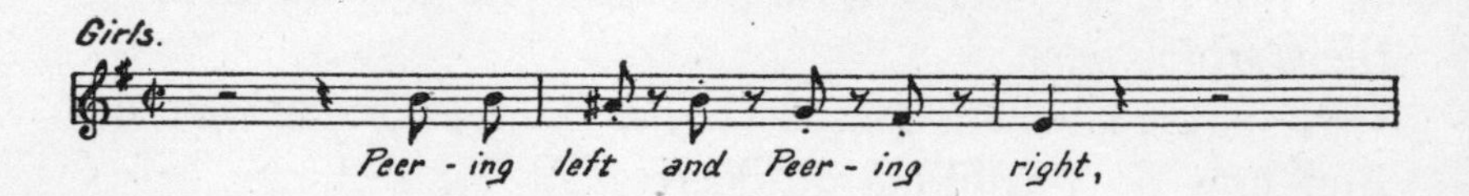

The timid girls and men of the guard proceeded fearfully into the dark night, and the road was empty. Then a dashing young horseman entered, singing *With cracking of whip and rattle of spur*. This was Alvarado, a swashbuckling baritone of the Madrid Opera and suitor to the ward of the Duke of Santa Cruz.

The audience gathered that Alvarado was something of a scoundrel, though a charming one. It had been necessary for him to leave Madrid rather hastily. Not only were his irate creditors on his trail but also a certain Yvonne, to whom the heedless young baritone had been engaged before he met and fell in love with the fair Dolores of Santa Cruz. Yvonne was the pretty and sprightly daughter of Colombo, a former grand-opera tenor. These two made a living by giving pantomime performances at holiday celebrations in the lonely Spanish castles of the mountains.

Back in Madrid, the Duke of Santa Cruz, himself in love with his ward Dolores, had been furious when he learned of Alvarado's attentions. Every night the young man sang a beautiful serenade under the girl's window:

The haunting melody of this song and the words "I love thee, I adore thee" drove the Duke nearly mad. The air became popular with everyone. It dogged the Duke wherever he went. The thing vexed him all the more because he had never seen Alvarado face to face, and no one would give him a hint as to the suitor's identity. To the enraged nobleman, every man who sang the melody was suspect. To get away from the hateful song, which had an uncanny way of making itself heard wherever Dolores happened to be, the Duke determined to take his ward far away from Madrid and keep her prisoner in his mountain castle.

Alvarado learned of the plan, and determined to outwit the Duke by arriving at the castle first. That is how he happened to be on the lonely road near Santa Cruz. At the conclusion of his song, Alvarado dashed away toward the castle, close on the heels of the Duke's servants and guard.

Again the road was empty and silent. Then off-stage shouting was heard. The Duke was making a tremendous racket, crying "Hola, Hola!" for his guard. He entered the scene with his humorous "Hola-ho, Hola-ho!" song.

This song succeeded in bringing the guard back to their places beside the Duke and Dolores. With comical excuses and explanations, they begged, "Forgive us!" And the Duke, who could see a joke on himself, broke into a merry song, *The funny side of that.*

The next scene was within the castle of Santa Cruz. Congratulating himself that he would at last be able to sleep in peace, far from unwelcome suitors and the detestable sound of Alvarado's serenade, the Duke retired to his own apartments. Dolores, gazing wistfully from her window, was too occupied with sad thoughts to sleep.

She drew back in alarm when she noticed a shadowy figure beneath her balcony. Then the strains of a guitar and the notes of the serenade reached her ear. The singer was unmistakably Alvarado. Dolores, overjoyed, began to sing, too. The duet *I love thee, I adore thee* provided a rare fairy-tale moment of romance for the listeners that night at the Knickerbocker, as it has done ever since for all lovers of romantic melody—for this song was one of Victor Herbert's best.

Later in the scene, a threatening storm and the terrors of the dark road drove three other travelers to seek the shelter of the castle. These three were Colombo and Yvonne, making one of their usual professional visits to the lonely castles of the region, and Gomez, a tailor, who had fallen in with them along the way.

The coming of this trio complicated matters in the castle, for Gomez fell madly in love with the beautiful Dolores, and Yvonne discovered that her beloved Alvarado was in hiding there. Saucy, pretty, daring little Yvonne saw in the tailor's infatuation for her rival a way to divert Dolores' attention from Alvarado. She informed Gomez that the only way he could win Dolores would be to learn to sing the serenade; and she persuaded Colombo to give the love-smitten tailor singing lessons.

In *The Singing Lesson* these three delighted the audience with the composer's lampoon of the current exaggerated styles of operatic singing. The heaving bosom, the interminable trill, the heroic posturings of the trio brought down the house on that spring night of 1897.

Impudent Yvonne sang:

> "The old Italian method grand
> Is what we practice,
> What we practice with éclat—
> Just ope your mouth widely, so
> And warble *Ah*, like this:
> Ah-h-h-h-h—"

Then Colombo sang *Ah-h-h-h-h* for a very long time. Gomez, bewildered (as well he might have been) with these vocal acrobatics, essayed a feeble *Ah* of his own, but Yvonne protested, "No, no, no, no, no, no, no, no!"

Colombo kept explaining to the poor fellow how he must hold the *Ah*, how he must smile as he did so, and how he must breathe at the proper time. He nearly knocked the wind out of the tailor with thumping him to indicate the diaphragm, and Yvonne broke down completely with laughter.

During this absurd lesson, the Duke came into the room. Since the song being practiced was Alvarado's serenade, the Duke jumped to the conclusion that Gomez was the hated rival and proceeded to lock him in one of the rooms of the castle. This was something which Yvonne had not foreseen. The threads of the plot were becoming well snarled, and Yvonne's chagrin delighted and charmed her audience.

"Who is it singing the rôle of Yvonne?" someone asked and peered at a program.

"Alice Nielsen," someone else answered.

"Absolutely wonderful voice," was the opinion of one of the newspaper critics. "Most charming young singing actress I've seen in a long time."

"I understand she's a protégée of Mrs. Herbert's," commented another writer.

"Sh-h-h!" Again that impatient silencing, and Yvonne, Colombo, and Gomez were off once more, grimacing and gesturing and singing with zest an encore of *The Singing*

Lesson. Colombo, the distracted maestro, and Yvonne, the impish conspirator, concluded with this opinion of their bewildered pupil and victim:

"The man who hath not music in his soul
All men should ban.
For such a man is full of sin,
And you, sir, are that man!"

While all these complicated doings were taking place within the castle, the brigand band from the neighboring castle were lurking without the walls, waiting for their leader to give the signal to attack the unsuspecting occupants. Lopez, the secretary to this Royal Madrid Brigandage Association, growing restless with inactivity, wandered into the castle courtyard. There he met Yvonne, who was mooning over a picture of her false lover, Alvarado. He who had come to conquer became a captive; without any preliminaries to speak of, Lopez fell head over heels in love with winsome Yvonne.

Gaze on this face so noble (Alvarado's picture) was Yvonne's next offering to an audience gone mad with delight. This she sang as a duet with the uncomfortable Lopez, coquetting and teasing and warbling like a bird while the brigand secretary made uncomplimentary remarks on Alvarado's features, saying he thought the baritone's eyes were crossed, and pleading finally, "Take, oh, take me, I am just as good."

Eventually, the bandits got round to attacking the castle. The stage was suddenly all action and noise—the brigands charging the Duke's men furiously, Dolores and Yvonne shrieking, the Duke himself yelling commands and dancing about like an excited marionette. Just at the moment when all seemed lost for the inhabitants of the castle, in came Alvarado muffled in a huge cloak.

"The specter of the castle!" cried the terrified brigands, remembering the blood-curdling stories they had heard of the murdered knight who haunted the Duke's castle.

With the appearance of Alvarado, the superstitious brigands took flight. The Duke should have been decently thankful for the rescue; but far from being grateful, he was more wrathful than ever to have the singer of the serenade meddle in his affairs. However, everyone else was pleased, none more so than the unhappy Gomez, released from his prison when the Duke realized that he was not Alvarado. The spirited *finale* brought even the Duke out of his sulks in time to sing:

> "The like of me you rarely see.
> Ha, ha, ha, ha,
> Ha, ha, ha."

The curtain closed to the sound of hearty "bravos" from the audience.

Like a good cake, a successful play or operetta is composed of many ingredients. None of them may be omitted, none may be inferior, if the work is to be acclaimed as art. For an operetta, there must be a good libretto and good music, of course. In addition, there must be a good audience, capable of appreciating both story and music. Above all, there must be good performers—orchestral musicians capable of interpreting the music of the instrumental score; singers capable of extracting every bit of meaning, whether serious or comic, from the words and music of the vocal score. Thus the critics, knowing well how important a singing star of genius is to a composer of music for the theater, busily compared notes on the outstanding performer of the show—the girl who sang the rôle of Yvonne. This girl for many years to come was destined to interpret brilliantly the leading soprano parts of the Herbert operettas.

"Who is this girl Nielsen?" one critic asked another querulously. "I mean aside from the few simple facts we all know—that she sang small rôles in the Bostonians' *A War-Time Wedding*, *Robin Hood*, and *The Bohemian Girl*, and Herbert's *Prince Ananias*."

One of the younger men spoke up mischievously. "Lads, lads!" He addressed the dignified elder journalists. "Where do you keep yourselves? And what do you read? Not my stuff, surely, or you would have read La Nielsen's biography in my review of *Robin Hood* these many moons ago. Listen and ye shall hear!"

It was James Gibbons Huneker speaking—a journalist who was, from the first day they met, one of Victor Herbert's stanchest admirers. Huneker was a clever writer, a musician himself, and a critic of good taste and sound judgment.

"The exquisite little Miss Nielsen was born in Tennessee," he told his fellow-journalists. "She was a very young child when her father died from wounds received as a Union soldier in the Civil War. After his death, her mother moved to Kansas City, Missouri, where she opened a boardinghouse to support herself and her children. Alice Nielsen ran errands and played with other little waifs as ragged as she.

"The child had some of her mother's Celtic spunk, it seems. (Her mother was Irish, her father, Danish, you know.) Once she was bedeviled past endurance by some rough boys who gathered to make fun of her bare feet while she was buying some things at the corner grocery. So the young gamin picked up a couple of eggs and let fly at her tormentors. She likes to tell how she made a lifelong friend of the grocer by this act; for he had suffered frequently at the hands of the hoodlums, but had never thought of eggs as the means of ridding himself of persecution.

"Well, she grew up, as girls will do, put on shoes eventually, and sang in the church choir. That was her whole musical training. Finally she went with her brother to San Francisco, California. She sang at a mass in St. Patrick's church there, and attracted much attention. Professional appearances at the Orpheum followed, and soon she went to the Tivoli Theatre, where she became a favorite and, finally, the prima donna. That is where singing comedian Henry Clay Barnabee, on tour with the Bostonians, found her, recognized her talent, and hired her for his company. The rest you know. She has made history tonight."

"Remarkable story," the critics were still murmuring as the curtain went up on Act Two.

The rest of the tangled plot unfolded to the tunes of many delightful songs, of which the audience never seemed to get enough, so insistent were they on encores. The discovery that Dolores' suitor and the hateful serenade had followed his ward to the castle determined the Duke to shut the girl away in a convent. There was such a school in a near-by mountain village. Acting immediately on this decision, he made arrangements for Dolores to stay for a while in the convent, and returned to his castle confident that he had finally outwitted his rival.

Alvarado was not to be so easily discouraged, however. He took refuge with the monks of a monastery next door to the girls' school, and thus continued to be near his loved one. Yvonne, not to be outdone either, disguised herself as a boy and persuaded the monks to let her stay at the monastery. By this ruse, she contrived to be near Alvarado, *her* loved one.

The monks, in true comic-opera style, proved to be a set of jolly fellows, who confessed in song that they dwelt in a cloister "peaceful as an oyster shell," but had no objection to taking a quick look at some of the more worldly doings of life. They rather enjoyed such pranks as singing a bolero *In Fair Andalusia* with the incorrigible Yvonne, who enjoyed immensely the business of fooling them all by passing herself off as a boy.

The monks looked on with pleasure at the games and dances of a village festival (a celebration in which Romero and his brigands joined heartily), and even added their splendid voices to that of the brigand chief in the rollicking *The Monk and the Maid*, with its sly mock-serious *Pax vobiscum*.

Pretty soon everyone else was singing, too. Indeed, all these intrigues of Dolores and Alvarado, the Duke, Yvonne, Gomez, and Lopez had the monks of the monastery and the schoolgirls of the convent in an uproar.

The Duke, who had returned to the convent when he learned of Alvarado's presence near by, was overcome by the proximity of so many lovely girls and burst forth with *Woman, lovely woman*. Dolores and the chorus of convent maids sang the plaintive *Angelus*, with its really beautiful accompaniment of organ chords and chimes.

As for Yvonne, she of the roguish eye and nightingale voice, entranced the characters of the play as well as the members of the audience with her graceful waltz song *Cupid and I*, astonishing music-trained ears with the remarkable cadenza:

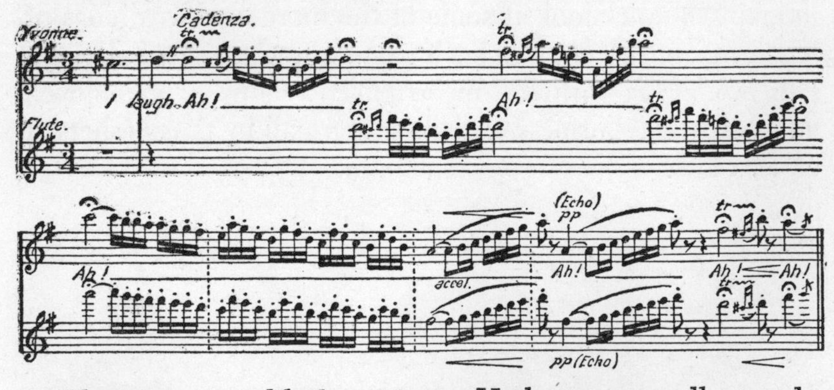

The story is told that Victor Herbert personally taught Alice Nielsen the song *Cupid and I*. At the "theatrical hotel" where the young singer was staying, the composer sat down at the tinny old piano and strummed an accompaniment.

"I practiced all afternoon, for we were to open that night,"

Miss Nielsen in later years recounted to a New York newspaper reporter.

The singer had been very nervous, eager to make a success of her part, fearful that she would forget the words of her songs. Herbert had laughed her fears away.

"If you forget the words," said Victor, "just make up something. If you forget the second verse, repeat the first!"

"If it hadn't been for his enthusiasm," declared Alice Nielsen, "I never could have got through that night's performance. Power and energy—and a dash of Irish pigheadedness—that's what he had."

Alvarado kept practicing his serenade, and the monastic brothers fell into the spirit of the thing and helped him out with their singing of *I love thee, I adore thee* in chant style. The schoolgirls in the convent learned the song, and even the convent parrot shrieked it.

The Duke could stand no more and made haste to take his ward away with him. But by this time Yvonne had given up hope of winning Alvarado and had decided to help Cupid bring him and Dolores together. She managed to exchange clothes with Dolores and slip into the convent while Dolores entered the garden of the monastery. When the Duke carried off his supposed ward, it was Yvonne (heavily veiled to conceal her face) who left the convent and Dolores who remained behind with Alvarado at the monastery.

But it is unthinkable to have an operetta end with matters in a snarl or with only one pair of lovers made happy. So it was that Alvarado appealed to the brigands, and found a ready supporter of his arguments in Lopez, who still loved the capricious Yvonne. The brigands settled the whole affair by going after the Duke, capturing his party, and exacting as ransom his promise to let the lovers have their way. Alvarado and Dolores flew into each other's arms, and Yvonne made the discovery that the dashing Lopez was not only "just as good" as Alvarado but even better.

And so all ended happily, with Dolores and Alvarado and

the chorus singing something about "Don José of Sevilla" and "Pif! Paf! Let her go!"

This hardly made sense, but who expects sensible conduct from lovers reunited after so much excitement? Lopez, delirious apparently at finding that Yvonne loved him at last, sang *I envy the bird.* Yvonne coaxed the Duke and Gomez (both of whom, all things being considered, were taking their disappointments in love rather philosophically) to join her in a trio, the rueful *Dreaming, dreaming:*

"Dreaming, dreaming,
Talking in my sleep,
Wandering in dreamland,
Where happiness is cheap."

In the finale which closed the operetta the whole company —the Duke and his servants and guards, Dolores and Alvarado, Yvonne and Lopez, Gomez and Colombo, Romero and his brigands, the monks, and the convent girls—took sides in a spirited dispute about the value of love. Some of them sang in derision:

"That for love, Pif! Paf!"

But the rest ignored the cynics and had the last word with echoes of the serenade and the words,

"I will love thee, dear, forever,
For my dream and my star thou art."

When the last echoes of the applause had died away, applause that told Victor Herbert and his librettist, Harry B. Smith, that their operetta was a success with a capital S, and everyone with a finger in the operatic pie had taken a bow, the house lights went on. The audience filed out well past midnight, chuckling over the jokes of the operetta, and humming snatches of the catchy tunes.

Backstage in the dressing rooms, the artists sighed happily though wearily as they went about the business of removing grease paint and costumes. The stage itself suddenly swarmed with waiters, who laid a festive supper on long tables. In their own street dress, the cast of the show assembled behind the curtain to celebrate with food and drink the triumphant opening.

William MacDonald, head of the Bostonians; librettist Smith; Victor and Therese Herbert; critics and reporters—everyone was invited and everyone, pretty nearly, remained for the "show after the show."

And what a show it was! Intoxicated with the excitement and success of the evening, the actors outdid themselves in telling jokes and presenting impromptu skits. Henry Clay Barnabee, incomparable comedian of the troupe, was persuaded to recite the absurd poem for which he had become famous, *The Cork Leg.*

Though the company many times had seen Barnabee go through his antics to illustrate the adventure of the animated leg, they laughed as uproariously as if the skit were new to them. The great master of comic art had a way of making each performance a shade different from previous ones. He seemed to unjoint himself, to separate from his leg entirely, as he recited in tragic tones:

"I'll tell you a tale now without any flam,
In Holland there dwelt Mynheer Von Clam,
Who ev'ry morning said,
'I am the richest merchant in Rotterdam.'

One day he had stuffed him as full as an egg,
When a poor relation came to beg,
But he kicked him out without broaching a keg,
And in kicking him out he broke his own leg.

A surgeon, the first in his vocation,
Came and made a long oration,
He wanted a limb for anatomization,
So he finished the job by amputation."

The song went on to tell how Mynheer Von Clam refused to use crutches after the amputation, but ordered a beautiful leg of cork from an artist who made such legs "as strong as an iron beam," with clockwork-and-steam mechanism for moving them. When he got this leg, the Dutch merchant was so delighted that

"He walked through squares and passed each shop,
Of speed he went to the utmost top;
Each step he took with a bound and a hop,
Till he found his leg he could not stop!

Horror and fright were in his face,
The neighbors thought he was running a race;
He clung to a post to stay his pace,
The leg, remorseless, kept up the chase.

He called to some men with all his might,
'Oh, stop this leg or I'm murdered quite!'
But though they heard him aid invite,
He, in less than a minute, was out of sight.

He ran o'er hill and dale and plain;
To ease his weary bones, he fain
Would throw himself down—but all in vain.
The leg got up and was off again!

He walked of days and nights a score,
Of Europe he had made the tour.
He died—but though he was no more
The leg walked on the same as before!

In Holland sometimes he comes in sight,
A skeleton on a cork leg tight.
No cash did the artist's skill requite,
He never was paid and it served him right.

My tale I've told both plain and free,
Of the richest merchant that could be,
Who never was buried—though dead, ye see;
And I've been singing his L.E.G."

The company was still rocking with laughter at Barnabee's outrageous nonsense when Victor Herbert rose to propose a toast.

"To actor Barnabee and the Bostonians!"

The toast was drunk with a will. For many years this group of players had been America's favorite light-opera troupe. They were in much the same class as the world-famous "Savoyards," the English company assembled by D'Oyly Carte and Gilbert and Sullivan.

The Bostonians derived their name from the fact that the nucleus of their organization had been formed (as early as 1879) in the Boston Theatre, Boston, Massachusetts. There they had perfected their comic art under the direction of one of the first women managers in America, Miss E. H. Ober.

Victor Herbert always declared that meeting William MacDonald, head of the Bostonians, in the spring of 1894 was the turning point in his career. This famous company provided the combination of sure artistry and careful management which contributed much to the early successes of the Irish-American composer.

More toasts followed, and finally the little singing star, Alice Nielsen, spoke up shyly.

"To a dear lady and a magnificent artist. Madame Therese Herbert-Foerster!" she proposed, using Mrs. Herbert's professional name.

"A song, a song!" The company clamored and Therese consented. She rose and made her way to a piano rolled in from one of the wings. As expert musician's fingers accompanied her singing, Therese's glorious voice soared up and up in an operatic aria. Alice Nielsen, who had lately entranced an audience with her own sweet singing, sat lost to the world, paying a comic-opera singer's homage to a singer of grand opera. One day, she too would sing grand opera. That is what she must have been thinking as she listened. Some years afterward, this little street arab from "the wrong side of the tracks," who had pulled herself up by the boot straps to the first place in operetta, was to surprise the world by studying with a famous European teacher until she was worthy to sing grand opera in New York's Metropolitan Opera House.

Mrs. Herbert came to the end of the aria and acknowledged the applause. Shaking her head when the company clamored for more, she returned to her seat. As the night wore on till morning, she contributed little to the lively talk, preferring to let her husband take the limelight.

Victor Herbert loved the exhilaration of gatherings like these. Indeed, how else could he have written so brilliantly and successfully for the madcap people of the theater? Therese, however, was happiest in the peace and quiet of her own well-managed home, where she played the rôle of devoted mother to her two children and capably looked to the cooking of appetizing meals and the smooth ordering of other household tasks.

She smiled fondly at her husband, who was amusing the diners with an Irish story.

"A tale from life it is," Victor was saying with (figuratively speaking) his tongue in his cheek. "Something that was seen with me own eyes on the old post road which leads from Dublin to a retired disthrict to the south of Ireland. A young Irish lad had bin to Dublin to see a land agint, to exchange 'the big rint for the little patch.' 'Tis a habit of the English landlords and their agints to wilkim the Irish kindly whiniver the rint comes due. So this darlin' av a lad wint to Dublin, as I say, and he was on his way home by post at the time I spake av.

"There was a passenger in the coach who seemed to take pleasure in making offensive remarks. He kept making remarks about how hard it was to make low fellows keep their distance, all the while looking with a meaning that could not be mistuk at the lad returning home from Dublin.

"Afther one av the stoppages on the road for refreshment, the passengers resumed their places, and the last av thim to do so was this same snobbish fellow I've bin telling you av. On taking his seat, he said 'Where's the coat I left here?'

"No one made answer to His Impudince, so the poltroon raised his voice and glared about him as he asked again, 'Where's the coat?'

" 'Your coat, is it, sir?' said the coachman.

" 'Yes, my coat! Do you know anything of it?'

" 'No, sir,' said the coachman; 'may be you tuk it into the house with you.'

" 'No, I did not; I left it in the coach. And by the by,' said he, looking at the Irish lad, 'you were the only person who did not quit the coach. Did you take it?'

" 'Take *what?*' said the lad.

" 'My coat,' said the other with extreme effrontery.

" 'I've a coat av me own,' said the lad.

" 'That's not an answer to my question,' said the other.

" 'I think you ought to be glad to get so quiet an answer,' was the lad's calm reply.

"At this moment a waiter made his appearance at the door av the inn, bearing the missing coat on his arm, calling 'You left this behind you, sir!'

"The other passengers turned indignant eyes on the man who had accused the lad. He scarcely knew what to do. Afther much stammering, and hemming and hawing, he took the coat from the waiter, and said to the lad, 'I see—I forgot—I thought that I left it in the coach, but—ah—I see 'twas a mistake.'

" 'Oh, make no apologies,' said the lad; 'we were both undher a mistake.'

" 'How both?'

" 'Why, sir,' said this darlin' av a counthry boy, 'you mistuk me for a thief, and I mistuk you for a gintleman.' "

"You rogue!" said Therese as Victor leaned back in his chair to enjoy the laughter which his story and his brogue had provoked. "Flying undher false colors, is it?" she mimicked, a sly twinkle in her eyes. "So! A tale from life, to be sure! A tale right out of your Grandfather Lover's book *Rory O'More!*"

"Whisht, woman. Be still. A man can't be original all the time!" Victor grinned good-naturedly.

When it was Alice Nielsen's turn, she chose to recall an amusing incident of the dress rehearsal.

At one point in the play, where Yvonne has to make one of her lightning-quick costume changes, the young star was still struggling to get into her boy's boots when her cue was given. The orchestra was launched into the music of her song before she had time to pull on the second boot.

"Come, come, little person. What's keeping you?" Victor Herbert, who was conducting the dress rehearsal, called out in sharp impatience.

Holding the boot that would not slip on quickly enough, Alice Nielsen hopped out comically to explain her difficulty. Herbert's look of annoyance fled, and a genial smile lighted up his face.

"Take your time, small one," he said kindly, as if the capable young singer had been a bewildered child. "I'll have them wait."

"And," finished Alice Nielsen dramatically, "if he didn't sit down at the edge of the stage and write a song for one of the characters so that there would be more time for me to dress!"

Therese was not a little pleased at this story. It illustrated not only the kindness and sympathy with the problems of his fellow-workers which made the composer beloved by all who knew him but also his uncanny ability to turn out music at a moment's notice. This facility made Victor Herbert particularly valuable to the theater. Every actor knows the value of successful "ad-libbing"—whether it take the form of improvising words to fill in an awkward pause, or of writing extra music the night before an opening.

Noticing Mrs. Herbert's glance of approval, the young singer smiled back in understanding.

More than a quarter of a century later, Alice Nielsen, married to Dr. Leroy R. Stoddard of Bedford Hills, and retired from the stage, paid generous tribute to Victor Herbert's wife. Looking back wistfully over the years which had passed since that first performance of *The Serenade*, she put her memories into words for a newspaper interview:

"Women, they say, are not creative in the arts." The puckish Nielsen smile flickered for a moment to indicate that she did not believe in what "they say." Then she added quite seriously, "Victor Herbert's devoted wife 'created' Victor Herbert."

She went on to explain this odd conceit, saying that Therese Herbert-Foerster, talented artist though she was, sincerely believed that her own creative abilities were inferior to those of her husband. Being honest and unselfish, she devoted herself to helping further the career of the one she considered to be the greater artist.

Alice Nielsen drove her point home by relating how Therese Herbert was ever on the lookout for talent which her husband's work needed:

"It was Mrs. Herbert who 'found' me for the part of Yvonne. I can see her kind face now, hear her eager voice, with its foreign pronunciation, as she exclaimed, 'You are the girl to be Victor's Yvonne! No one else will do.'

"She would have had the same manner if she had discovered a special sort of overcoat or a new dish or a bar of melody that would help this man whom she so loved. She put no sentiment into it, made no complimentary speeches. I was the type that was needed—she must have me.

"If Victor had had for his wife a less devoted and less competent woman, I doubt if he would have been so great. As it was, he had his struggle and was forty or more when he made his real success."

When the composer and his wife rose to say good-by to the cast of *The Serenade* and the other guests, everyone called out some affectionate word to them. Making their way to the exit beyond the "props" and sets in one of the wings, they passed the critics' end of the table. Victor slapped the shoulder of a handsome blond fellow, who stopped a quick, brilliant flow of talk long enough to rise and say good night. This was "Jimmy" Huneker, who had taken so much delight earlier in the evening in informing his maturer colleagues about the singing star of the show.

When Victor and Therese had opened the outer door and stepped into the gray light of the early dawn, the rest of the newspapermen pounced on Huneker.

"Jimmy, you know Vic better than the rest of us. Who is he, anyway? Never mind this musical comedy stuff. We all know he's the Crown Prince of Operetta. And everyboy knows that he's an outstanding 'cellist. But what about this Irish brogue he pulled on us tonight? And where did he meet Therese Foerster of Vienna? And is it true that he has spent most of his life in Germany?"

Jimmy Huneker's lazy eyes sparkled with sudden animation. "All right, fellows, I'll tell you. But it's a long tale, mind you, and it begins in Dublin, Ireland, where this darlin' av a lad, Victor Herbert, was born February 1, 1859 . . ."

Sevenoaks

1861-1866. These were the Civil War years in the United States. In England, Arthur Seymour Sullivan (of Gilbert and Sullivan operetta fame) was making a start with strictly serious music. *Dixie, In the Land of Jubilo,* and *When Johnny Comes Marching Home* were new songs. Ladies of fashion in Paris, London, and New York walked abroad in stiff crinoline or hoops to keep their skirts ballooned out. Hair was parted in the middle, looped over the ears, and caught into a shapeless mass in a silk net (snood) worn low on the neck. Whiskers were very much the fashion for men, and the well-dressed gentleman wore trousers without a crease, with bands of braid down the sides, and broadcloth coats so stiff that they would stand alone.

DUBLIN was the prologue to Victor Herbert's story, but "The Vine" at Sevenoaks was the real beginning. It was one spring day at the market town of Sevenoaks, twenty miles southeast of London, that a lively-mannered little gentleman with a gray poll and black eyes as bright as a magpie's waited eagerly for the public coach which had just made its appearance in a cloud of dust on the Dover-to-London road. Neighbors and townspeople called out cheerily to him.

"A happy day for you, eh, Sam Lover?" A bluff, red-faced man in baggy, expensive tweeds smiled his greeting.

And a man in workman's clothes commented for all to hear, "Who'd know of 't, if 'twas otherwise with Sam Lover, I'd like to know, that's what! Did any of *us* ever see him glum?"

The neat little man smiled happily at this affectionate banter. Genial Samuel Lover, that Irishman "so cursed with versatility" (as one of his contemporaries put it) that he was poet and composer, singer, novelist, painter, dramatist, humorist and lecturer, all in one skin, was pleased in the knowledge that he was as popular with those who did the world's work as with those who hired it done.

The carriage for which Lover waited was bringing his widowed daughter, Fanny Herbert, and her young son, Victor, to live at "The Vine," Lover's beautiful estate in Sevenoaks. As the big horse-drawn coach pulled up smartly to discharge passengers, Sam Lover hurried forward to greet the slender young woman in black traveling cloak, and the small boy dressed (in the fashion of the day) much like his elders, in long trousers and waistcoat, with a jaunty sailor's hat on his curls.

Everyone smiled to see how Sam Lover bustled about and got underfoot as he called out excitedly:

"Fanny, my dear! Welcome home! And Victor! Don't know your old grandpa, eh? Sure, he won't eat you, darlin'," he added as Victor, bewildered by all the clamor and confusion, drew back uncertainly.

"How good to see you again, father. How good!" There was a little catch in Fanny's voice. "And how is Grandma Mary Waudby?"

"Hearty, my dear. Hearty, as always. Wanted her to come along with me, but you know how women are. Had to stay home to get the tea things ready, she said. She'll be waiting for us at 'The Vine.' But mercy on us," he broke off. "What a lot of luggage. All yours, Fanny? Here, porter! Porter! Take this luggage, will you? The carriage is right over there," he explained to Fanny. "We'll stow the boxes and bags in somehow. Let me see, I had better ride up here." He indicated the seat beside the coachman, who was holding in the restive horses and trying to touch his cap to Mistress Fanny.

Fanny nodded a greeting to her father's coachman and took her place in the carriage. Victor, quite overwhelmed by the new impressions rushing at him from all sides, was as still as a mouse as he sat beside his mother.

Leaning her head wearily against the back of the seat, Fanny closed her tired eyes. "Home, home!" she was thinking. So much had happened since she had seen her father a few years before.

The bags were stowed safely at last, and the horses started up briskly at the smart flick of the coachman's whip. As the carriage rolled along the country road which wound its way among the downs of the valley of the Darent River, Fanny's thoughts reviewed the troubled events of the recent past.

Just two years before, in 1859, Fanny Lover Herbert had looked out wistfully from her bedroom window, which commanded a view of the River Liffey in Dublin, capital and ancient seat of the government of Ireland. Her week-old son was lying in his cradle, rocked by an Irish nurse who crooned an old *husho*, a soft, monotonous lullaby-chant, to soothe him to sleep. In the library, Fanny's husband, Edward Herbert, was sorting papers and packing law books in boxes preparatory to quitting Ireland as soon as his wife and son could travel with him. He expected to take up his residence and his practice on the Continent.

Fanny's father, Samuel Lover, had been born in Dublin, and educated there. There, too, he began his career as painter, married charming Miss Berrel, daughter of a Dublin architect, and established a home where men and women of wit and progressive thought were always welcome. In that home, two daughters had been born, of whom Meta was the elder, Fanny the younger.

From her father's anecdotes as well as from her own knowledge of the town, Fanny had grown to understand and love the turbulent city. Dublin was vivid and a trifle terrifying for its tradition of Irish rebellion against British rule. It was a beautiful city, with wide streets along the river, proud of the time-mellowed buildings of Trinity College. It was proud, too, of its sons of genius—men like Jonathan Swift, who wrote the acid political satire *Gulliver's Travels;* Richard Steele of the *Spectator* papers; and Richard Sheridan, the playwright. All of them lay, after life's fitful fever, in the little cemetery of Glasnevin.

Fanny's thoughts turned to her little son, and she wondered if someday he would attend Trinity College, where hotheaded young Robert Emmet had planned and plotted for a free and united Ireland; and gentle Thomas Moore, Emmet's good friend, had dreamed his poet's dreams and gathered the impressions which later went into the wistful *Irish Melodies.* These thoughts brought a frown to Fanny's brow. Would the day ever come when Ireland would be rid of poverty and freed from strife and dissension?

In 1861, far away from Dublin, in a modest *pension* (family hotel) in Paris, Fanny Herbert's husband died, and it was Fanny who kept candles burning late in the library as she sorted over papers and books in preparation for the journey to England and her father's home at Sevenoaks. All unaware of sorrow and anxiety, two-year-old Victor slept in his small bed.

And now the carriage was coming to a stop before a spacious two-story brick house on the commons. This was Sam Lover's hospitable home, "The Vine."

"Mary! Mary!" Lover called out as he jumped down from his perch. "They have arrived!"

A neat little lady, some years her husband's junior, hurried through the doorway.

"Sam, dear! Don't excite yourself so! La, la! Let me have some of those boxes. You go help Fanny."

"Let me help you down, child," he called, hurrying back to the carriage. And then over his shoulder to his wife: "Are you sure the tea things are ready, Mary darlin'? Everything must be right, you know. This is an occasion! Fanny and Victor home to stay!"

Grandma Mary threw up her hands in a gesture of mock despair. "Tea things! Indeed! And why is it I didn't go with you to meet the coach? And what is it I've been doing all this while? Sam Lover, I think—"

But what she thought can only be guessed, for Grandpa Lover was already holding young Victor in his arms, the coachman was urging the horses to the stables at the rear, a young serving lad was wrestling with the traveling bags, cases, and boxes, and Fanny was crying on Grandma Mary's comfortable shoulder. Victor was crying, too, because to him Grandpa Lover was a stranger, and to the child this little old man who made funny noises of welcome was thoroughly frightening.

"Let me take that boy, Sam!" Grandma Mary commanded.

Mary Waudby was not actually mother and grandmother to Fanny and Victor, the real Grandma Berrel having died years before; but kindly, energetic, wholesome Grandma Mary was a most satisfactory step-grandma. She and Sam Lover had been married following the death of Lover's elder daughter, Meta. Meta had been his constant companion after the death of his first wife and the marriage of his younger daughter, Fanny. In losing her, he had lost a fellow-artist as well as a daughter-companion. Samples of Meta's skill in etching and making pen-and-ink drawings were preserved for years in Sam and Fanny Lover's famous scrapbooks, later in the collections of Victor Herbert and his daughter, Ella Herbert.

Young Victor soon felt very much at home at Sevenoaks. In the early mornings, before his mother was awake, he would creep downstairs to his grandfather's study, where he received what help he needed with the complicated business of dressing. Then the two of them—the stooped little old man with the merry dark eyes, and the chubby boy with the crisp, curling dark hair—walked out into the spring sunshine. They looked first to see if the snails were in the garden and to discover the first spring blossoms. They stopped to pet the dogs in the kennels, took time at the stable for Victor to sit for a moment astride one of the beautiful horses impatient for their morning workout. Sometimes they went into the fields beyond the common, to listen to the song of the English lark and to look at the woolly Shropshire lambs.

For the next five years this was Victor's life. He learned to know and love the English countryside. In summer, he followed the prim hedgerows to meadows dotted with daisies. He learned to look eagerly for the flowers which had taken root in the thatched roofs of the cottages, where country folk greeted him with the quaint speech of Kent. In fall, when the first frost had crisped the leaves of the trees, the sound of the hunting horn and the baying of the hounds at full cry across the brown stubble of the fields made his heart beat faster. And in winter, when the cold fogs rolled in from the North Sea, or a fall of snow powdered the trees for a white Christmas and piled feathery drifts against the bare shrubs in the garden, he was content to gather his storybooks and toys together and play by the fire in his grandfather's studio. There the artist would paint the portraits for which he was famous while Fanny busied herself with sewing and Grandma Mary read to them out of some late book—George Eliot's *Silas Marner*, perhaps, or Charles Dickens' *Our Mutual Friend*.

Victor came to love the pleasant North Downs of the valley of the Darent. His rambles with his grandfather took him often to the village of Sevenoaks, where quaint half-timber shops with little dormers and mullioned windows lined the pleasantly shaded streets. They visited the old church of St. Nicholas, which had been built and added to for three centuries beginning with the thirteenth; and the grammar school and almshouses founded in 1418 by Sir William Sevenoke. Once or twice they drove out to Knole Park, a magnificent old English residence owned in the time of King John by the Earl of Pembroke.

Best of all, Victor loved his grandfather's home, with its spacious, high-ceilinged rooms, comfortable furnishings, cheerful fireplaces, and verdant steaming conservatory. It was pleasant to see the gleam of fine old silver and bright glassware when generous feasts were set out for guests in the paneled dining room, mellow and cheerful in the yellow candlelight.

As he grew older, the boy took a keen interest in the talk that accompanied the meals at the oak table in the dining room. Samuel Lover was an educated Irishman, fervent in his love of his native country. Because of the general poverty of his fellow-Irishmen, however, he was forced to live and work in England, where enough people had the money to buy books and music and to attend the theater to make an artist's profession pay.

The very fact of this "exile" of culture from Ireland served but to deepen Lover's pity and love for his homeland. His home at Sevenoaks was a Mecca for the Irish intelligentsia of the day. All sorts of Irishmen—politicians, revolutionaries, poets, novelists, actors, playwrights—came to talk and laugh at "The Vine," and frequently to weep for the sad land of the Emerald Isle.

In Dublin, too, and in various other places where Lover had lived before taking the house at Sevenoaks, Irish artists had always delighted to gather. Genial Thomas Moore had been a frequent guest, and Lover liked to recall their first meeting. It was at a dinner given in the famous poet's honor. Samuel Lover was at that time just a boy, making a modest beginning with painting, singing, and song-writing. Lover had been so grateful for the chance to be at the same table with the great Irish poet that he sat down and composed a song in Moore's honor. Imagine his amazement and delight when he found that he had been seated next to his idol. It so happened that the arrangers of the program had forgotten to prepare the customary tribute in song. Anxious whisperings and a worried "What shall we do?" attracted Lover's attention. He produced his little song and volunteered to sing it.

The offer was accepted, and, though stage-fright nearly overcame him, Lover managed to sing well enough. Moore was delighted with the compliment and became Sam Lover's lifelong friend from that moment.

Theatrical and musical people were always welcome in Lover's home, and among his favorites was handsome Tyrone Power (founder of the distinguished theatrical family of which the present-day Tyrone Power of Hollywood is a member). For one hundred nights at the Adelphi Theatre in London, Power had played in *Rory O'More*, the dramatized version of Lover's novel of Irish life during the days of the Napoleonic Wars.

Another stanch friend was enchanting Madame Vestris, an actress who was manager of her own theater. It was for her that Samuel Lover wrote his operetta *The Greek Boy*.

An old scrapbook of Fanny's (actually Samuel Lover's personal scrapbook) was the basis of an article which she wrote in later years for *Century Magazine*. That was during her visit to the United States, when Victor was a man grown and eminently successful as a composer in his adopted country. This book of Fanny's contained autographs and pencil sketches of many of the famous men and women that came often to visit the Lovers. It was given to her by "Grandma Mary" Lover in 1878, and in 1897, Fanny brought it to her son Victor. The book is now the property of Victor Herbert's daughter. The first autograph in the scrapbook is that of Thomas Moore, written in 1830, which might well be a tribute both to Samuel Lover and his illustrious grandson, Victor Herbert:

"The Dead are like the stars by day,
Withdrawn from mortal eye,
But not extinct, they hold their way
In glory through the sky."

Daniel O'Connell's face is there—a sketch drawn by Lover on the back of a letter as he sat breakfasting with O'Connell, member of Parliament from the city of Dublin. Lord

Brougham (after whom the carriages were named) looks out from under his curled wig.

Ten-year-old Johnny Millais (later Sir John Millais, famous English painter) contributed a sketch of a gallant and his lady. Violinist Paganini and poets Thomas Campbell and Lord Byron provided autographs. Oriental traveler Wilkinson set down in hieroglyphics Mrs. Lover's name and social status.

Among other friends of the family listed by Fanny in her article were Dickens, Cruikshank, Sir Edwin Landseer, Thackeray, Bulwer, and the "Jessamy bride" of Oliver Goldsmith, Mrs. Gwynn. Lover painted Mrs. Gwynn's portrait when she was very old.

Of her father, genial Sam Lover, who attracted all these people to him, Fanny wrote:

". . . although distinguished by an enchanting amiability and cheerfulness, yet he had an iron will, an untiring industry, and perfect self-dependence."

Fanny told how, after leaving his Irish home because of a disagreement with his father over the choice of a career, ". . . he managed to support himself by executing for physicians drawings, which were destined to appear in anatomical works, and had, of course, to be remarkably accurate. It is the more extraordinary that he was able to do this, as he had never been taught to draw, and had up to that time practiced the art only for his amusement in leisure hours."

Fanny went on to tell how, out of hard-earned wages, he paid for French lessons. French was a necessary accomplishment if one was to deal with the aristocrats of the day. And "with patient industry, he daily improved himself in miniature painting, and was soon able to establish himself as a portrait painter in Dublin."

But the people who had enough money to pay for the luxury of miniature portraits were limited in Dublin. Fanny tells us why her father had to leave his beloved Ireland:

"Having painted everybody in Dublin who wished to be painted (as he himself used to express it), after the lapse of a considerable time he decided on shifting the scene of his efforts to London. The groundwork of all his future activity had in the meantime been laid in Dublin.

"The first song which he succeeded in selling to a publisher he would not take money for, but arranged to take a guitar in exchange, as he had long wished to possess such an instrument, but had not as yet been able to buy one.

". . . he played both the piano and the guitar exceedingly well, although he had never had a lesson on either of these instruments."

Lover's working methods were a reflection of his easy-going nature. Fanny recorded:

"Many artists are as dumb as fishes at their easels; but he could converse charmingly while he was painting. . . ."

He liked to have his wife read to him as he worked. In this way he could keep up with the latest news and the best literature of the day, and his work would not suffer from time lost.

In the early days of his career, when he was making his way with painting portraits, Lover received a commission to make a miniature of the violinist Paganini. Bored with posing, Paganini had presented an almost expressionless countenance for the painter who was striving for life and character in his portrait.

Quite casually, Lover began to hum part of a difficult composition of Paganini's, a composition which the violinist had played but once in England and but twice anywhere.

"Where did you get that?" the musician asked in amazement.

"Oh, I heard you play it once."

That was the end of dull eyes and sagging posture for Paganini, and Lover chuckled to himself as he painted just the expression he had been trying to get. His remarkable musical memory had served his painter's art admirably.

After the Paganini miniature was completed, a letter arrived from the chamberlain of the Duchess of Kent, summoning the artist to London at once to paint the portrait of

Princess Victoria (later Queen Victoria). But one of his children was soon to be born, and Lover answered that he would have to paint the picture at some later time. Fanny recorded with dry brevity, "Unfortunately, Courts are easily offended, and the order was never renewed."

When Victor and his mother lived at Sevenoaks, one of the most colorful guests was swashbuckling Charles Lever, witty author of many novels, notably *Charles O'Malley*, a hair-raising story of adventure. In his youth, Lever had composed the famous convivial song *The Pope He Loved a Merry Life*, patterned after the German-type student *Lied*. Lever was a spinner of droll Irish yarns, too. One of his best—*Con Cregan's Legacy*—is a gem of storytelling.

Lever was an old friend, with whom Samuel Lover had been associated in a literary way when both were young men. Four bright young enthusiasts—Lover, Lever, Petrie, and Carlton—are listed by Lover's biographer, A. J. Symington, as among those who founded the brilliant monthly periodical, the *Dublin University Magazine*. Lover's quaint yarn, *The Story of Barney O'Reirdon*, appeared in an early number of this magazine.

Charles Lever had been educated in German schools, and this circumstance, curiously enough, affected the life and career of Victor Herbert. It was due in large measure to Lever's bright reminiscences of his student days in Germany that the decision to educate Victor abroad took form in the minds of Grandpa Lover and Fanny.

Education in the German states (at that time they were not yet united into one country under a Kaiser, and the ugly days of the Nazi Reich were even more distant) was progressive and thorough. In addition, German schooling was financially within the reach of people in moderate circumstances.

Lever was fond of recalling his gay student life, where "work when you work, but *play* when you play, and learn something from both" had been the motto. Serious study was taken for granted, and there was no admiration for the shirker or dullard; but when holidays came, fun was the order of the day. There were student jaunts through the mountains of Bavaria and Switzerland, where the boys traveled in merry groups, rucksack on back, resting at picturesque inns when night overtook them.

As they walked, the students joked, argued politics and philosophy, and sang boisterous school songs. At the inns, they danced with the rosy-cheeked peasant girls from the villages, to the music of lusty zither orchestras twanging out old folk tunes.

To perpetuate this bright memory, Lever had organized a club in London. It was called the *Burschenshaft*, the name given in 1815 in Germany to associations of students banded together for liberal political purposes, advocating at that time the supposed democracy of Napoleon Bonaparte. In the English club, it was the liberal aims of the "Irish in exile" that were kept alive; but the songs and convivial gatherings of the members were the kind that kept green the memory of the German student adventure.

Samuel Lover was a member of this club. In fact, because he was a composer and writer of verses, he held the official post of "Minstrel of the Burschenshaft." Members of the club told him little known facts about German educational methods, the best in the world at that time. It was natural, therefore, that his mind should turn to Germany when he and Fanny discussed young Victor's future.

"We haven't the money we once had," he told his daughter. It must be remembered that free public schools were not in existence in England when Victor was a child.

"Yes, I know," said Fanny thoughtfully.

"Unhappy Ireland is not our solution, either," said Lover sadly. "No schools there, except the little village schools with their sorry equipment and ill-paid teachers. And fine men like Emmet being expelled from Trinity for holding an opinion on Irish rights!"

"Take the lad to Germany," Lever advised again and again.

These discussions took place off and on as Victor passed his third, fourth, fifth, and sixth birthdays. Unaware of the earnest planning on his behalf, he went adventuring in the countryside around Sevenoaks. He spent whole days in the fields, lying on his back in the fragrant grass, watching the lazy clouds create their gigantic sculptures. He went visiting, dropping in at the stables of the village to talk "horsey" talk with the grooms, or stopping to pass the time of day with the cottagers of the neighborhood. He enjoyed rough-and-tumbles with his grandfather's dogs, and liked to help the coachman drive the sleek horses of the family carriage. Sometimes it was almost nightfall before he returned to his grandfather's house, where guests were sure to be assembled in the drawing room.

As is the way of children, Victor seemed to take little notice of the adult conversations; yet it is certain that he missed very little of the talk of the Irish Nationalists who assembled at "The Vine." The boy was allowed to stay at table when Fanny and Grandmother Mary, in conformance with the custom of those days, retired to allow the men to smoke their cigars and drink their wine. That was when the real talk began, the kind of talk that made the heart beat faster.

Victor heard many reminiscences of "the old days," stories as colorful and romantic and full of hair's-breadth escapes as any adventure novel. A good many of these stories were repeated solely for Victor's benefit, so that the boy might learn something of Ireland's history and the men who made it.

"I remember," Grandpa Lover would say in that pleasant Irish accent of his, not quite a brogue, yet "flannel" enough to remind the hearer that an educated Dublin man was speaking, "I remember the way we used to listen with such pride and fear and dread to the talk about Emmet's doings. I was six when the poor boy led his unsuccessful revolt against the Viceroy at Dublin Castle. When the revolt failed and Emmet had to go into hiding, his friends tried to persuade him to flee to France, but the romantic fellow would not leave his beloved

Irish sweetheart. His love for the colleen was his undoing. On one of his visits to her home, he was taken prisoner. A mortal grief to dear Thomas Moore it was, too. Moore's song, *She is far from the land where her young lover sleeps,* is in memory of this ill-fated love.

"And, oh, the keening when valiant young Emmet was hanged. It was a thing to make a child remember his native land's sorrows. Emmet's last words were: 'When my country takes her place among the nations of the earth, then, and not till then, let my epitaph be written.' The poor boy and the gallant martyr that he was, to be sure!

"I tell you, I saw things to make the hair stand straight on your head and make the flesh to crawl when I was a green *gossoon* (boy). We lived near Marlborough Green and the dark buildings where infamous John Claudius Beresford put Irish political prisoners through a brutal inquisition to try to get them to inform on their comrades. Th' dirty divil! (Sam Lover always lapsed into broad Irish when his emotions were thoroughly roused.) Many's the tale of the pitch cap and the cruel whip I heard along with the other *childher,* and on our way to school we ran past that black place as fast as our feet could take us!"

Victor's eyes grew round with wonder as he listened to these tales of Irish rebellion. He came to understand the burning desire for economic and political freedom which no famine or persecution could quench.

As he listened, not only many of the ideas but also the very manner of speech of these educated Irish people were absorbed by Victor. In spite of his education in Germany and the later years in America, where he became a citizen of the United States, Victor Herbert maintained to the end of his days the fascinating tripping speech of the land of his birth.

Victor's mother was full of Irish lore, too, telling her son tales of Leprechaun and banshee and other Irish "little folk"; singing for him mournful Irish lullabies; or reciting for him fanciful little poems similar to those which Samuel Lover sprinkled lavishly through his novel *Handy Andy*. One of Victor's favorites from *Handy Andy* was the ballad of the pious Quaker and Jim Barlow, the outlaw, with its refrain "Heighho! Yea thee and nay thee."

Fanny Herbert, like her sister Meta, was artistic, but her talents leaned mainly toward music. She was an accomplished pianist, of whom it has been said that, had she so desired, she could have had a successful concert career. She chose instead to practice her art for herself and her family and friends. At "The Vine" she contributed her share to the musical evenings, of which there were many.

Musicians were always among the visitors. Of the famous men who brought their music to Sevenoaks when Fanny and Victor stayed there, two are of special interest: Michael Balfe, Irish composer of *The Bohemian Girl*, that blithe operetta which holds charm for modern audiences as it did for the audiences of the early nineteenth century, was one. The other was Alfredo Piatti, famous Italian 'cellist. Who knows how much these two men and their art may have influenced a boy's early impressions, a boy destined to become famous both as 'cellist and composer of operetta?

Fanny's love of things Irish was reflected in her music. Always on the piano was a familiar book—a collection of traditional Irish airs edited and arranged by Sir John Stevenson, with words written by poet-musician Thomas Moore. This was the book of *Irish Melodies*, as well known and well loved today as it was nearly one hundred fifty years ago.

Recalling his early delight in these Irish songs, composer Victor Herbert once spoke of how he missed folk music in the United States:

"I long for music which shall have the intensity of appeal of the folksong. It was not for nothing that my mother kept Moore's *Irish Melodies* on the piano and played and sang them until they were part of my being."

The composer recurred again and again in later life to the

debt he owed the influence of Irish folksong. Proudly he pointed out:

"Ireland presents a rich field for the musician. . . . Musically, the Irish are descended from the harpists who played and sang their melodies at Court and throughout the towns and cities of the country. The harp, indeed, came to symbolize Ireland. Certainly, no other land ever placed its musical instrument on its flag."

Others were quick to sense the Celtic charm of some of Herbert's music. Alice Nielsen tried to describe this quality:

"It had a lilt born of the Irish in him," she said; "the same quality in music that the Irish have in their eye. . . . A sort of minor key thing with a bit of an eerie catch in it. . . ."

By way of illustrating her point, the singer sang a few bars from one of Herbert's operettas, *The Fortune Teller.* She might have cited any number of themes. *Eileen,* for example, is filled with quaint Gaelic conceits. But surely no better example exists than Herbert's treatment of an old Irish air, *The Red Lark.* The composer's arrangement for 'cello and piano contains phrases of haunting beauty:

The child Victor was not slow to learn that his grandfather was a famous teller of tales, with many published novels to his credit. His *Legends and Stories of Ireland* alone would have secured his literary fame.

"Tell me a story," was a familiar request of Victor's. "One of *your* stories, grandfather. Please."

"A tale is it?" Samuel Lover's eyes would twinkle, and he

would begin some story from one of his books or plays, like his famous *Tale of the Gridiron.*

"The gridiron," he explained, "is the favorite cooking utensil of the Irish poor, who live in sod huts with only a turf fire on the hearth, some three-legged stools, a prized dresser, perhaps, with a few bits of Delft ware for display, and maybe a cracked mirror for the women folk to look into on Sunday mornings to see their bonnets.

"But this is no tale of the Irish countryside, mind! This is a tale"—and here Lover lapsed playfully into his Irish brogue—"of a stout boy who wint to say and was shipwrecked along av siv'rel av his fellow mariners, not to overlook the captain av the ship. They got into a small boat whin the big boat wint to Davy Jones' Locker, and in the words av the darlin' av a lad who's the hero av the tale:

" 'We prepared for the worst and put out the boat, and got a sack av bishkits, and a cashk av pork, and a kag av wather, and a thrifle av rum aboord, and any other little matthers we could think av in the mortial hurry we wor in. . . .'

"So—" Sam Lover continued. "Days and days they drifthed, with nothing to be seen but the sun and the say and the sky, and though the say and the sky is mighty purty things in thimsilves, Victor, throth they're no great things whin you've nothing else to look at for a week together. . . .

"Afther a time, the crew in the boat caught sight av land, and by the captain's reckoning it had to be the coast av France.

" 'We have pork left, Captain,' said our Irish hero. 'With your lave, I'll be landing here and seek the loan av a gridiron to cook it on.'

" 'But can ye speak French?' inquired the captain.

" 'Parlay voo Frangsay!' said Paddy proudly.

"So he was set ashore, and made his way to a cottage where a family of French were eating their meal outdoors on a long table. Paddy addressed himself to an elderly fellow who sat at the head.

" 'Parlay voo Frangsay, sir. And God go with you kindly. We're a sthranded boatful av saymen as ever wor shipthwrecked on the coast av France. We have a cashk av pork aboord our small boat, but nothing to cook it on. So plaze, sir, will you have the kindness to lind us the loan av a gridiron?'

"The old Frenchman and his family, who understood not a word of this request, stared wonderingly. Poor Paddy, who thought his 'Parlay voo Frangsay' enough French for anybody, repeated his request in a louder tone, fearing that the old gentleman was deaf.

"Again and again he made his polite request for 'the lind av a loan av a gridiron.' Each 'Parlay voo Frangsay' brought forth a vigorous nod of assent from the family, which actually guessed that the strange sound meant 'Do you speak French?' But the rest of his speech was a mystery to them; so they sat still and looked puzzled.

"Paddy's temper was rising (as Irish tempers are likely to do), and finally with a few eloquent remarks concerning what he thought was an inhospitable reception, he stalked back to the crew on the beach.

" 'Well, sir,' he reported to his captain. 'The divil a bit av a gridiron the ould Frenchman would gi' me. And so with that, "The curse av the hungry on you, you ould negarly villain!" says I. "The back av me hand and the sowl av me fut to you, that you may want a gridiron yourself yit!' "

"And in truth, this incident always remained a source of wonder to poor Paddy. In recalling the incident in afther times, he would shake his head wonderingly and say solemnly, 'Often sense it is that I've thought it was *remarkable!*' "

Sam Lover had used the story of the gridiron to good advantage during his lecture tour in the United States in the years 1846-1848. His lectures were really humorous entertainments called *Irish Evenings*. Nathaniel Hawthorne, author of *Twice Told Tales, The House of the Seven Gables, The Scarlet Letter*, had sponsored this clever Irishman who was a whole show with his songs, dances, and stories in Irish brogue.

Samuel Lover's first appearance was at the Stuyvesant Institute in New York. An enthusiastic audience (all of whom could afford the enormous admission price of one dollar—enormous, that is, for the year 1846) assured Lover of the success of his venture.

The critics were kind, too, and the *New York Herald* next day reported:

"All the songs were of his own composition and, indeed, all new to this country except two or three. *The Widow Machree, The Low-Backed Car, Rory O'More,* and others created a perfect storm of laughter and applause.

"The story of the Gridiron was a rich treat, lighted up by the inimitable drollery which marked its recital."

One of the songs *(The Low-Backed Car)* which made such a hit at these *Irish Evenings* was a favorite of Victor's, too. Many years later, when he was known as a famous composer, he liked to play this little song for his friends. Many a visitor to his New York studio was treated to a singing 'cello interpretation of this beloved song, words and music of which were written by Sam Lover:

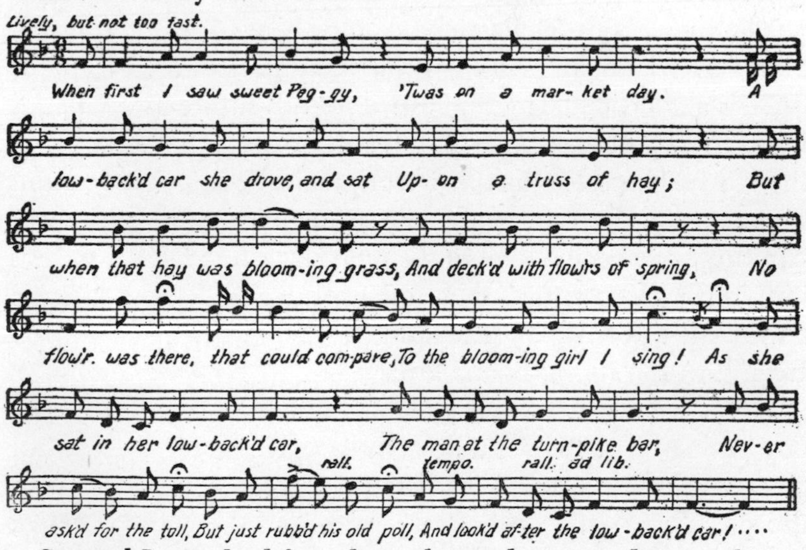

Samuel Lover had found much to admire, and some things to laugh at, in the United States and Canada. Natural wonders like Niagara Falls made their impression, and after he had described these falls, he was always sure to remark seriously, " 'Tis a power of wather is in it, darlin', to be sure!"

He liked the people of America, too, even though he sometimes did not understand their ways. "Sure, whin you're standing before one of thim restrained audiences in New England it's like being a voyager among icebergs!" was one of the observations he made in his *American-Irish Evenings*, which he presented profitably throughout England on his return home.

March 17 was a day of celebration at "The Vine," when all the Irish friends came in carriages from London to smoke a pipe over the "Patrick's bowl." Grandfather Lover was careful to explain to Victor the significance of the day.

"March 17 is the day dedicated to Patrick, patron saint of Ireland. Around the name, Victor, legends and tradition have gathered like clusters of Irish moss; and every good Irishman, Catholic or Protestant, has a warm place in his heart for the old saint and the shamrock, which together are a sort of symbol of *Erin go bragh* (Ireland forever!)."

"Tell me about St. Patrick," Victor begged. And, as usual, Sam Lover launched with zest on the telling of an Irish tale:

"It's a good tale, lad, and as full of adventure as a Charles Lever novel. It has been put together piece by piece from the old Irish and English manuscripts in the monasteries, and some parts of it are missing still. A deal of varnish and overpainting have been added to the picture with the years, but we know enough to scrape those off until we find the authentic parts of the portrait of that human, vigorous man who loved Ireland with a warm, poetic love.

"Patrick was born a long while ago, maybe in what we now call Wales. His mother must have been from Gaul (modern France), since it is believed that she was related to the great St. Martin of Tours. Patrick's father was a native Briton, a man of some influence in his community, a friend of the Roman conquerors of Britain, and a Christian. Patrick spoke the language of the Celts and the Latin of the Romans.

"When Patrick was about sixteen years old, he was taken captive by some of the wild tribesmen from the north, who made frequent raids on the Roman settlements in Britain. The boy was taken to Dalaradia, the present county of Antrim in Ireland, where he was sold as a slave to a chieftain named Milchu. For six years he tended his master's sheep in the valley of the Braid and on the slopes of Slemish, a black basalt hill of scanty verdure near the modern town of Ballymena.

"During his years as a slave in Ireland, Patrick learned to speak the dialect of the Irish Celts. He became familiar also with the pagan rites of Druidism, of which his master was a high priest. The druids worshiped the sun and the mistletoe, and may have offered up human sacrifices on their stone altars. You can be sure that they ruled their people in matters of government as well as religion.

"In his twenty-first year Patrick fled his servitude. Turning his steps toward the west, he walked to the coast, and became one of the crew of a ship ready to sail with a cargo of Irish wolf-hounds. Where he landed on the Continent and how long he wandered afterward we can only guess; but he made his way finally to Tours, where for some years he studied with his kinsman, St. Martin. Later he went to Auxerre to study under St. Germain. Here Patrick was promoted to the priesthood, and here came to him a vision. He seemed to see the children of the land by the Western Sea crying, 'Come back to Erin and walk once more amongst us.'

"With several companions, Patrick set out for the land of the Irish. The little band of missionaries landed at the mouth of the Vantry River, and Patrick set out at once for Dalaradia, where he had once been the slave of Milchu. On the way, he was very successful in converting the people to Christianity. News of his triumphs preceded him to the fort of Milchu. In a frenzy, the old Druid gathered his treasures together within the fort, set fire to the buildings, and threw himself into the flames. The ancient record states:

" 'His pride could not endure the thought of being vanquished by his former slave.'

"He knew full well, this Patrick, how to turn the ceremonies of the Druid faith inside out and use them for his own purposes. When the chieftains assembled at Tara to celebrate a special Druid feast, Patrick commanded the attention of the people by a daring stroke.

"It was the custom for the Irish to extinguish their hearth-fires and not relight them until the ceremonial fire at Tara had been kindled. The Druid priests had convinced them that terrible punishment would overtake anyone who disregarded this custom.

"Patrick challenged this superstition by lighting an early fire on a hill in plain view of the hill called Tara. Nothing terrible happened to him, of course. The people, being reasonable, began to question other things their priests told them, and listened with greater respect to this new priest who had come among them.

"There followed a battle of wits at Tara. During his speech, Patrick is said to have plucked a leaf of the shamrock to illustrate with its triple leaf on one stem the idea of the Trinity. That is how the shamrock became the emblem of Christian Ireland.

"Patrick must have been the better man that day; for he came away from the council with the permission of the Druid chieftains to preach his faith unmolested throughout Ireland. He did not always go unchallenged, however. Once he was loaded with chains and condemned to death. Somehow, he always managed to escape.

"After a long, busy, and successful life, Patrick died somewhere in Dalaradia, the district where he had been a slave-shepherd. His wanderings through Ireland always brought him back to this locality. There he must have felt happy and at home.

"It is not known exactly where he was buried. Several towns claim his grave—and a good many Irish heads have been cracked in disputes over the matter. Tradition has it that his bier was laid on a wagon to which four white oxen were yoked. The oxen were allowed to move without human direction. Where they came to a stop, Patrick was buried; and this place was henceforward called Downpatrick.

"Patrick came to Ireland to instruct his adopted people, but he stayed to learn much from his pupils. The poetry of the Celt crept into his bones. It was a true Irishman who blessed the people of Munster thus:

> 'A blessing on the Munster people—
> Men, youths, and women;
> A blessing on the land
> That yields them fruit.
> A blessing on every treasure
> That shall be produced on their plains
> Without anyone being in want of help.
> God's blessing on Munster.
> A blessing on their peaks,
> On their bare flagstones,
> A blessing on their glens,
> A blessing on their ridges.
> Like the sand of the sea under ships,
> Be the number of their hearths;
> On slopes, on plains,
> On mountains, on hills, a blessing.'"

Such happy times as these, when his grandfather spoke eloquently of Ireland, its history and its culture, were surely in Victor Herbert's mind when in later years he composed the music for *Sweet Harp of the Days That Are Gone.* The words of this song are a poem by Samuel Lover. Herbert's beautiful setting for them was a tribute both to his grandfather and to the Irish folk, who were dear to Lover's heart.

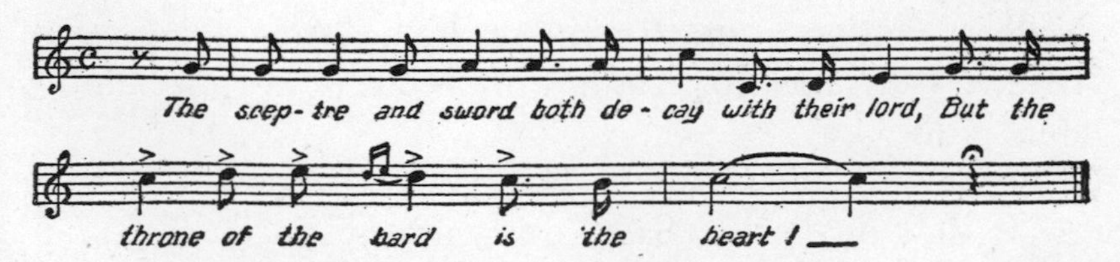

Land Beyond the Rhine

1866-1875. In these years, dynamite was invented by Alfred Nobel, donor of the Nobel Peace Prize. The United States bought Alaska from Russia. The Trans-Atlantic Cable was laid. The Franco-Prussian War came to an end with the surrender of Paris, and Bismarck succeeded in uniting the German states into the German Empire. The Suez Canal was opened. Chicago was swept by disastrous fire. The last spike was driven in the Union Pacific Railroad. The typewriter became practical. Bell was about to patent his first telephone. Ulysses Simpson Grant was President of the United States. Blackface minstrels had just discovered the song *Shoo Fly, Don't Bother Me.* Harrigan and Hart were making *The Mulligan Guard* famous. Dame Fashion decreed that women should wear bustles. Men began to wear colored shirts with their business suits. In 1867, in Vienna, Strauss' *Beautiful Blue Danube* was played for the first time.

FANNY LOVER'S usually serene young face was earnestly thoughtful as she poured tea for her father and stepmother one chilly spring afternoon.

"Victor worries me, father," she was saying. "I am not at all easy in my mind about him."

"Victor?" Grandpa Lover looked up with the energetic, birdlike motion characteristic of him. "Are you serious, Fanny? Why, that boy is as healthy as one of my prize Shropshire rams!"

Both Fanny and Grandma Mary laughed at this remark.

"It isn't his health, Sam," his wife explained. "Fanny is

concerned about Victor's education. Now that he's seven, he ought to have some formal education, and be with boys his own age."

"And I am determined to take him abroad for his schooling," added Fanny.

Grandpa Lover sat up even straighter in his chair, so that he looked like an eager and somewhat mischievous child, who had just overheard something not meant for his ears.

"Well, Fanny! I always said you were a girl of more than ordinary common sense. I didn't want to meddle, but I have been hoping!"

Grandma Mary chuckled. "Meddle! Why, that's all you've been doing, you old humbug. You and all that fine talk about the German schools. How many hours have I heard you and Charles Lever go on about that man—what's his name? You know, the one who grew children in a garden like Contrary Mary."

"Whisht, woman! A man must havc his opinion!" Sam Lover smiled at his wife. "And it's positively irreverent ye are, too. Contrary Mary, yourself!" Then he grew quite serious as he explained, "The man you speak of so freely is Froebel—Friedrich Wilhelm August Froebel, dead these last fourteen years, God rest his soul, to be sure! And the garden you mention is the *Kindergarten*. And mark my words, both of you. This kindergarten idea will spread all over the world; for it's a fine method of teaching young children, since it's based on kindness and common sense, not to mention science.

"And then there's Herbart (pretty close to your name, eh, Fanny?). Johann Herbart made a wonderful contribution to education. He saw that all studies are related, that you can't have much knowledge of history, for example, if you don't know geography and literature and music and—"

"Enough, father!" cried Fanny, laughing. "You have had me convinced of all this for years! Behold! In me you see a disciple!"

Lover curbed his enthusiasm and kept smiling at his daughter over his teacup while she talked.

"Yes, father, I have gone over the whole thing, and my mind is made up. Victor shall not go to school in this country. And all things being considered, entering Victor in a German Gymnasium seems the best way."

The *Gymnasium* Fanny spoke of was a sort of preparatory school, corresponding to upper-grade and high schools in the United States.

"Good girl, good girl," said her father approvingly.

Grandma Mary found one flaw in the scheme. "But to let them go so far away from us, Sam! Just a young woman alone, and a child! Do you really think it wise, Fanny?"

Lover smiled as he looked at his daughter, so calm, independent, intelligent. Firmness of will was in every line of her handsome face, and the very way she sat and walked seemed to speak to the onlooker, saying, "I know where I am going, exactly how to get there, just what I am going to do when I arrive, and I need no help, thank you."

Fanny patted Grandma Mary's hand reassuringly. "Don't you worry, dear. Victor and I shall be able to look after ourselves nicely. We have a little income of our own, and I know something about the Continent, remember. It does seem the best way, when all is said and done."

"And I sincerely hope all is said, if not yet done," declared Grandpa Lover. "Is it decided then, Fanny?"

"Decided!" Fanny jumped up briskly from her chair. "I believe that I shall go up and sort over our clothes right now. Then if I may have the carriage this afternoon, I shall make a few calls and arrange to have two portable baths sent down from London. There is absolutely no way to get a proper bath when you're traveling on the Continent, and—well, English or Irish, we must have our daily tub!"

"I declare, I never saw anything like that girl!" Grandma Mary stared after her stepdaughter, who was crossing the room with that athletic, swinging walk of hers that never seemed to go with the long skirts and corseted waist. "She'll be on her way before the week is out!"

"Sensible girl. No frilly *can't-do-this, can't-do-that* about her." Sam Lover smiled and poured himself another cup of tea.

Just as Grandma Mary had foreseen, Fanny's energetic preparations went forward without delay. Letters to the Continent were written, passports procured, tickets bought. Dressmakers arrived with pins, scissors, and tape measures, and the serious business of turning yards of silks and suitings into traveling clothes was begun. In due course, the portable baths arrived from London.

With the exception of this added pleasant excitement, life went on much as usual at "The Vine." Victor had his daily piano lesson from his mother, and practiced his simple exercises. Grandma bustled about, tending to her many household duties—seeing to it that every room was dusted and aired and provided with spring flowers from the garden; making sure that lavender was tucked away with the freshly laundered linens; not forgetting to supervise the basting and seasoning of the savory roasts of beef and mutton in the kitchen. Samuel Lover worked serenely in his studio, creating the delicate miniatures so much in demand in English society.

In the music room, the Lover family and their dinner guests gathered as usual round the piano, where Fanny played softly and somewhat sadly. Now that it was settled that she was to take up her life in an alien land, she was finding it none too easy to say good-by to the pleasant home in Sevenoaks. To cheer her up, Sam Lover would sometimes take up his guitar and strike bright, metallic chords to accompany a gay song or jig tune. Victor liked to watch his grandfather strumming melodies from the guitar. Very early in his life, the music of stringed instruments appealed to him more than the music of the piano.

Charles Lever arrived one evening to join in a send-off party for Fanny and Victor. He was in high spirits and entertained the company with one of the droll yarns for which he was famous.

With infectious humor, no less delightful because it comments with devastating honesty on the ugly theme of human deceit and avarice, the story tells of a really unique deal in real estate. Charles Lever chose to tell it in the first person, making believe that he himself was the Irish boy who had observed with mingled dismay and amusement the strange doings of the tale.

Con Cregan's Legacy

I was born in a little cabin on the borders of Meath and King's County; it stood on a small triangular bit of ground, beside a crossroad; and, although the place was surveyed every ten years or so, they were never able to say to which county we belonged, there being just the same number of arguments for one side as for the other—a circumstance, many believed, that decided my father in his original choice of the residence; for while, under the "disputed boundary question," he paid no rates or county cess, he always made a point of voting at both county elections! This may seem to indicate that my parent was of a naturally acute habit; and indeed the way he became possessed of the bit of ground will confirm that impression.

There was nobody of the rank of gentry in the parish, nor even squireen; the richest being a farmer, a snug old fellow, one Henry M'Cabe, that had two sons, who were always fighting between themselves which was to have the old man's money. Peter, the elder, doing everything to injure Mat, and Mat never backward in paying off the obligation. At last Mat, tired out in the struggle, resolved he would bear no more. He took leave of his father one night, and next day set off for Dublin, and 'listed in the "Buffs." Three weeks after, he sailed for India; and the old man, overwhelmed by grief, took to his bed, and never arose from it after.

Not that his death was any way sudden, for he lingered on for months longer; Peter always teasing him to make his will, and be revenged on "the dirty spalpeen" that disgraced the family: but old Harry as stoutly resisting, and declaring that whatever he owned should be fairly divided between them.

These disputes between them were well known in the neighborhood. Few of the country people passing the house at night but had overheard the old man's weak reedy voice, and Peter's deep hoarse one in altercation. When at last—it was on a Sunday night—all was still and quiet in the house, not a word, not a footstep could be heard, no more than if it were uninhabited, the neighbors looked knowingly at each other, and wondered if the old man were worse—if he were dead!

It was a little after midnight that a knock came to the door of our cabin. I heard it first, for I used to sleep in a little snug basket near the fire; but I didn't speak, for I was frightened. It was repeated still louder, and then came a cry: "Con Cregan; Con, I say, open the door! I want you." I knew the voice well; it was Peter M'Cabe's, but I pretended to be fast asleep, and snored loudly. At last my father unbolted the door, and I heard him say, "Oh, Mr. Peter, what's the matter? Is the ould man worse?"

"Faix that's what he is! for he's dead!"

"Glory be his bed! when did it happen?"

"About an hour ago," said Peter, in a voice that even I from my corner could perceive was greatly agitated. "He died like an ould haythen, Con, and never made a will!"

"That's bad," says my father, for he was always a polite man, and said whatever was pleasing to the company.

"It is bad," said Peter, "but it would be worse if we couldn't help it. Listen to me now, Corny, I want ye to help me in this business, and here's five guineas in goold if ye do what I bid ye. You know that ye were always reckoned the image of my father, and before he took ill ye were mistaken for each other every day of the week."

"Anan!" said my father; for he was getting frightened at the notion, without knowing why.

"Well, what I want is, for ye to come over to the house, and get into the bed."

"Not besides the corpse?" said my father, trembling.

"By no means, but by yourself; and you're to pretend to be my father, and that ye want to make yer will before ye die; and then I'll send for the neighbors, and Billy Scanlan, the schoolmaster, and ye'll tell him what to write, laving all the farm and everything to me—ye understand. And as the neighbors will see ye, and hear yer voice, it will never be believed but that it was himself that did it."

"The room must be very dark," says my father.

"To be sure it will, but have no fear! Nobody will dare come nigh the bed; and ye'll only have to make a cross with yer pen under the name."

"And the priest?" said my father.

"My father quarreled with him last week about the Easter dues: and Father Tom said he'd not give him the 'rites': and that's lucky now! Come along now, quick, for we've no time to lose: it must be all finished before the day breaks."

My father did not lose much time at his toilet, for he just wrapped his big coat 'round him, and slipping on his brogues, left the house. I sat up in the basket and listened till they were gone some minutes; and then, in a costume as light as my parent's, set out after them, but by bad luck I fell into a bog hole, and only escaped being drowned by chance. As it was, when I reached the house, the performance had already begun.

I think I see the whole scene this instant before my eyes, as I sat on a little window with one pane, and that a broken one, and surveyed the proceeding. It was a large room, at one end of which was a bed, and beside it a table, with physic bottles, and spoons, and teacups; a little farther off was another table, at which sat Billy Scanlan, with all manner of writing materials before him. The country people sat two, sometimes three deep round the walls, all intently eager and anxious for the coming event. Peter himself went from place to place, trying to smother his grief, and occasionally helping the company to whisky—which was supplied with more than accustomed liberality.

All my consciousness of the deceit and trickery could not deprive the scene of a certain solemnity. The misty distance of the half-lighted room; the highly wrought expression of the country people's faces, never more intensely excited than at some moment of this kind; the low, deep-drawn breathings, unbroken save by a sigh or a sob—the tribute of affectionate sorrow to some lost friend, whose memory was thus forcibly brought back: these, I repeat it, were all so real, that, as I looked, a thrilling sense of awe stole over me, and I actually shook with fear.

A low faint cough, from the dark corner where the bed stood, seemed to cause even a deeper stillness; and then in a silence where the buzzing of a fly would have been heard, my father said: "Where's Billy Scanlan? I want to make my will!"

"He's here, father!" said Peter, taking Billy by the hand and leading him to the bedside.

"Write what I bid ye, Billy, and be quick; for I haven't a long time afore me here. I die a good Catholic, though Father O'Rafferty won't give me the 'rites'!"

A general chorus of muttered "Oh! musha, musha," was now heard through the room; but whether in grief over the sad fate of the dying man, or the unflinching priest, is hard to say.

"I die in peace with all my neighbors and all mankind!"

Another chorus of the company seemed to approve these charitable expressions.

"I bequeath unto my son, Peter—and never was there a better son, or a decenter boy!—have you that down? I bequeath unto my son, Peter, the whole of my two farms of Killimundoonery and Knocksheboora, with the fallow meadows behind

Lynch's house, the forge, and the right of turf on the Dooran bog. I give him, and much good may it do him, Lanty Cassarn's acre, and the Luary field, with the limekiln; and that reminds me that my mouth is just as dry; let me taste what ye have in the jug." Here the dying man took a very hearty pull, and seemed considerably refreshed by it. "Where was I, Billy Scanlan?" says he. "Oh, I remember, at the limekiln; I leave him—that's Peter, I mean—the two potato gardens at Noonan's Well, and it is the elegant fine crops grows there."

"Ain't you gettin' wake, father, darlin'?" says Peter, who began to be afraid of my father's loquaciousness; for, to say the truth, the punch got into his head, and he was greatly disposed to talk.

"I am, Peter, my son," says he, "I am getting wake, just touch my lips again with the jug. Ah, Peter, Peter, you watered the drink!"

"No, indeed, father, but it's the taste is lavin' you," says Peter; and again a low chorus of compassionate pity murmured through the cabin.

"Well, I'm nearly done now," says my father, "there's only one little plot of ground remaining; and I put it on you, Peter —as ye wish to live a good man, and die with the same easy heart I do now—that ye mind my last words to ye here. Are ye listening? Are the neighbors listening?"

"Yes, sir. Yes, father. We're all minding!" chorused the audience.

"Well, then, it's my last will and testament, and—give me over the jug"—here he took a long drink—"I bequeath the little plot at the crossroads to poor Con Cregan; for he has a very heavy charge, and is as honest and as hard-working a man as ever I knew. Be a friend to him, Peter, dear; never let him want while ye have it yourself; think of me on my deathbed whenever he asks ye for any trifle. Is it down, Billy Scanlan? the two acres at the cross to Con Cregan, and his heirs in *secla seclorum*. Ah, blessed be the saints! but I feel my heart lighter after that," says he; "a good work makes an easy con-

The Red Mill

science; and now I'll drink all the company's good health, and many happy returns—"

What he was going to add, there's no saying, but Peter, who was now terribly frightened at the lively tone the sick man was assuming, hurried all the people away into another room, to let his father die in peace.

When they were all gone, Peter slipped back to my father, who was putting on his brogues in a corner: "Con," says he, "ye did it well; but sure that was a joke about the two acres at the cross."

"Of course it was, Peter," says he. "Sure it was all a joke for the matter of that. Won't I make the neighbors laugh hearty tomorrow when I tell them all about it!"

"You wouldn't be mean enough to betray me?" says Peter, trembling with fright.

"Sure, ye wouldn't be mean enough to go against yer father's dying words?" says my father; "the last sentence ever he spoke"; and here he gave a low wicked laugh, that made myself shake with fear.

"Very well, Con!" says Peter, holding out his hand, "a bargain's a bargain; ye're a deep fellow, that's all!" And so it ended; and my father slipped quietly home over the bog, mighty well satisfied with the legacy he had left himself.

And thus we became the owners of the little spot known to this day as Con's Acre.

Grandma Mary was inclined to think that dishonesty like Con Cregan's and his scheming neighbor's was hardly a subject for humor, but her husband chided her gently for her view.

"Whisht, woman! Ridicule is the best scalpel to lay bare the bones of the ugly in life. Better to laugh an idea to death than to burn it at the stake."

And so it was, with Irish music and story the last evening at Sevenoaks was spent. Victor was not too young to sense that a door was about to close gently but finally on something very rare and very beautiful in his life.

On a brisk, windy day in the early summer of 1866 young Victor stood beside his mother and their luggage waiting to board a channel boat which was to take them from Dover, England, to Calais, France. From Calais, they would travel by easy post stages through Belgium and Luxemburg, and then into the land beyond the river Rhine—the Black Forest region of the Duchy of Baden and the Kingdom of Württemberg. These German provinces touched on Lake Constance, on the shores of which Fanny proposed to settle for a time.

The little boat crossed the English Channel in rough seas. The spray that wet the decks was cold, but Victor and his mother were warmly bundled up in their woolen tweed cloaks. Toward the end of the crossing, they stood eagerly by the rail, straining their eyes for a view of the shore of the Continent. The wind-blown fog whipped even higher color into their pink cheeks and added a brighter sparkle to their eyes.

Fanny had need of her Irish sense of humor many times on that trip. To begin the series of awkward incidents (nearly all of which had to do with Fanny's portable bath), there was a baffling delay while the port officials and customs officers at Calais consulted each other on the subject of why an Englishwoman and a child should have so much luggage. A Europe which is usually either at war or on the point of war is inclined to be suspicious.

"These bags, bags, bags, and more bags! And leather trunks! And these other strange affairs—portable baths, you say? How do they work?"

Fanny, a woman of spirit, became exasperated. "I'll show you!" And to the amazement of the customs officers and the amusement of her fellow-passengers, she insisted on having her collapsible wood and canvas tubs uncrated. She herself set up one of the baths and plumped astonished Victor into its dry interior to give the officials a sketchy idea of how a lad and lady from England took a bath.

The Frenchmen were amazed, and frankly delighted, with this determined Irish colleen, who, many years later, was to make a visit to her son in New York and (to Victor's huge enjoyment) proceed to shock and amuse the people of Manhattan by smoking cigarettes in public—this in the nineteenth century, when women who smoked did so behind the closed doors of their bedrooms. There is no doubt that Fanny was a woman who dared to do as she pleased, a trait which her son inherited and turned to good account in his later musical career.

Victor's eager eyes widened with excitement on that Continental journey. Their way took the two adventurous Herberts north from Calais to Lille and Brussels and across Belgium to the Duchy of Luxemburg. The trip down the Moselle River to Metz and historic Strassburg brought them into the sunny vineyard country.

The city of Strassburg recalled to Victor's mind a folk song which he had heard in his grandfather's house:

> "O Strassburg, O Strassburg, du wunderschöne Stadt!"
>
> (O Strassburg, O Strassburg, you wonderfully fair city!)

Crossing the Rhine River, Fanny and Victor were in the region of the Black Forest, which lies in Baden, one of the independent states which made up the Germany of that day. There were about three hundred of these little states in all, and not until 1871 would they be united under one ruler. Meanwhile, there was a bewildering crazy quilt of little Courts, presided over by kings or princes, archbishops, or electors. It was during Victor's schooldays in Stuttgart that all these states became dominated by the powerful military province of Prussia and agreed to form one nation, Germany, with an emperor called a kaiser (the German equivalent of Caesar or Czar).

In a tiny village in Baden, the travelers from England remained to rest for several days. The Black Forest, Victor soon learned, was a region rich in folklore, a fairy-tale land of song and story. This was the land beyond the Rhine, with its legends and tales of

> ". . . days of old
> When knights were bold,
> And barons held their sway."

Like most of the German states, Baden was curiously placid, even sleepy. Though this very sleepiness was the principal charm of the German villages for travelers of the day, who mistook inertia for repose, it was not a healthful condition. Powerful and devastating forces were already in motion, and instead of facing and overcoming them, the German people, like ostriches, buried their heads in sand and pretended that there was no danger.

There were some thinkers among them who saw and pointed out the dangers ahead for sleepwalkers. One of these was Heinrich Heine, a great poet with a pen more caustic than the French Voltaire's. A delightful satire, reminiscent of Dean Swift's *Gulliver's Travels,* poked fun at the incompetent rulers and their placid subjects, all of whom refused to see the danger of Bismarck's policy of "blood and iron" and the shadow of Prussian militarism. Heine's words are frequently charged with bitter irony:

"Our Elector," wrote Heine, "was a fine gentleman, a great lover of the arts, and himself clever with his fingers. He founded the picture gallery at Dusseldorf, and in the Observatory in that city they still show a very artistic set of wooden boxes, one inside the other, made by himself in his leisure hours, of which he had twenty-four every day.

"In those days the princes were not overworked mortals as they are today. Their crowns sat very firmly on their heads, and at night they just drew their nightcaps over them and slept in peace, while peacefully at their feet slept their peoples; and when these woke up in the morning they said, 'Good morning, Father,' and the princes replied, 'Good morning, dear children.'"

However, for a boy, unaware of the grim political plots hatching in the minds of power-mad politicians and generals, only the charm and peaceful beauty of winding streets, gabled houses, and Old World shops mattered. Through many-paned windows set in dormers, like and yet unlike the shop windows in faraway Sevenoaks, Victor peered at the wonderful wood carvings. These had been made on cold winter nights by peasant families living on small farms in the Black Forest.

Many of these carvings were mechanical toys for which the craftsmen of Baden are noted. The cleverest of these were the little wooden men dressed like hunters, nodding their heads when a spring was wound. Their pursed lips seemed to whistle the tunes which really came from music-box bodies.

One of the favorite tunes of the "whistlers" was *Wandrers Nachtlied* (Wanderer's Night Song), a melody which Friedrich Kuhlau had written for a poem by Goethe:

> "Über allen Gipfeln ist Ruh;
> In allen Wipfeln spürst du
> Kaum einen Hauch;
> Die Vöglein schweigen im Walde."

> (On all mountain peaks, silence reigns;
> In all the treetops you can perceive
> Hardly a stir.
> The little birds are quiet in the woods.)

Several of the little men whistled measures from the German Christmas songs—*O Tannenbaum* (*O Fir Tree*) and the well-known *Die heilige Nacht* (*Holy Night*). A jolly fat fellow delighted his listeners with

"O du lieber Augustin, Augustin, Augustin,
O du lieber Augustin, alles ist hin!"

(Oh, beloved Augustin, Augustin, Augustin,
Oh, beloved Augustin, all, all is lost!)

There were clocks set in frames with intricate acorn and oak-leaf designs. Their busy little pendulums swung back and forth dizzily. There were toy windmills, sets of miniature furniture, and tiny replicas of the villages of the Black Forest. These villages were complete with farm houses and dairy houses displaying little churns and shelves of round cheeses, and landscaped with little black fir trees, copies of the big black firs from which the forest region takes its name. Dolls and puppets, wooden soldiers and small carts, wagons and carriages were carefully made and brightly painted. Victor studied them all with delight.

The boy's German education was already begun. These early impressions were most important to Victor Herbert, whose Irish and English heritage was greatly modified by the German environment of his youth. He always preferred the substantial German foods. He loved German and Austrian music, particularly the gladsome three-four rhythm of the waltz, which the Strauss family made known to all the world. Many of composer Herbert's most successful compositions were like Viennese songs and dances; and he never wrote an operetta without including a waltz or two.

Victor learned German industry and pride in good workmanship, too. These traits stood him in good stead in later years when he was turning out his more than forty operettas and long compositions for 'cello and orchestra, and numerous pieces for piano and voice.

Above all, Herbert added to his Irish wit and humor that tremendous zest for life which the Germans call *Gemütlichkeit*. The composer's love of good company, good food, good jokes made him a pleasant co-worker and business associate.

Many of the shops in Baden displayed books for children. Many of these contained stories about Hänsel and Gretel, Rumpelstilzchen, the Goose Girl, Tom Thumb, Snow White, and the Bremen-Town Musicians. Not a few of these quaint folk were "natives" of the Black Forest. For hundreds of years the peasants had told fanciful tales about them, but none of these stories was written down until two sober old scholars decided to go from farm to farm and listen to the old grandmothers repeat the old fairy tales. The brothers Grimm published their collection, and soon translations were made into English and many other languages.

Several shops displayed violins and 'cellos, and a miscellany of bows, chunks of resin, and catgut strings. Victor stood for a long time looking at these things. For him some special magic lurked in the mute strings, which needed only the touch of a skilled hand and bow to send beautiful sounds, joyous or sad, quivering on the air.

At this stopping place on the Rhine, as at all the others along the way, Fanny astonished the innkeeper by bringing out her portable baths.

"These English and Irish and Scotch!" the landlord exploded. "There never was such a race for bathing! A hot tub at night! A cold tub in the morning!"

The next stage of the journey took Fanny and Victor south along the Rhine winding between vineyard-covered hills. They went farther east and south, crossed the upper waters of the mighty Danube, and came at length to the shores of

Lake Constance, where Fanny chose the village of Lungenargen for her temporary home.

Settling themselves in a comfortable inn on the outskirts of the village, they prepared to rest a bit and then explore the hamlet and countryside. Their kindly landlord and his jolly wife did their best to make the travelers feel at home by helping with the unpacking and making little jokes in their broken English about Fanny's and Victor's attempts at German.

Victor was quick to explore the lake shore near the inn. Taking off his shoes and stockings, he waded in the cold blue water of this lake through which the River Rhine flows.

A little lateen-rigged excursion boat docked twice a week just below the inn. Sometimes Fanny and Victor took a lunch basket and boarded the boat along with other merrymakers. All day they would sail lazily just offshore, following the contours of the huge lake, which is more like an inland sea. To the south were the magnificent snow-covered peaks of the Swiss Alps.

Victor's mother told him that already the goats and cows were being driven down from the summer pastures to the winter shelter of the valleys. During the summer, the herd boys and girls lived all alone in crude mountain huts high in the mountains. There the herds and flocks pastured on the luscious green grass of the upland meadows. For "company" these herd boys and girls had their zithers and accordions, and for food they had cheese and bread, and milk warm from cow or goat.

With the evening, the excursion boat turned back to Lungenargen. With a moon making a silver path on the dark water and other little boats passing silently, there was a special magic about these night-time hours on the water. Then someone would take up an accordion, and play for the others to sing. The songs were folk melodies, as old and mellow as the farmsteads which dotted the fir-clad shores of the lake.

"Du, du liegst mir im Herzen" (Thou, thou, dear to my heart) was a favorite:

"Wenn ich ein Vöglein wär, und auch zwei Flüglein hätt" (If I were a little bird and had two little wings, I should fly to you—so the song stated) had a merry lilt and sly humor.

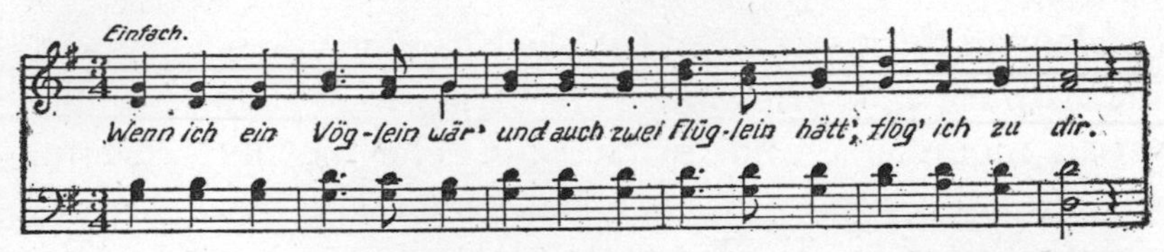

Of the "composed" songs, *Die Lorelei* was ever popular. Heinrich Heine's words and Friedrich Silcher's music told the story of the Rhine maidens, who sat on a rock in the river while they combed their golden hair and sang sweet music to lure unwary boatmen to their death.

There was another favorite, too—Goethe's *Mignons Lied* (Mignon's song), set to music by Friedrich Himmel:

"Kennst du das Land
Wo die Zitronen blühn . . . ?"

(Knowest thou the land
Where the lemon trees bloom . . . ?)

Sometimes Victor and his mother made longer trips—into the neighboring Austrian Tirol and the German state of Bavaria. In these regions, German farmers came into town wearing short leather breeches and hats with flowers stuck in the bands or a feather at the back. They came in horse-drawn carts piled high with food to be sold at a local fair: poultry, eggs, butter, cheese, milk, and cream. The boys and men brought wood carvings which they had made while the storms of the previous winter whistled round their sturdy timber houses; the girls and women brought fine lace and embroidery.

The women came to the fairs dressed in holiday costumes—full skirts with embroidered aprons, caps of net, and silver coins making a belt or necklace. Each locality had its own particular style of cap and dress, so that anyone might tell at a glance which of the towns and valleys the wearer came from.

Many of the men carried flat black cases which held zithers, the harplike folk instrument of the Austrian Tirol, the Bavarian mountains, and Switzerland. The metallic, cheerful music of the zithers in some Bavarian home where friends were gathered made Victor want to skip and caper in the street. The old folk tunes were dance melodies, full of mirth and good spirits. One of these songs that Victor heard on a market day was the jolly *Tiroler:*

"Tiroler sind lustig,
Tiroler sind froh."

(The Tirolese are hearty,
The Tirolese are gay.)

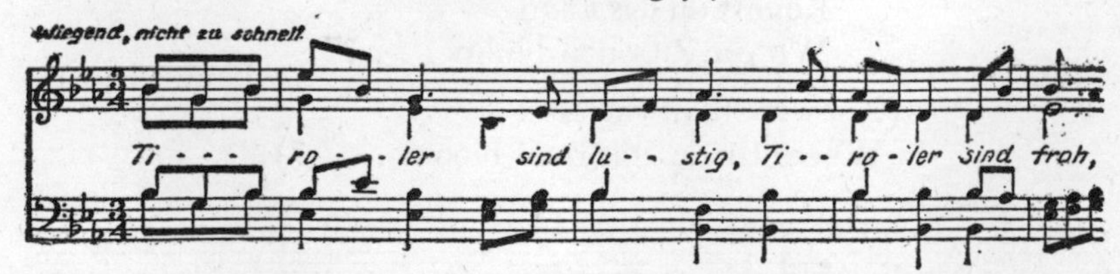

Melodies like these played an important part in Victor Herbert's development as a musician. They were beautiful and yet simple—true folk music—and from such music the best artistic inspiration has ever sprung.

As a child, Victor Herbert was lucky enough to absorb what was best from the folk song of two great peoples, the Irish and the Germans. The riches from the German storehouses were by no means the least.

As he reached manhood, Herbert became acutely conscious of the debt he owed the singing peasants of Europe, and once commented on the difference between the musical heritages of Europe and America:

"The reason we do not get a higher grade of music, why we don't get music typically American, is because our farmers don't sing. How can we get good folk songs like Europe when the folk don't sing?"

The village of Lungenargen soon came to mean "home" to Fanny and Victor. There was hardly a man, woman, or child who did not greet the lively Irishwoman and her handsome son as they took their walks along the lake or through the shop-lined streets of the village.

"Guten Morgen, Frau Herbert! Guten Morgen, Victor!" everyone called out to them.

Summer gave way to the brisk days of autumn, and these to winter's wind and snow. Still Fanny lingered with her son in the pleasant village by Lake Constance. The reason was soon apparent.

One voice that called out the invariable cheery "Good morning!" did not altogether please Victor. This was the voice of Dr. Carl Schmid, a physician. Gradually it dawned on the boy that his mother was in love with this doctor, and he with her. Before long, Victor was trying to accustom himself to the idea of having Doctor Schmid as a step-father.

Fanny and the doctor were married quietly in Lungenargen, and shortly afterward they decided to move to the town of Stuttgart, capital of Württemberg, where the doctor hoped to establish a larger practice. Victor's brief twinge of jealousy was gone by this time, and he settled with content into the new home at Stuttgart. It is true that he did not accept wholeheartedly the idea of becoming a doctor, as Fanny and her husband decided he should, but he had no alternative plan at the time, and he liked his preparatory studies very well.

The new life was happy and interesting. Victor was a good

student. He learned, before many months had passed, to speak German fluently. Soon it came as naturally to him as the English which he and his mother spoke at home.

The rules in the *Gymnasium* were strict. Victor and the other pupils were taught to speak clearly and to the point, to learn accurately, to excel in one subject and to know something about all branches of knowledge. These were the days, it must be remembered, before false and terrible political ideas grew up out of war and hunger to warp the good humor of the German people and twist to evil purposes their former praiseworthy pride in a task well done.

Victor began to learn about the famous men of Germany, the painters, composers, scientists, and philosophers. He learned to appreciate the skilled brushwork of Albrecht Dürer's paintings and to understand why it is that this artist's engravings are considered works of genius. Of Dürer it has been said, "He cut into the copper with the hand of a workman, the heart of a poet, and the brain of a philosopher." Victor learned also about Germany's second ranking artist, Hans Holbein the Younger. Holbein was of special interest to Irish Victor; for this artist, once painter to the king at the English Court of Henry VIII, had painted a remarkable picture depicting St. Martin of Tours, that famous kinsman of St. Patrick.

The German hero saga called the *Nibelungenlied* was fascinating legend. Victor read again and again the story of Siegfried's struggle with the dragon and Brunhilde's strange sleep on the enchanted flame-ringed rock.

Victor read from the works of the great writers of the eighteenth and nineteenth centuries, Schiller and Goethe and Heine. Every concert spoke of the genius of German composers—Mozart, Beethoven, Händel, Haydn, Bach, among the early group.

And of course Victor learned about the philosophers—Kant, Hegel, and Nietzsche. Karl Marx, the socialist, was mentioned with some caution. Men were already being exiled and imprisoned for endorsing this man's studies in economics.

It was not all work for the pupils, though. When school let out, they went their carefree schoolboy ways through the town of Stuttgart. They loved the sights and sounds and smells of the old part of the city, where craftsmen carried on the time-honored trades of printing and bookbinding, tooling of leather, manufacturing of jewelry, making of cigars. Sometimes they walked along the broad avenue which cuts the city in two—the Königstrasse or King's Street—past squares and parks and the fine old buildings which housed the royal theater, the museum of antiquities, and the royal library. They looked with childish interest at the palace of the Crown Prince. Expeditions among the woods and vine-covered hills as far as the banks of the Neckar River were even more to their liking.

Victor's home life was the happy, ordered life which every child deserves. His mother was a good and energetic housekeeper, who saw to it that her husband and son always had clean shirts to wear and wholesome meals at regular hours. In addition, she was a charming and cultured hostess, and evenings in the Schmid household were not unlike those at Sevenoaks, with friends congregating for stimulating conversation and good music.

Very soon after the family moved to Stuttgart, Fanny's second son, William, was born. The years proved William Schmid to be talented, though in a different way from Victor. William became an actor of some renown. Unlike Victor, who eventually emigrated to America, William spent his entire life in Germany, where he died shortly before Herbert.

One cloud darkened the early years in Stuttgart. Victor and his mother had been looking forward to a visit from Grandfather Lover in 1868. For many a month, Victor had gone about telling his classmates of his grandfather's talents, the good fun he was, the clever games he knew how to play, and the funny stories he could tell. Then one day Victor came home to find his mother in tears. A letter had arrived to inform Fanny and Victor that Samuel Lover was dead.

Grandfather Lover's death was like a door closing on the old life at Sevenoaks. With the passing years, Victor's mother, as wife of Doctor Schmid, settled more and more contentedly into the life of Stuttgart. Victor almost forgot how it was to be with English-speaking people, and among his friends few ever thought of him as an Irish lad, accepting him rather as a typical German student.

Victor's introduction to a serious study of music came during these school days in Stuttgart. Of course, he had always loved the little Irish songs which his mother and grandfather taught him, and he continued to practice his piano lessons. But he had not once given a thought to making music a profession. His first step in that direction was made almost by accident.

The school orchestra was scheduled to play Donizetti's *The Daughter of the Regiment* when lo! the piccolo player fell ill and there was not another to take his place.

One of Victor's friends, with the confidence of rash and optimistic youth, suggested that Victor act as substitute. Though Victor did not play the flute or piccolo (or any other orchestral instrument) he had an ear for music. He had a stout pair of lips which, it seemed logical to his friend, ought to produce music from the piccolo.

Would Victor try to master the part in two weeks? To youth all things are possible. Victor positively *would* enter the breach and save the day for the school orchestra!

"Oh, dear, dear!" wailed Fanny. "He sounds like all the dreadful banshees in Ireland!" There was no way to escape the noise made by her son, who sat in his room and produced weird noises as he played the piccolo (small flute pitched an octave higher than the regular flute).

"What!" thundered Doctor Schmid, entering the house tired and irritable from a hard day with his patients. "Is that boy still playing that infernal flute? Tell him to take it somewhere else for a while!"

Guests lifted inquiring eyebrows as Victor, grown to be large for his age, retired after a brief "Gruss" (Greetings!) and gave himself up to his arduous task. On these occasions his mother would look both pained and amused. "I wish he would learn the violin or 'cello," she would say. "Somehow, the piccolo, for such a big strapping boy as Victor, is funny!"

Victor shut his ears to all the protests and played and squeaked steadily for two weeks. When the night of the concert arrived, he took his place proudly with the other members of the orchestra. Unfortunately, he had a little solo part in the overture, and the fact that all eyes were turned on him at that point quite overwhelmed him. He was stricken with stage fright. Instead of the tolerably accurate notes which his lips had brought forth at home, the solo was in the nature of a variation on the original score, and a sadly distorted variation into the bargain.

Shortly after Victor's disastrous appearance in public as a flute player, his mother bought him a 'cello. After a few lessons, he made such progress that his teachers procured him admittance to the Stuttgart Conservatory.

Then well-meaning friends stepped in, as such friends often do, and suggested that music was a poor profession. Surely Victor was not giving up the idea of becoming a surgeon? Victor's mother was undecided, but by this time Victor was not. He added his arguments to those of his teachers and fellow-students, and their combined pleas carried the day.

Victor continued his studies in Stuttgart until his sixteenth year. Throwing himself fervently into his new study, he proved that his was no ordinary talent. Recognition of his ability, and amazing progress in a very short time, came when he was accepted as a pupil of Professor Bernhardt Cossman of Baden-Baden.

Professor Cossman was one of the best concert 'cellists

of the day. He was also a teacher of genius, who took only such pupils as showed promise of virtuosity.

Much of composer Herbert's most effective music was written for the 'cello, which he played with skill and artistry. Even in the songs and entr'acte music for his operettas, a mellow, singing quality reminiscent of the low-voiced 'cello was often apparent.

Moonbeams, one of the Herbert songs, has in late years been transcribed for the 'cello, an instrument which ideally suits this yearning melody from *The Red Mill.* A tender, almost caressing phrase in the *Andantino* of the transcription has a haunting beauty:

A Wandering Minstrel

1876-1886. During these years, Thomas Alva Edison invented the phonograph, and helped Manager Steele MacKaye make theater history by personally installing overhead lighting in the Madison Square Theatre. *H.M.S. Pinafore* was produced in England. The West was still wild: "Please refrain from shooting from car windows" was the request posted in all Union Pacific Railroad stations. Popular songs of the day included *White Wings,* by Banks Winter. Women were wearing the boned basque and the looped polonaise. Only elderly men stuck to beards, but mustaches were so important that they were christened with names like the "heavy cavalry," the "waterfall," the "wax-end," and the "up-curled end."

FROM the moment that Victor took up the 'cello, he became absorbed in music somewhat to the detriment of his other studies. In later years he told about this change in his interests:

"Up to that time I had been one of the first five in my class of fifty, but from the time I began the study of the 'cello, I took a drop in my work at the *Gymnasium.* Soon after, there were financial troubles and while my mother did not wish me to become a professional musician, she was told that I had a great deal of talent, and through the influence of the father of my violinist friend, I became the only pupil of Professor Cossman, of Baden-Baden. Cossman wrote a great deal for the instrument and was one of the best concert 'cellists of his day."

So it was that Victor placed his 'cello in its large black case, packed a few modest belongings in a traveling bag, gave half an ear to the advice of his mother, and went on his way blithely to the town of Baden (called Baden-Baden to distinguish it from other mineral-bath resorts).

Victor did not feel at all strange in his new surroundings; for he was once more in the Black Forest region where he and his mother had stayed a while on the way to Lake Constance. Baden-Baden was a picturesque town. Its principal industry (aside from wood carving) was catering to tourists. Tourists were the real life of the town. They came from all corners of the world to take the hot baths in the mineral waters from the famous springs. Hotels, cafés, the grand-duke's summer residence, an old castle, the baths, and numerous private homes with rooms for paying guests—this was Baden. Round about were the beautiful black fir trees and the rustic farm buildings typical of the Black Forest region. Serenity, order, a pleasant isolation, combined with a cosmopolitan air of being in touch with the outer world—what better environment for a young student who had come to apply himself diligently to the study of music?

Professor Cossman and his wife lived in an old-fashioned house with a little shop at the front. This shop displayed fine old laces, and was Mrs. Cossman's special care.

A customer had just closed the door behind him when Victor walked up the street toward his new home. A short, energetic man with amazing eyebrows shading keen, knowing eyes, he glanced at Victor, then at the 'cello case.

"So! A music pupil for Herr Professor Cossman, eh?" he remarked pleasantly, and in his speech there was a trace of accent which Victor could not place. "Um," the stranger went on, "you've got the build for it. Good stout fingers. Look to your bowing, boy. Herr Cossman can teach you a thing or two about that, I promise you."

With a cheery nod, the stranger passed on his way, leaving a puzzled and amused Victor to stare after him. Mrs. Cossman, who had witnessed the little scene, opened the door of the shop.

"Welcome, Victor Herbert. I don't blame you for being surprised, getting all that advice before you crossed the threshold! Do you know who that was?"

Victor shook his head.

"That was the great Anton Rubinstein from St. Petersburg, Russia," Mrs. Cossman told him. "He comes here nearly every year for a few weeks, to take the baths."

Victor was impressed, as any boy with a knowledge of music would have been. Anton Rubinstein was one of the greatest composers and conductors of the day, a man of genius to whom other men of genius looked up, musically speaking. He was also a great teacher, and the famous Peter Ilich Tchaikovsky had been his pupil.

Mrs. Cossman had a quiet, motherly way that made Victor feel at home, and Professor Cossman commanded his respect and admiration. After the evening meal, served by a quiet girl in the costume of her particular district of the Black Forest region, the Cossmans asked Victor to play for them.

When Victor had played one of the little compositions which he had learned in Stuttgart, Professor Cossman nodded his approval. "Good! Very good! You have an aptitude for it. You shall learn something here."

Later, when Mrs. Cossman showed Victor to his room and wished him a kindly good night, she hesitated a moment and then whispered, "Whatever you do, you must apply yourself. Nothing so angers my husband as to have a good pupil show laziness. You will remember? Professor Cossman was much impressed with your playing, Victor. He will take much pride in helping you to perfect your technique."

Mrs. Cossman need have had no fears for this new pupil. Without complaint, Victor buckled down to difficult lessons. In fact, the professor set him such rigorous tasks at the very beginning that if Victor had not been a boy of stubborn determination, he would surely have cried quits and rushed home to take up a less arduous trade or profession.

Victor Herbert appreciated to the full this opportunity to study with a great teacher. In later years he said:

"I spent a year and a quarter in Professor Cossman's household. I had exceptional advantages. My lessons were no fifteen-minute affairs and then away at something else. I was under the constant eye of my master, and I could not help making rapid progress."

It was Victor's good fortune, too, that most of the famous concert artists, conductors, and composers of the day came regularly to Baden-Baden for the mineral-water baths. Sooner or later, they always found their way to Mrs. Cossman's lace shop and Professor Cossman's study. The young student met, in this way, men like Franz Liszt and Camille Saint-Saëns.

Kindly, laughter-loving Brahms was always a welcome guest. Victor Herbert, in later years, liked to tell an amusing story about this composer. At a neighboring resort town, Brahms lived for several months out of every year. The master was a man of rigid habit. Every day at the same hour he walked solemnly and sedately to the same little inn for his stein of beer. Learning his habit, tourists made a point of walking out at the same time to catch a glimpse of the famous composer. Brahms' beer hour soon took on all the gayety of a village festival.

The Rubinsteins, Anton and Nicholas, were guests of the Cossmans at least once a year. They brought with them news of the sensuous, disturbing music of their native Russia. Tchaikovsky, Rimsky-Korsakov, Moussorgsky, Balakirev, Cui, Borodin were the names sprinkled through their talk.

The spirit of genius was in all these men. They had in common several attitudes—respect for craftsmanship, acceptance of hard work as art's companion, appreciation of what is fine and beautiful, rejection of the trivial and slap-dash. Victor, sitting quietly in his "apprentice's corner," listened to them and learned much.

These men and others were responsible for a veritable outburst of inspired music. It was the "golden age" of European music, with great composers in every country writing great music.

The Hungarian Liszt was making brilliant adaptations of the colorful dances of his people. His *Czardas Obstiné* and *Czardas Macabre* introduced to the world the fascinating rhythms of the *czardas,* an Hungarian peasant dance superbly rendered by native gypsy orchestras.

Sensitive always to the folk-music content of art forms, Victor studied compositions such as these and played 'cello adaptations prepared for him by his teacher. How well he absorbed the spirit of Hungarian music may be seen in a work of his own, composed many years later. *Romany Life,* a song from *The Fortune Teller,* is actually a *czardas.*

The typically slow, melancholy introduction of the dance has its counterpart in the music of "We have a home 'neath the forest shades":

The startling change from slow to fast tempo, a characteristic of the dance, is accomplished with the phrase "Thro' the forest wild and free":

Brahms' "Pastoral" Symphony (inspired by the composer's visit to Pörtschach on the lake of Worth in Austria) was completed during the years of Victor's stay in Baden. "All rippling streams, blue sky, sunshine, and cool green shadows," this was a work which reflected a love of nature in its friendly aspects. The music of this symphony had an enthusiastic disciple in young Herbert, who instinctively rejected the fatalistically sad and morbidly gloomy in art. His own compositions were records chiefly of the sunny hours.

Brahms' *Academic Festival Overture* was another composition which held a special place in Victor Herbert's heart. The traditional student songs, which Victor had sung and loved just as every German schoolboy sang and loved them, were the inspiration for this work. Four of the best-known songs were ingeniously interwoven in the music of this rollicking fantasy.

1876 saw the publication of Tchaikovsky's nature pieces for piano, *The Seasons*. The Russian's interpretation of nature's moods differed from those of Brahms in his "Pastoral" Symphony. Even the gayest phrases of *The Seasons* were tempered by an undercurrent of melancholy. Victor's 'cello was the ideal voice for the poignant music of the Slav composer, whose sadness, it has been said, was not the voice of despair but rather an understanding comment on the tragic in life. The young 'cellist at Baden was quick to learn of other exciting compositions turned out by the Russian genius—*The Tempest, Romeo and Juliet* (symphonic poems based on the Shakespeare dramas), and the delicate *Swan Lake* ballet music.

Tchaikovsky was one of the famous conductors who came to Germany to conduct their own works. It was not in the Baden months, but not very long after, that Victor Herbert was in the audience when Tchaikovsky conducted a performance of the famous *Fifth Symphony*.

In the year 1918, Victor Herbert, himself a conductor of note, was rehearsing the Cincinnati Orchestra in Tchaikovsky's *Fifth Symphony*. The orchestra played a certain movement in a tempo which did not please Herbert. He rapped his baton on the conductor's stand to silence the instruments.

"That movement will have to be played in this tempo," he said, indicating the proper time. "I heard Tchaikovsky play it myself."

Later in the rehearsal, the orchestra was laboring, but without much spirit or fire, at one of the smashing climaxes of the symphony. Herbert rapped for quiet.

"That will have to be played wilder and faster," he said. Then with a merry twinkle in his eyes and an impish smile hovering about his lips, he added, "Remember, it was written before Russia prohibited vodka drinking!"

Edvard Grieg, the Norwegian, was another contemporary of Victor's. Grieg was interpreting the old Norse rhythms and harmonies into the "world language," just as Tchaikovsky was interpreting the music of the Slavs.

Victor was familiar with Grieg's *Concerto for piano and orchestra*, in A minor, which had been presented four years before in Leipzig. He was aware, too, that the year 1876 saw the completion of the brilliant *Peer Gynt* music, and the magnificent *Ballade*.

César Franck, the odd little Belgian organist, was writing some of his most inspired music. Saint-Saëns' *Carnival of Animals*, "Grand Zoological Fantasy for Orchestra" was first heard in 1886. Charles Gounod, whose opera *Faust* was always a favorite of Victor's, was still writing music, though of a serious churchly character in those latter years.

As for Wagner, he was a living presence in nearly every musical household of the day. The old revolutionary, who had been banished from the German states for many years, had returned to favor with the princes and was established in a comfortable home, with a theater all his own (built by contributions from music-lovers all over the world), in the town of Bayreuth. Ludwig II, King of Bavaria, sometimes called Mad Ludwig, had taken the composer under his wing.

Wagner ranked with Mozart among Victor Herbert's favorite composers. Herbert never wavered in his opinion that the "Nibelungen Ring" was, to quote his own words, "one of the rocks of ages upon which time will dash its waves in vain."

The tremendous task of writing the music for *Der Ring des Nibelungen* had occupied Wagner from 1853 to 1874. In 1876, the cycle of four dramas was at last produced in the *Festspielhaus*, the festival theater in Bayreuth.

Musicians came from all over the world to Wagner's theater in Bavaria the summer of 1876, to hear what Grieg described as "the work of a giant, equaled perhaps in the history of art only by Michelangelo." In quiet Baden, Victor listened to the opinions of those returning from the Bayreuth festival.

There was something to set the imagination on fire in the story and music of *Das Rheingold*, *Die Walküre*, *Siegfried*, and *Götterdämmerung*. Victor could hardly have escaped the magic of such music as *Forest Murmurs* from *Siegfried*. The story has it that Siegfried lies on the grass contemplating all the sounds of nature. He has just slain the dragon Fafner. One of the hero's fingers, stained with the dragon's blood, touches his lips, and suddenly the youth realizes that he can understand the language of the birds. The descriptive music for this episode is inexpressibly charming.

Bohemia was producing music, too. Antonin Dvořák (who was to be a dear friend in later years) and Friedrich Smetana were the famous names among the Bohemian Czechs. By

1876, Dvořák had composed his *Moravian Duets*, two comic operas, *King and Collier*, and *The Pig-headed Ones (The Blockheads)*, several symphonies, overtures, and concertos, numerous songs, and considerable chamber and choral music. In that same year, Smetana's symphonic poem *Die Moldau* from the cycle *Ma Vlast* (My Country) was two years old. Like his opera *The Bartered Bride*, *Ma Vlast* is rich in folk melody.

Both Dvořák and Smetana drew on the folk music of their people for inspiration, and this element in their work attracted Herbert like a magnet. In America, he frequently complained that composers were handicapped by a lack of folk-song background. If you wrote any sort of music, he said, you would be handicapped from the start. You never sang folk songs. You never had been a peasant singing as you pitched the hay to the top of the load. Consequently, you were not to be blamed if you wrote music out of your head and not out of your heart.

Victor Herbert felt that folk songs were the source of all melody, and he believed melody to be essential to good music. For that reason, he was never converted to the ideas of the extreme modernists, who achieve their impressionistic effects through strange harmonies, and do not know melody at all in the sense that Mozart, for example, knew it. Of Richard Strauss (not a member of the family who produced the waltz kings), Victor Herbert had this to say the year that Strauss appeared as guest conductor of the Pittsburgh Orchestra, of which Herbert was permanent conductor:

"Richard Strauss is a great composer, but in his *Elektra* I think he is a great man gone wrong." Comparing Strauss' strange harmonies and dissonances with the melodious writing of Beethoven and Wagner, Herbert concluded: "They always have a definite idea in mind, a theme which people can recognize and take pleasure in. But the extreme modernist seems to regard melody with hatred."

Out of Austria was coming a charming, popular rhythm,

the waltz; and Johann Strauss the Younger was already the Waltz King. The Strauss family and the music for which their name stood influenced Victor Herbert tremendously. At the height of his career, many of his most successful compositions were waltzes in the Strauss tradition. Sylvia's song, from the operetta *Sweethearts,* is a typical Herbert waltz in the manner of old Vienna, where youth danced the nights away to the strains of *Roses of the South* and *The Beautiful Blue Danube.*

In France, Jacques Offenbach was writing gay light operas like *Les Contes d'Hoffmann* (Tales of Hoffmann) and *La Vie Parisienne* (Parisian Life). From across the Channel, echoes of a musical travesty *Trial by Jury* reached the Continent. This Gilbert and Sullivan farce, like those which followed it (*The Mikado, Iolanthe, The Yeoman of the Guard, The Gondoliers,* etc.), contained tuneful music set to droll lyrics. Despite his preoccupation with serious music in the early part of his career, Victor Herbert was to show himself a master in the field of comic opera or operetta. It is on his more than forty romantic, gay operettas that his fame rests most securely.

With such a wealth of musical impressions as background, and the careful teaching of an inspired tutor, any boy would have made progress. But it was Victor's native ability which was largely responsible for a rapid mastery of 'cello technique little short of the miraculous. After less than two years of study with Professor Cossman, Victor was ready to take his place with the musicians of the professional world. Before he was nineteen, he was making his living by playing with orchestras throughout Germany and the rest of the Continent.

The Cossmans watched their young pupil with fond and anxious eyes as he waved them a blithe good-by one day and set out with all the confidence of youth to play his first engagement as 'cellist with an established orchestra. Like parent birds, they feared for and yet never doubted the ability of their fledgling to make use of his own wings. The apprentice was now a journeyman, beginning his *Wanderjahre* like any other German tradesman.

The *Wanderjahre* (wander years) were an interesting custom in Europe. When an apprentice had completed his time of service (known as the *Lehrjahre*, or "learning years"), he became a journeyman, wandering from place to place. He took the tools of his trade with him and became for the time being a vagabond workman, plying his trade for a few weeks here, a few weeks there, and a few weeks farther on. This "journey" was undertaken to broaden the craftsman's experience; for in other cities and other countries workmen were likely to have developed methods and skills superior to those he had learned.

After his years of wandering, the workman chose some likely town, city, or village in which to settle down. There he either "hired out" or set up his own establishment; in either case he was, by virtue of his skill and experience of the *Wanderjahre*, a master mechanic.

A professional musician followed much the same pattern. Taking up his violin or 'cello or horn, the apprentice player left his teacher's home and set out to gain experience by playing an engagement now with a large, established orchestra, again with some small group of popular musicians making music for dancers in a beer garden, or perhaps with a band of strolling players who, like the minstrels of old time, performed at chateaux and castles for wedding celebrations, or in public squares at fairs and festivals.

Victor had been looking forward eagerly to this time of youthful vagabondage. What fun to take his 'cello and go from town to town all over Europe, playing for his supper, absorbing new impressions, enlarging his repertory, meeting adventure at every turn.

Victor's mother smiled confidently when she heard the news that Victor was "on his own." "The boy will be successful. I am not worried," she told her friends.

For the next four years, Victor "wandered," playing in the smaller orchestras of Germany, Italy, France, and Switzerland. East, west, north, and south in Germany he went, to small communities near Hamburg, Berlin, Breslau, Mannheim, and Munich. Across the Belgian "low country" of level fields and windmills with huge sails he traveled. This was the country made famous by Ouida (Louise de la Ramée) in *A Dog of Flanders*, the story of a peasant child, Nello, who wanted to be an artist, and his faithful friend, the cart-dog Petrasche. Salzburg in Austria, birthplace of Mozart; Arles and Tarascon in France; Bergamo, Cantania, Milan in Italy; Lugano, Bern, Montreux in Switzerland—happily the young 'cellist moved from city to city, a wandering minstrel with mischief in his smile, youth in his heart, and genius at his fingertips.

During this four-year period of Victor's *Wanderjahre*, he became a member of a private orchestra of a fabulously wealthy Russian baron, Baron von Dervies. Hundreds of toiling serfs in the land of the Czars created with their slave labor the wealth of this baron "who maintained a grand opera company, solo singers, orchestra, chorus—and all for his family solely. Wherever he went he took with him a symphony, ready for the tapping, and comprising from fifty to seventy instrumentalists.

"Von Dervies had a summer villa, or palace, at Lugano, and a wintering place at Nice. Victor Herbert spent a year with him, but seems to have gotten tired of it all. Probably it was too soft." (Stanley Olmsted in *The Morning Telegraph*, 1914.)

So Victor went his independent way again. There were "downs" as well as "ups" in such a life, of course; but these mishaps were merely sources for humor in later years. A year or more after Herbert left the Russian Baron, he became involved in a concert tour which ended with the stranding of the players in Montreux, in the French part of Switzerland.

"Everybody in Montreux regarded me with suspicion," Victor Herbert said. "Because I seemed to play the 'cello so well and yet was so unmistakably dead broke."

A musician of Montreux, Herr Klemm, took the boy into his home and helped him make a new connection with a concert group. Herbert never forgot this act of kindness, and years later, when Herr Klemm was in need of help, the composer procured him a position in the Thomas Orchestra in Chicago.

Finally, Victor landed in Vienna. There in that madly gay capital he became solo 'cellist in the orchestra conducted by the violinist Eduard Strauss, brother of the Waltz King, Johann Strauss.

One of Victor Herbert's favorite stories was about Eduard Strauss, who, though he came from so celebrated a musical family, was no great shakes of a violinist. Johann and his father before him had made it a custom to lead the Strauss orchestras while playing first violin. Eduard must needs follow this family tradition, but none was quite so aware of his deficiencies as a violinist as Eduard himself. He devised the scheme of playing with an unrosined bow—in other words, of playing inaudibly, merely going through the motions to fool the audience.

Being of a theatrical turn of mind, Eduard knew that it would not do to let his audiences guess the true state of affairs. In order to bolster the illusion, he always arranged for one of the players to make a huge to-do of rosining the bow of the Strauss violin just before the first waltz.

"When I was solo 'cellist," Victor Herbert told his friends, "it was the regular duty of an old chap who played at the first desk of the second violins to rosin the bow for Eduard; that is, to pretend to rosin the bow. . . .

"Eduard used to go through all the motions, but very little music did that bow produce, for the old chap had his instructions. One evening this man was sick. A young player new to the orchestra sat in his place. Eduard came out, bowed to the applause which greeted him, and then handed his violin to the new man for the usual stage business to be gone through.

"He was an earnest, conscientious young man, and he certainly got more dramatic effect out of rosining the bow than his older colleague had. The overture finished, the new man handed the violin back to Eduard with the bow, for the first waltz was next on the program, and, as was the custom with the Strausses, Eduard was to lead, playing the violin.

"He struck an attitude with the bow poised; he raised his head; he nodded, and he swept the bow across the strings with a picturesque gesture. But—the new young man had not been told! There was some very real rosin on that bow.

"The introduction to that waltz was supposed to begin in the softest of pianissimos, but Eduard's unexpected raucous scraping sent both orchestra and audience into roars of laughter."

Herbert liked to recall the time that Léo Delibes came to Vienna to conduct the music of his *Sylvia Ballet* music. The Frenchman was delighted with the Viennese turn which the Strauss orchestra gave his music.

"The same notes, everything the same, and yet everything different—and delightfully so. The lighthearted spirit of Vienna added to my score!" Thus marveled Delibes.

Composer Victor Herbert was always fond of "talking shop." One of his favorite topics was this matter of interpreting a score.

"It is almost impossible to transfer to paper certain rhythms," he would say. "How write down a gypsy air as a gypsy plays it in the light of a flickering campfire when the caravan is camped at night? Impossible! And take the *Habañera* from Bizet's *Carmen*. Any musician knows that it is never played as it is written, and so it is played in as many different ways as there are orchestras to play it. Same thing with the spoken word. What a difference when a schoolboy reads the soliloquy from *Hamlet*, and when actor Edwin Booth recites 'To be or not to be. . . .' The same words, as Delibes would say, and yet everything is different!"

Four years of experience had made of Herbert a superlative performer. Rating him "a 'cello virtuoso of great technical skill, real power and delicate, sympathetic quality," a critic of the day remarked that he "was placed by some critics at the head of all living 'cellists." As an acknowledged master of his instrument, Herbert played in all the finest orchestras of the Continent. Guest conductors under whom he played included Liszt, Brahms, Rubinstein, Saint-Saëns, and, of course, Delibes.

During these years of work and travel, Herbert picked up information which was to prove of the greatest practical value. Languages were, of course, an inevitable acquisition. French and Italian were added to his English and German. It is said that he spoke all four fluently, and when he became a conductor, he always made it a point to address each musician in his native tongue, passing easily from one to another language as occasion demanded. His varied experience with many orchestras gave him a wide knowledge of music and musical instruments. Performers who were masters of violin, oboe, clarinet, flute, etc., were able to show him the scope and limitations of every instrument of the orchestra. For a composer, this information is vital.

Among the stray bits of information which he picked up, stored away in his mind, and used to great advantage later in America, was knowledge of the copyright laws and systems of Europe. A French organization—Société des Auteurs, Compositeurs et Editeurs de Musique (Society of Authors, Composers and Editors of Music)—was actually the model for the American Society of Composers, Authors and Publishers, of which Victor Herbert was the founder. The successful methods employed by the French society to protect the performing rights of members were adopted by ASCAP, as the American group is usually called. Today, thousands of men and women of music receive benefits and protection from this non-profit organization.

As soloist, Victor Herbert came back to Stuttgart for one of the Liederkranz concerts. He had left this city of his boyhood school days with all the doubts and hopes that accompany the amateur undertaking a career. He returned, a confident artist, with a measure of fame. Fanny and William and Doctor Schmid welcomed the wandering son and brother home, their hearts warm with an added glow of pride.

But before his return to Stuttgart, a happening, seemingly of small importance at the time, was to influence Herbert's whole life. At Dresden, where Herbert was appearing with an orchestra as 'cellist, he wandered early one evening to the deserted auditorium where the concerts were given. Setting aside his 'cello, he opened the piano and began to run his hands idly over the keys. Thinking himself alone in the theater, Herbert let his fancies take wing and succeeded in improvising some delightful little tunes. He was lost in his dreaming and did not notice the entrance into the dimly lit auditorium of a fellow-performer, a man of middle age who had taken an interest in the talented young man.

This man—also a 'cellist—listened in some surprise to the gossamer fancies Herbert's fingers were weaving.

"Why, you should compose, Herr Herbert!" he burst out excitedly.

Victor looked up, surprised and sheepish at having been caught trying his hand at composing.

"I doubt if I have the ability." Victor Herbert shook his head, but his eyes questioned the elder musician.

"But you have, boy! You have! You *must* study composition!" declared Victor's friend.

Victor remembered this advice when he returned to Stuttgart. After the Liederkranz concert, Herbert was offered a permanent position in the Royal Court Orchestra. He was not slow to accept the offer, for it gave him his chance to play

Mlle. Modiste

under the baton of the celebrated Hof Kappellmeister, Max Seifritz. He became a student again, too, learning orchestration and the principles of composition from Seifritz himself.

Seifritz was a man who believed with the Russian Tchaikovsky that the more talent a composer had, the harder he ought to work. He set Herbert the task of absorbing the principles of harmony, counterpoint, and orchestration. At the same time he had his pupil arrange a book of old melodies for 'cello and orchestra, to put his newly acquired knowledge to the test. When the arrangements were completed, he had Herbert write a suite in five movements for 'cello and orchestra.

It is truly remarkable that Herbert finished this *Suite for Violoncello and Orchestra*, Opus 3, in three months from the time he began his studies with Seifritz. The suite was played shortly afterward at one of the concerts of the Royal Court Orchestra and was received with enthusiasm.

"If Grandfather Lover could have heard it!" Fanny congratulated her son, and dabbed at her eyes with a bit of lace.

This first major work of a young composer with three months of music theory to his credit is now played by all leading solo 'cellists. The fourth movement, the *Serenade* (Andantino grazioso), contains a melody with which nearly everyone is now familiar:

Herbert did not forget the musician who had encouraged him to become a composer. Many years later, he remembered the kindly old 'cellist of the Dresden orchestra with a unique gift. Expressly for this man who had discovered Victor Herbert's composing talent, the first—and only complete—set of recordings of *Mlle. Modiste* were made.

"In Old New York"

1886-1887. These were the years of the unveiling of the Statue of Liberty, a gift from the people of France to the people of the United States. The first Sears, Roebuck catalog was issued. America was singing *Where Did You Get That Hat?*, *Down Went McGinty*, and Reginald De Koven's *Oh, Promise Me*. The shirtwaist for women was coming into popularity. Every well-groomed man carried a cane in his thickly gloved hand, and American and English hallways showed an assortment of walking sticks—Malaccas, Irish blackthorns, ebony canes, cherry-wood sticks, odd sticks of snakewood, vine, ash, even of horn.

BY 1886, Victor Herbert had been five years in Stuttgart. Those years were happy and carefree, for the most part, and productive. After the suite for violoncello and orchestra, Victor tried his hand at composing a concerto. His *Concerto for Violoncello and Orchestra, in* D major (the first 'cello concerto, Opus 8, never published) was played by the Royal Court Orchestra of Stuttgart; its success brought modest fame to the young composer.

Short pieces for 'cello—*Berceuse* and *Scherzino*—followed the suite and concerto. Herbert discovered he had a gift for writing songs, too, and turned out a number of popular pieces in the manner of Schubert. Two male choruses were an ambitious contribution to vocal music. Almost before he realized it, Victor Herbert was a composer of prominence, his works for orchestra being known by most of the musicians of the Continent. His songs and choruses were bringing in regular royalties, proof of their popularity.

Most of Herbert's early works were published first in Germany, later in the United States. There is no record, however, of the publication of the first 'cello concerto anywhere. This work, wholly in the writing of the composer, has been deposited in the United States Library of Congress by Victor Herbert's daughter, along with a number of holographs and manuscript copies of other Herbert music. Immediately after the Pearl Harbor incident, the Herbert manuscripts were included with the "important and highly prized manuscripts" in the Library collection, and were "evacuated from Washington for safekeeping for the duration of the war." As soon as peace comes, they will be back in their old places.

Victor Herbert was a popular young man, too—none of the pale-student-in-a-cold-attic business for this composer. He and his musician friends were welcome everywhere. Hardly an evening passed without their gathering for lighthearted fun at the home of some well-to-do family of Stuttgart. Indeed, handsome Victor was a most eligible young man in the eyes of many a parent. And where was there a daughter in a Stuttgart household who would not have said "yes" to a proposal of marriage from the witty Irish musician who played the 'cello with the touch of genius and composed songs that some people were likening to those of Schubert?

All unspoiled by flattering attentions, Victor went his merry way, always ready, as a friend of those days once declared, for a bit of music and a stein of Pilsener in some jolly German beer garden. Money came and money went. Though Victor was earning a substantial wage as first 'cellist of the Court Orchestra, and picked up additional sums from the sale and performance of his music, his generous spending kept him perpetually short of cash. An amusing story is told of his washing his underwear in great secrecy at night and hanging it from his window to dry—an undignified procedure forced upon the first 'cellist of the Royal Court Orchestra whenever he could not dig up the few coins necessary to pay a laundress.

The climax to this busy, happy, heedless life came in the year 1886. In that year, Victor Herbert met a beautiful young singer from Vienna, Therese Foerster. She came from the Vienna Opera House, where she had been prima donna of the Royal Vienna Opera Company, to sing in the Stuttgart Opera. Victor took one look at this blond girl on the stage and was in love.

"Who *is* she? What do you know about her—not her career, but the girl?" Victor went about asking.

He learned that her mother and father were Austrian. She had studied music both in Vienna and in Stuttgart. And she had already sung in most of the music centers of the Continent.

Victor was not slow to get an introduction to the lovely young singer, but Therese was merely coldly polite. Undaunted, Victor went often to the opera just to hear Therese sing. Finally he scribbled a note and sent it to her dressing room. He asked if he might come to her home, help her with her rehearsing, perhaps. Therese's reply was a polite refusal. But Victor persisted. Surely she needed a bit of coaching? Surely a skilled musician might be of help to her? Therese was amused, and relented enough to invite him to call. The two young musicians spent a happy afternoon together.

Soon after this first meeting, Therese was asking, "Who *is* he? But of course I mean the man, not the musician. I know that he plays the 'cello divinely and that he composes. But he's not German. So! I thought there was just the least trace of accent in his speech. Not accent, either, for he speaks perfect German. He's Irish, you say? Well, then, that explains it. He plays the 'cello like an angel!"

And of course everyone smiled. Mixing up 'cellos and angels in her speech was a sure sign that her mind dwelt on neither, but rather on a personable young man who had just fallen in love with her.

Well, naturally Fräulein Foerster needed considerable

coaching, she discovered, and Victor knew that no better coach than he lived in the whole of Stuttgart. Hours spent together going over operatic arias at the piano fostered the romance, and very soon these two clever artists, both on the road to fame, announced their betrothal. That was the spring when Herbert was twenty-seven and Therese twenty-five.

That same spring a man arrived from America who was to play the part of fate for these two. That man was Frank Damrosch, son of Dr. Leopold Damrosch, brother of Walter Damrosch of the Metropolitan Opera, New York.

The Metropolitan Opera Company had been running in the red, and it was hoped that a change from Italian opera to the more robust German opera would bolster the box office. Dr. Leopold Damrosch had died before he could realize his dream of German opera for the company of which he was Director. Walter was assistant to the conductor at the Metropolitan and could not be spared. The management decided to send Frank Damrosch, who was Dean of the Institute of Musical Art (later the Julliard School of Music), to Europe to look for talent.

In search of the required talent for the proposed German operas, Damrosch came to Stuttgart just before the end of the opera season. He liked Therese immediately. She had a good voice, a good stage personality, youth, and beauty.

At the end of one of the Stuttgart performances, when Therese had shone like a bright star in all her blond beauty, Damrosch went backstage. With him he took a Metropolitan contract.

Not for a moment did he think that Fräulein Foerster would refuse to sign it; for the contract carried with it a salary far greater than any Therese could hope to get in Europe. Imagine his surprise when she did refuse!

"But Fräulein Foerster! You do not understand! This is a rare opportunity. How many young players long for just this chance to sing before the audiences of the Metropolitan. It will make you world-famous. And then the salary! It is a big one, you know."

"I know," said Therese unhappily. "But all the same, I must refuse your offer. You see—well, I am engaged to be married, and I could not leave my sweetheart to go so far away. I could not!"

"Who is he? One of the singers?" asked Damrosch.

"No. He plays the 'cello."

"Tell me who this 'cello player is," said Damrosch with a sigh. He would go to see the fellow, he decided, though he was of the opinion that his visit would be a wild-goose chase.

Damrosch was to receive his second surprise that day. Far from being "just some 'cellist that Therese had chosen to fall in love with," this Victor Herbert proved to be an artist of outstanding ability. Damrosch listened to Herbert play several compositions and immediately saw the value which this artist would have for the Metropolitan.

"Will you go to America, as 'cellist in the orchestra of New York's Metropolitan Opera House?" he asked bluntly. "I like your playing," he went on. "We need talent like yours. As for you, this engagement will give you the opportunity to play under the baton of one of the greatest conductors of our day, Anton Seidl."

Victor Herbert's eyes brightened. He was more than a little familiar with the career of Anton Seidl, the Hungarian conductor born at Budapest and trained at Leipzig Conservatory. Seidl had been assistant to Wagner at the first festival at Bayreuth, in 1876. Wagner had been so impressed with Seidl's work that he recommended the Hungarian for the position of conductor of the Stadt Theatre of Leipzig, where Seidl established himself forever among the great by his masterly presentation of German opera. There he proved that he could reach "the ultimate heights"; there he "summoned the elemental ground-swell from the vasty deep" (as critic James Huneker expressed it later in America).

In 1882, Seidl had presented Wagner's Trilogy in London,

arousing enthusiasm where formerly the English had been indifferent to Wagner's music. In 1885, he succeeded Dr. Leopold Damrosch as conductor of German opera in New York.

Seidl was a man of unusual appearance and striking personality. James Huneker was to write the classic description of this pale, long-haired, ascetic-looking man with the compelling eyes:

"I saw much of Seidl. His profile was sculptural. So was his manner. But a volcano beneath. He was a taciturn man. He smoked to distraction. I've often seen him with Antonin Dvořák, the Bohemian composer, at the Old Vienna Bakery Café, next to Grace Church. There the coffee and the pastry were the best in town. The conductor and composer would sit for hours without speaking. It was Seidl who introduced the New World Symphony by Dvořák. . . .

"He never seemed a happy man to me. . . . His Gothic head I've seen in medieval tryptichs . . . or else among the portraits of Holbein. His shell was difficult to pierce, but once it was penetrated, his friends found a very warmhearted human."

Victor made his decision: "If Fraülein Foerster is willing—you see we are engaged to be married—yes, I shall be glad to go."

Damrosch smiled to himself and rushed back to Therese. Would she go to America if Victor went along as 'cellist in the orchestra of the Metropolitan?

Therese was all smiles. But certainly!

So it was that Victor agreed to play for a modest sixty dollars a week at the opera where his wife would receive a somewhat staggering salary for singing leading rôles.

The young couple were married that spring and set sail for America in the summer.

"Don't forget to see Niagara Falls," said Victor's mother as she kissed her son good-by in Stuttgart. "You owe it to Grandpa Lover to see that 'great power o' wather!' And," she added, her eyes misting over with tears, "when you are very famous, and very wealthy, perhaps I shall visit you in America."

When Victor and Therese arrived in New York, they settled immediately to work. They lived in a "pension" north of Gramercy Park, one of those old-style family hotels, where the food was good and the company mostly German-speaking artists.

There was little time to get acquainted with the city or its people, however, for rehearsals were long and rigorous. Anton Seidl and Walter Damrosch were determined to present perfect performances, if possible. For Victor and Therese, there were few hours for anything but work until the opening night of the 1886 season.

There was a story behind this almost frantic effort to make a success of German opera. The Academy of Music, in the old neighborhood of 14th Street and Irving Place, had for years been the home of opera in New York. Dissension had broken out, however, among those who favored Italian opera and those who preferred German. So Anton Seidl and Leopold Damrosch broke with the old staff, moved bag and baggage to the Metropolitan, sold the idea of German opera there, and set to work. If the current season should be a failure, how the supporters of Italian opera would crow! Walter Damrosch felt that failure would be a betrayal of his father. Anton Seidl felt that failure would be betrayal of art itself.

Opening night arrived, and backstage at the Metropolitan, that badly designed "diamond horseshoe," Therese took a last-minute look at her pale face reflected in the mirror of her dressing table. She was nervous, but not for herself. She knew her rôle, and she could sing. She was nervous because of Victor—Victor who was so proud, and who would be sitting in an obscure seat in the orchestra pit while she held the eyes of critics and audience in her dazzling rôle of the Queen of Sheba. How she hoped that everything would turn out well for them both in this bewildering rich country of the United States. Was Victor nervous? Perhaps not. After all, he knew how to play!

Out front the huge crowd which had assembled to greet the artists from across the Atlantic was a daunting one even for experienced singers. Critics whose newspaper articles could make or break a performer were sprinkled among the fashionable society crowd which was waiting to pass judgment on this experiment of Seidl's and Damrosch's second season.

Victor Herbert in the 'cello section of the orchestra kept wondering if Therese felt nervous. No, surely not. She was an artist, that girl! He himself felt unusually calm. He was going to like this vigorous big country. Of course, he intended to do more than play 'cello in an orchestra—even a great orchestra like this one.

A murmur of interest greeted Anton Seidl's commanding figure. Herbert forgot everything else in his desire to play his deep-toned 'cello well for this great Hungarian conductor.

Karl von Goldmark's opera *The Queen of Sheba* had been selected for the gala opening night, partly because of the magnificence of its scenery and costuming, partly because of the glorious mezzo-soprano voice of Therese Herbert-Foerster (as she chose to call herself professionally), which was ideally suited to the queen's part.

Founded on the Biblical story of the Queen of Sheba's visit to Solomon's Court, the drama takes place in Jerusalem. The cast consists of King Solomon; Solomon's favorite courtier, Assad; a High Priest; Sulamith, daughter of the High Priest; and Astaroth, a woman slave of the Queen of Sheba.

On this night in 1886, when Therese sang the rôle of Queen, she was in famous company. The great Lilli Lehman was Sulamith, and Marianne Brandt was Astaroth. With all the poise and confidence of the well-trained artist, Therese sang gloriously throughout the exotic opera, which is rich with Eastern color and barbaric beauty. It is reported that the mounting of this opera cost $80,000. An army of supernumeraries, real black and brown men, women, and children, made an awe-inspiring spectacle.

Act One opens with preparations going forward for a wedding in Solomon's palace. Assad, favorite courtier of the King, is to wed gentle Sulamith, daughter of the High Priest. Solomon has ordered that no expense be spared; for Sulamith and Assad are loved by him as if they were his daughter and son.

Word comes that the Queen of Sheba plans to make a visit of state to Solomon's Court. Assad is sent to escort the Queen on her journey.

Assad returns to Solomon in despair. When the King asks the reason for his sadness, Assad confesses that his love for Sulamith is dead. On his journey to the Queen of Sheba's Court, he caught a glimpse of a beautiful woman bathing in a stream. Though he does not even know her name, he cannot forget her exotic Eastern beauty.

While Solomon is pondering this alarming confession (for it would be no light matter for Assad to break his vows with Sulamith), the Queen of Sheba makes her appearance. She is in gorgeous array, and moves proudly and majestically forward to take her seat beside Solomon. When she removes her veil, Assad is struck dumb with dismay. *She* is the unknown beauty who has won his heart!

Assad involuntarily moves toward her, but the Eastern Queen refuses to recognize him. She makes it plain that she considers him too far beneath her in rank to be acknowledged as a suitor, and Assad falls back in dismay. His heartbreak goes unnoticed in the color and barbaric splendor of the palace scene, where brown-skinned slaves and guards stand beside Solomon's peacock throne, and richly dressed courtiers line the pillared hall.

Therese's singing was superb. All the imperious pride, cruelty, and sensuousness of the Queen were in those velvet tones. There was a subtle suggestion of sharp claws hidden in velvet paws.

The first scene of Act Two is an oriental garden by moonlight. The Queen and her slave girl Astaroth are sitting at the edge of a fountain. The Queen seems restless, almost distrait. Suddenly she commands her slave to sing—something which will lure Assad into the garden. Though the Queen cannot bring herself to acknowledge her love for Assad before the world, she has no scruples against a secret intrigue.

Astaroth's song, a tender melody, mysterious and compelling, and Assad's poignant reply are the memorable prelude to the love-scene between the Queen and Assad. They are interrupted by Solomon's guard, and in the angry scene which follows the Queen learns to her dismay that the wedding preparations in the palace are for Assad and Sulamith. She cries out in wounded pride. Avowals of love give way to outbursts of passionate jealousy.

Therese skillfully unsheathed the barbaric Queen's claws. The critics in the audience nodded appreciatively.

The next scene of the opera is laid in a temple. Solomon and the Queen of Sheba bring gifts to lay before the altar of the priests. Assad is there, too. Unable to control his feelings any longer, he throws himself at the Queen's feet and proclaims his undying love for her.

The Queen turns away in pretended disgust. Solomon watches the scene in utter amazement, for he is beginning to understand that the proud Eastern beauty with whom Assad had fallen in love on his journey is the Queen herself.

The priests see in Assad's conduct only an act of blasphemy, and sentence him to death. But Solomon, taking pity on Assad, has him led away by his own guards.

Act Three is set in the Festival Chamber of the Palace. A reception for the Queen of Sheba is in progress, and graceful oriental dancers present elaborate dances for her pleasure.

The Queen's thoughts are with Assad, however. She suddenly bursts forth with an imperious demand that Solomon release him. Her manner angers the King, and he refuses.

Therese sang the Queen's threats of vengeance on Solomon for his refusal with frightening sincerity. Danger and evil were in the music.

Following the dramatic exit of the savage Queen, Sulamith came forward to plead with Solomon for her loved one. Touched by the girl's devotion, Solomon comforts her and tells her that Assad shall not die.

Act Four is a desert scene. True to his word, Solomon has interceded for Assad with the High Priest. Banishment from the Court, not death, is to be his punishment.

Realizing at last the Queen's ugly nature, Assad no longer feels any love for her. He wanders aimlessly in the desert, bewildered and suffering, thinking only of his gentle sweetheart, Sulamith.

Into this desert wilderness, the Queen of Sheba follows him. Assad turns from her in disgust, and she is left alone, a frustrated, tragic figure, humbled at last.

Assad wanders on, hopeless, caring nothing for the burning desert sands and winds. Sulamith comes to him, as he somehow knew she would, and Assad dies in her arms, content in the knowledge that he is forgiven for his betrayal of their love.

Next day, New York newspapers printed enthusiastic notices. The *World* praised Therese's sensitive interpretation of the leading rôle:

"Frau Herbert-Foerster is a singer from the royal opera houses of Dresden and Stuttgart. . . . She has a fine stage presence, and a dramatic soprano voice of great beauty and power. She was in every way well suited to the rôle allotted to her. Her rendering of the great dramatic scene opening the second act revealed many beauties not brought out last year, and the success gained by Frau Herbert-Foerster during the evening leads us to look forward with pleasure to her appearance in other great dramatic rôles during the season."

There were, of course, no such reviews mentioning Victor;

but he found immense satisfaction in the fact that the great Anton Seidl had taken particular notice of him, and had come over after the final curtain to shake hands and express appreciation of Herbert's fine 'cello playing.

Victor Herbert always had an intense respect and real affection for Seidl, who for his part had the greatest confidence in the young composer. Seidl put many opportunities in the way of his young friend, and Herbert was always grateful for the famous conductor's interest and help. When Seidl died, some twelve years later, Herbert was deeply affected, as this tribute to a lost friend shows:

"When I came to the United States, in 1886, I had known Anton Seidl by his great reputation as a Wagner disciple. . . . He was at that time in the second year of his work at the Metropolitan Opera House. The musicians comprising his orchestra had readily come to appreciate his profound knowledge of Bayreuth tradition, alike of the stage and the orchestra. They found in Seidl a man thoroughly imbued with Wagner's ideas, both in general conception and in the smallest detail of each opera. He fairly bristled with animated energy and was ever on the alert to right the minutest of errors. His thorough knowledge of this work, which with him was a life passion, enabled Seidl to make incredible progress with both players and singers in preparation of his superb productions. The great presentation of 'Tristan and Isolde' at the Metropolitan Opera House in the year of my arrival was accomplished with but five rehearsals with the orchestra, including the one set apart for the correction of orchestral parts.

"But our conductor never took to himself any credit for such remarkable achievements. Always anxious to ascribe honor where honor was due, he attributed this, the greatest success of the season, to perfection of discipline in the orchestra, and the ready perception of its members and their fine routine in orchestral work. To his soloists he was ever anxious to accord full measure of praise. In 1885, for instance, the principals included Lehman, Auguste Kraus (Seidl's wife),

Marianne Brandt, Niemann, Robinson, Anton Schott, Alvary, and Herbert-Foerster, whose artistic contributions to these great operatic performances were graciously recognized by the conductor, his characteristic modesty placing them and the orchestra before himself.

"The musicians frequently saw that the music affected Seidl most profoundly. He was a man of deep emotion. Certain passages in 'Siegfried,' and the wonderful closing scene of 'Tristan,' always made him cry like a child, so that by the time the curtain dropped he would be in a state of emotional collapse.

"Seidl was universally admired and loved by the members of the orchestra. He never showed the faintest trace of false pride. His players were his companions, his helpers; he was simply one of them. It was through this strong bond of fraternity that he came to acquire personal influence over the instrumentalists which was entirely distinct from the musical magnetism exerted in rehearsals and public performances. This all-powerful, impelling yet unfathomable power of control imperiously commanded his followers in the orchestra by first awakening their entire interest and then spurring them on to efforts that they could make under the baton of no other master. The graceful, incisive, clean-cut movements of his stick were intelligible at all times. And, for his part, Seidl always relied implicitly upon the quick perception of his musicians, never wasting time in unnecessary explanations of what was to be brought about in this bar, or avoided in that. We always knew by a glance from his eye what was expected of us.

"Mr. Seidl was a man little given to words. As it was so aptly remarked of Von Moltke's position in the realm of scientific warfare, so may it be said of Anton Seidl, as a musician and composer, that he was 'der grosse Schweiger' (the great silent one). Yet he never failed to say the right thing in the right place and many anecdotes are related of his quick wit and dry humor. When he talked, it was because he had something to say. . . .

"He was known to be very fair in his judgment of men and their works."

Seidl admired Victor Herbert both as man and artist. It was a real tribute to Herbert's ability when Seidl asked him to be his assistant conductor at the Brighton Beach concerts, the resort where Seidl's orchestra played every summer. Seidl's recognition of the 'cellist's composing talents took a practical turn with the placing of the young musician's Stuttgart works on the concert programs. It was Seidl who requested that Herbert compose a typically American piece for the orchestra. Herbert's *American Fantasy* was the prompt and tasteful answer to this request.

Herbert's wholehearted adoption of the life of the United States, where the hustling, get-ahead attitude quite suited his intensely ambitious temperament, was expressed in two significant acts. He had been in the country but a short time when he took out citizenship papers; and his first composition on American soil mirrored his quick understanding of United States idiom and mood. Herbert, like many another Irishman before him, became the most American of Americans.

It is an interesting and revealing fact that he never returned to Germany or to his native Ireland, and made but one brief visit to England. He simply became too busy to travel abroad. When he took a vacation, he went to Lake Placid, where he could keep in touch with business associates in New York. He became a part of his new home, and never had the feeling, common to many naturalized citizens, that he was an exile from dearer and more familiar scenes.

For the school days in Germany, of course, it was natural that he always had a special place in his heart. As for Ireland, he would not have been a true Celt if he had not loved fervently the customs and songs of Erin. But, sincere and loyal in everything he did, Herbert found it proper to place the land of his adoption first. As for New York, the "old New York" which he saluted so fondly in one of his later songs, it became his real home, a pleasant, congenial home where he was to work happily and profitably, and make hundreds of friends.

Therese followed her success in *The Queen of Sheba* with three more important and brilliant rôles that season of 1886: Elsa in *Lohengrin;* Aïda; and Irene in *Rienzi.*

Therese was the first person in this country to sing the rôle of Aïda in German. She is remembered in music circles best for her portrayal of Verdi's heroine.

In *Aïda,* as in *The Queen of Sheba,* Therese sang an exotic rôle against a background of ancient splendor, in this case Egypt in the time of the Pharaohs:

Act One is set in the Egyptian king's palace at Memphis. Aïda, a captive Ethiopian girl, is a slave among the Egyptians. She has fallen in love with the Captain of the Guard, Radames, who loves her in return. His *Romanza* "Celeste Aïda" is a gloriously beautiful love serenade, known to all music lovers.

Pharaoh's daughter, Amneris, also loves Radames. When she discovers that he has eyes only for the little slave girl, she is hurt and her thoughts are vengeful.

Radames learns from the High Priest that an army is about to be sent against the Ethiopians. Radames is to command the expedition. Not knowing that his beloved Aïda is the daughter of Amonasra, the Ethiopian King, Radames is glad of his commission; for he wants to make Aïda proud by winning a glorious victory.

When Aïda hears the news, she grieves for her people and her father. She is torn with conflicting emotions; for she loves Radames, too. In Aïda's poignant *Return Victorious* Therese's golden voice grieved and exulted, despaired and hoped.

The act closes with a solemn prayer in the Temple of Ptha.

Radames receives the blessings of the priests and leaves to lead his soldiers in battle against the Ethiopians.

Act Two opens in Amneris' chamber. The Egyptian girl has had word that the Ethiopian campaign has been victorious. Thinking to trick Aïda, however, she tells her that Radames has been killed. Overwhelmed, Aïda pours forth her grief in song, *O love, O joy, tormenting.* The Egyptian princess thus confirms her fear that the love of Aïda and Radames is deep and abiding, no passing fancy.

Aïda is overjoyed when she sees Radames returning alive and victorious, but she is grieved when she watches the procession of captives. Among them is her father, Amonasro. He makes a sign that she is not to betray his rank.

The sorrow of the helpless slave girl is deepened by the King's bestowal of his daughter's hand on Radames. In Therese's singing, there were deep pathos and gentle, pitiful pleading. With great art, she made Aïda warm and human and understandable.

Act Three is played near a Temple of Isis, on the banks of the Nile. Radames and Aïda meet for what they both believe to be the last time. As they sing their poignant duet *Again I see thee,* Princess Amneris listens jealously from the temple.

Aïda is heartbroken at having to part from Radames, and distracted with the knowledge that her father is hiding near them, hoping that Radames' conversation will betray to him the position of the Egyptian army, so that a new Ethiopian army may surprise them in battle.

Radames does unwittingly betray the secret. He is stunned when Amonasro reveals himself and begs that Radames desert the Egyptians and return to Ethiopia with Aïda. At this point, Amneris, who has heard everything, takes her revenge by rushing out of the temple and denouncing Radames as a traitor. Aïda flees with her father, but Radames remains to be taken by Pharaoh's soldiers.

In Act Four, Radames is tried and sentenced to death. He

is to be walled up in a burial chamber—buried alive! Amneris, aghast at this verdict and method of execution, goes to Radames and promises to save him if he will renounce his love for Aïda, but Radames refuses.

When Radames is entombed in a burial place in the temple, he finds the faithful slave girl, who has come to die with him. Gazing at her with pitying eyes, he sings, *To die, so pure and lovely.* Aïda and Radames perish in each other's arms as the priests and priestesses of the temple sing "Almighty Ptha" and repentant Amneris says a prayer.

The simplicity of the slave girl, her devotion and her all-consuming love—these Therese conveyed to her audience. The rich, sweet voice of Therese Herbert-Foerster gave to Aïda's lonely figure the dignity of high tragedy.

When this one season at the Metropolitan closed, Therese, for reasons of her own, retired from professional life. She was confident that Victor was destined to become famous. She also knew, and accepted the fact gracefully, that Herbert had to be first, in his work and in his home.

Herbert was made happy by her announcement. The fact that two young people getting a start in a strange country could have used Therese's salary to good advantage was not even considered. It was true (as the composer later confessed to a friend) that he was sometimes hard put to it to pay their modest rent, but he was proud to be head of his family in every sense of the word. His new responsibility caused him to redouble his efforts to make his music pay.

Magic in a 'Cello

1887-1891. Edward Bellamy's idealistic book *Looking Backward, 2000-1887*, was a best seller. The French built the first naval submarine. The Eiffel Tower was completed in Paris. The disastrous Johnstown flood occurred. Montana, Washington, and the Dakotas were admitted to statehood. Popular songs were *Little Annie Rooney* and *Molly O*. Frilly summer parasols and long white kid gloves were the fashion for women. Every home had a "mustache cup" for the convenience of the man of the family at mealtime.

HERBERT began to hustle about in search of work to supplement his income from the Metropolitan and the Brighton Beach concerts. In addition to the three nights a week and a matinée at the opera, he was soon playing with the Philharmonic Society of New York, under the baton of Theodore Thomas. As a soloist, he played for benefits and musicales, organized concerts of his own, and accepted offers to assist other concert artists. Wherever he played, audiences were enchanted by his 'cello magic.

Frederick Kraft of the publishing house of Schuberth, the first music publishers on Union Square (1872) and the first to publish a Victor Herbert composition in this country (*Prince Ananias*, 1894), recalls being present at one of those early concerts. It was a small vocal program, where a 'cellist was needed for variety. Victor Herbert, then almost unknown to American audiences, was the 'cellist. The concert took place in old Chickering Hall, Eighteenth Street and Fifth

Avenue, a rival of Steinway Hall on Fourteenth Street.

In those days, New York's musical activities clustered around Fourteenth Street and Irving Place. In this neighborhood stood the old Academy of Music, where the first operas were presented and which lost out eventually to the uptown Metropolitan Opera House. There, also, stood Steinway Hall, where the principal concerts were given. Between the two, facing historic Irving Place where Washington Irving's house still stands, Lüchow's was a famous rendezvous at mealtime for the musical crowd. Even Chickering Hall was within this "old city" of music; for the homes and hotels housing the musical talent of the city extended past that newer hall as far as Gramercy Park and Twentieth Street.

There was a good deal of excitement for the composer in this new life of his, and just the amount of activity that Herbert liked best. The novelty of new scenes and new faces, the sound of a vigorous English spoken in jaunty, careless American fashion, the friendliness of a group of men who combined real ability and love of art with the cheerful bonhomie of Bohemian life—no environment could have suited Victor Herbert better.

Chief among his early acquaintances that ripened into lifelong friendship was that with James Gibbons Huneker, the critic. "Jimmy" had his own circle—clever, artistic, up-and-doing young men, for the most part, whose robust health seemed not to know fatigue. Jimmy's crowd began to live after midnight, when the final curtains had gone down in the theaters and the reviews had been written for the morning papers. Then they foregathered in certain snug restaurants where the food was Hungarian, Italian, French, or German, the wine good and the beer plentiful; and they talked and talked and talked as only youth and belief in the future, mutual admiration and bubbling health can talk.

Jimmy Huneker was a remarkably attractive person, a young blond god who played the piano well and was something of an authority on Chopin. He had a genius for conversation, and in the "wee sma' hours," when all good Manhattan burghers were asleep, Jimmy would be sitting in some dim corner, smiling out from under the lazy lids of his eyes, talking of cabbages and kings and caviar.

Sometimes it seemed to Herbert that there never had been such talk before, certainly not since Shakespeare and Ben Jonson made the Mermaid Tavern ring with their laughter in Good Queen Bess' day, or Samuel Johnson and Addison and Steele and Pope had set minds awhirl in the London coffee houses of the eighteenth century.

The interesting and colorful people who made up this New York Bohemia, and their happy-hunting ground (Irving Place, Union Square, and Fourteenth Street) were all mentioned in Huneker's autobiographical book *Steeplejack*.

"I breathed an atmosphere ozone-charged," he said of his first days in New York. "The idols of my youth were to be seen perambulating Irving Place, Union Square, Fourteenth Street. At Lienau's you might see William Steinway in the flesh, an immense political influence, as well as musical. Theodore Thomas lived on East Seventeenth Street, opposite the Garrigues. William Mason would alight from the little blue horsecar which ran across Seventeenth Street at Union Square. He lived in Orange, New Jersey, and always stopped at Brubacher's where he met X. B. Mills, before beginning his lessons at Steinway Hall. A polished pianist, a delightful raconteur, Mr. Mason could discourse by the hour about Franz Liszt, with whom he had studied. And then there were to be seen at Lienau's, Anton Seidl, Mr. and Mrs. Charles F. Tretbar, Nahum Stetson, Joseffy, Sternberg, Rummel, Scharwenka, Lilli Lehman, Van der Stucken, Krehbiel, Mr. and Mrs. Victor Herbert, Rosenthal, Mr. and Mrs. Ferdinand von Inten, Charles S. Steinway, and of course Max Hinrich. A few doors down was Augustus Lüchow's restaurant, which outlasted Lienau's and a host of other hostelries.

"A small family hotel at the northeast corner of Irving Place and Seventeenth Street, kept by an elderly couple, was noted for its cooking and cheerfulness. Werle's, too, was an artistic rendezvous and its table-d'hôte dinners saw many celebrities. There were always entertaining companions. It was one of those houses where at any time before midnight the sound of pianos, violins, violoncellos, even the elegiac flute, might be heard, and usually played by skilled musicians. . . . Across the street was, and still is, the pretty Washington Irving house and at another corner lived Victor Herbert. From the vine-covered entrance of Werle's I often heard string music made by Victor Herbert, Max Bendix . . . and others.

"Steinway Hall was once the resort of our crowd, composed of Harry Rowe Shelley, Harry Orville Brown, Henry Junge, John Kiehl, Joseffy, Friedheim, Max Bendix, Victor Herbert, and, when in town, the witty Moriz Rosenthal."

Somewhat farther afield, a well-known gathering place for the musicians was Knirim's, frequented also by the ship reporters from their headquarters at Battery Park. Frederick Hackenburg, friend of Huneker and Herbert, once described this rendezvous:

"Down at Hanover Square, across from India House, a vicinity rich with historical associations of early New York merchants, among towering office buildings and ramshackle old warehouses scented with the odor of Old-World drugs and Oriental spices . . . a queer place, roomy, dark, comfortable, frequented by the cosmopolitan crowd from the neighboring shipping offices. . . ."

There was a music college called the National Conservatory of Music at 110 East Seventeenth Street, an institution founded in 1881 by Jeannette M. Thurber. The school had a charter from the United States Congress, and conferred the degree Doctor of Music. Young people who showed an outstanding aptitude for music were welcomed, and tuition was free to some of the poorer students. Among the talented pupils was Harry Burleigh, a Negro boy who became one of America's outstanding composers of songs and a distinguished arranger of the folk tunes of his people.

James Huneker taught piano to a class of Negro students at the Conservatory. He spoke about his work to Herbert, and it was not long before the Irish composer added his name to the faculty as teacher of 'cello.

"What a list of artists the faculty comprised!" Huneker wrote of this remarkable venture. "Antonin Dvořák, the great Bohemian composer in his prime, was musical director; Rafael Joseffy and Adele Margulies—a fine pianist and founder of the Margulies Trio—headed the piano department; Camilla Urso, greatest of women violinists; Victor Herbert, then a leading solo violoncellist; Leopold Lichtenberg, formerly of the Boston Symphony Orchestra . . . Anton Seidl, Otto Oesterle . . . conductor Frank Van der Stucken, Emil Paur, C. P. Warren, organist; Bruno Oscar Klein, Horatio Parker, Wassili, Safonoff, Gustav Hinrichs, John Cheshire, the harpist, Sapio; Fritz Geize, great Dutch 'cellist of the Kneisel Quartet; Leo Schultz, first 'cellist of the Philharmonic; Julia Wyman, all these and others were teachers at this institution. . . ."

Antonin Dvořák was director of the Conservatory when Victor Herbert joined the faculty, and the two artists soon became fast friends. There is ample proof that Dvořák appreciated Herbert's composing talent. He had various subtle and graceful ways of showing this approval. Once, for example, when the Bohemian composer was conducting an important concert, he motioned to Herbert, who was in the audience, to come forward and take the baton. If a great singer suddenly requested his understudy to sing in his placc, the gesture would be similarly generous and flattering.

A letter written by Victor Herbert to some unknown "Doctor," in the characteristic hurried pencil scrawl in which the composer wrote the letters to be typed by his secretary, has recently been found among the family papers. This letter gives a number of charming vignettes of the lovable Dvořák, and seems to settle once and for all the moot point as to the source of some of the "spiritual" themes of Dvořák's *New World*

Symphony. Herbert indicates that the talented Harry Burleigh hummed these Negro folk melodies for the Czech composer.

"Dear Dr.

"Mr. Carl Engel (Chief of the Music Division, Library of Congress, Washington, D.C.) has asked me to give you some details as to my recollections of my association with Dr. Antonin Dvořák.

"I was head of the 'Cello Class of Mrs. Thurber's National Conservatory when this enthusiastic lady managed to persuade Dr. Dvořák to accept the directorship of this Conservatory. It was my pleasure to see the doctor practically every time I gave lessons at the Conservatory. He took great interest in my pupils as he was most anxious to have them join the orchestra class, which he directed, although it was, to my mind, the 'enfant terrible' of the institution. With the exception of some excellent violin pupils of that master Leopold Lichtenberg, few of the players were advanced enough to play in the orchestra—and what they 'didn't do' to Mendelssohn's 'Midsummer-night's Overture' (the Dr. might have chosen a simpler piece) is beyond description. However, Dr. Dvořák seemed to enjoy these orchestral orgies.

"One of my pupils, a very charming girl and not an advanced player, acting as Solo-'Celliste, often had fainting spells when the Dr. got very excited.

"Dr. Dvořák, when he was not teaching composition, was always busy composing and often I heard him playing, even singing, in the front room of the Conservatory. I had the pleasure of playing the 'cello part of his beautiful Trio 'Dumbka,' which he had just completed, with him. . . . Dr. Dvořák was not a great pianist, but his playing was intensely musical, of course.

"We liked the composition immensely and I asked him what 'Dumbka' meant in Bohemian. He thought for a while —shook his head—and said, to our surprise, 'It means nothing! —What *does* it mean?'

"Dr. Dvořák was most kind and unaffected, took great interest in his pupils, one of which, the very talented Harry Burleigh, had the privilege of giving the Dr. some of the thematic material for his Symphony—'From the New World.' I have seen this denied—but it is true. Naturally, I knew a good deal about this Symphony, as I saw the Dr. two or three times a week, and knew he was at work on it.

"The first orchestral rehearsal of it took place under the great Anton Seidl, then Conductor of the Philharmonic Society of New York, in Chamber-music Hall in Carnegie Hall, and I was Solo-'Cellist.

"A few years afterward, after I had played my (2nd) 'Cello-Concerto in one of the Philharmonic concerts, Dr. Dvořák came back to the 'Stimmin-Zimmer'—threw his arms around me, saying before many of the orchestra—'famos! famos! gang famos!'

"We all loved him, for he was so kind and affable—his great big beautiful eyes radiated warmth—and of such childlike simplicity and naturalness—and when he left us, we lost not only a great master musician, whose presence had had a marked influence on musical activities in New York, but a most admirable, lovable friend.

"V. H."

"P. S. Dear Dr.

"Mr. Harry Burleigh (one of Dr. Dvořák's best pupils in composition) probably knows much about him. I have asked him to send you a 'résumé' of his recollections.

"Burleigh (a Negro) was thought much of by Dr. Dvořák and has written many beautiful songs, etc., etc.—showing the Dr.'s judgment was right.

"Wishing you success—

"V. H."

Dvořák sincerely admired Herbert's playing of the 'cello. One of the Czech composer's most famous compositions for this instrument is now known to have been inspired by Victor Herbert's sensitive playing.

In program notes written for a Washington, D. C., performance of Dvořák's *Concerto in B minor for Violoncello and Orchestra*, Opus 104, Edward N. Waters (Assistant Chief, Division of Music, Library of Congress) made a statement based on facts furnished him by the daughter and son-in-law of Victor Herbert, Mr. and Mrs. Robert Stevens Bartlett:

"The B minor 'cello concerto is one of the great works that Dvořák wrote in this country. . . . Curiously enough, there does seem to be an American origin beyond that of mere geography. There is evidence to show that Dvořák was prompted to write the concerto after hearing a 'cello performance of Victor Herbert . . . , by far the best loved of our operetta composers. Herbert was at that time a truly remarkable 'cellist, playing principal 'cello under such conductors as Thomas and Seidl at the Metropolitan Opera House, and frequently making solo appearances. In March, 1894, he played his own second 'cello concerto, a major work in the repertoire, and apparently made a lasting impression upon Dvořák."

Work of this sort could come out of no humdrum environment. It required a congenial artist's world, and found it in this little old New York of the late eighties. Old Steinway Hall on East Fourteenth Street . . . rows of modest three-story dwellings and comfortable lodging houses on Irving Street . . . the old German restaurant two blocks from Gramercy Park (the Rheinschlösschen of O. Henry's stories about his Bagdad-on-the-Subway) . . . Gramercy Park surrounded by its gracious old houses . . . Washington Irving's home . . . Union Square . . . Old Moretti's, where spaghetti (then a novelty in America) was served . . . Lienau's . . . Lüchow's . . . Knirim's. . . .

Harrigan, of Harrigan and Hart fame, was still writing and acting in boisterous plays about Irish politicians and policemen and the German neighborhoods, and the proletarian parties where someone "threw the overalls in Mrs. Murphy's chowder." Herbert was genuinely delighted with the robust humor and rollicking music (furnished by Harrigan's father-in-law, Dave Braham) of the Harrigan songs. He called the Harrigan-Braham travesties folk plays and would have liked to provide the musical settings for pieces somewhat like them, if he could have found the right person to furnish a libretto and lyrics. Thoughts like these crossed his mind more and more frequently, even as he was composing.

All his works at this time were of a serious nature. They were presented either by Anton Seidl and his summer-concert orchestra, or by Herbert in his own concert work. *Serenade for Strings*, performed by Seidl's orchestra, impressed the reviewers favorably. Critic Krehbiel wrote:

"Mr. Herbert's composition was written for strings and the performance was conducted by him. It won for him the heartiest applause of the evening. . . . The vivid and varied splashes of color which Mr. Herbert threw into the score, notwithstanding that he had only five stringed instruments at his command, were most effective."

In the third movement of this serenade, Herbert's special talent for creating an atmosphere of youthful romance (an outstanding characteristic of his later work in the field of operetta) was apparent. Critic Krehbiel noticed it and commented that this movement, called appropriately "A Love Scene," could well have been taken out of the quintet and expanded for full orchestra.

For the 'cello, Herbert wrote *Berceuse and Polonaise*, which he played at a private concert in 1887; and *Bagatelle and Scherzo*, performed at a benefit concert. Several songs were written for the Mendelssohn Glee Club and the Brooklyn Männerchor. Just a year after his arrival in New York, Herbert completed his second 'cello concerto, in E minor, Opus 30. This work was written for and dedicated to the New York Philharmonic Society. It was played by the Philharmonic orchestra in 1894, Anton Seidl conducting, Victor Herbert interpreting the solo part. The composition is today a standard piece of solo 'cellists' repertoires.

One of the *World* critics wrote:

"Victor Herbert, the 'cellist, came forward as a composer and soloist and in both showed his ability as an artist. His work, a Concerto for violoncello, presented extreme difficulties for the solo instrument. This Mr. Herbert played with rare skill and finish; his tone is mellow and sympathetic and his playing of his own composition gave such pleasure to the audience that he was twice recalled."

This concerto, which pleased both public and critics, and which Dvořák had called "gang famos!," was provided at a later date with interesting program notes by Victor Herbert himself:

"After a tempestuous prologue in triple and duple measure, now fast, now slow, the first theme swings into a striking five-bar rhythm—a scherzo-like movement—which is yet impassioned and dramatic. Though highly complex in rhythmic structure, the movement produces such an effect that it appears to be merely the natural expression of musical fantasy under the force of inspiration, moving with a freedom and spontaneity almost like improvisation.

"At the transition without pause into the Andante, the first movement changes its character in a delicate coda and through a short *lento* reminiscent of the opening measure of the orchestra, modulates into B major. The theme, now tranquil and flowing, interrupted as it is by an episode, forms a contrast to the former movement. It is not long, however, before the first movement reasserts itself with fresh energy and new complexity including simultaneous combination of the three principal ideas and a close of brilliant figuration for the solo instrument."

No words, of course—not even the composer's—can give an idea of the sound of a musical composition. Even short excerpts from the music fall woefully short of this goal, especially where a long work like a symphony or concerto is concerned. A hint of the delicate melodies and dramatic harmonies is all that a few bars can give. From an arrangement for 'cello and piano, a tender phrase sings *molto più lento.* The 'cello part is played softly and sweetly against hushed piano chords which represent the orchestral score:

For the Worcester, Massachusetts, music festival of 1891, Herbert composed a massive cantata called *The Captive.* This work was performed at the same concert at which Edward MacDowell's *Orchestral Suite in A minor* was heard for the first time.

And yet, with all this activity, Herbert was not achieving what he wanted most—a chance to write music of a light, humorous, romantic turn for the theater. His busy mind was alert for the opportunity which was soon to present itself.

Some of Herbert's friends among the "serious" musicians sincerely believed that anything truly popular was bound to be trash. They pleaded with the composer to give up his plan to write music for the stage. They felt that he was betraying his own talents by turning away, ever so little even, from the high standard he had set with his second 'cello concerto.

It took no small amount of courage to go against them—but courage and belief in his own ideas were always Herbert's. He defended his position by asserting that there were but two kinds of music. Not heavy music and light music, as many declared. Not "classical" music and "popular" music. There was, in his opinion, only *good* music and *bad* music.

Herbert would argue that a poem by Bobby Burns was certainly not a serious work like Shakespeare's *Hamlet*, say, but in its way, Burns' poem shared a claim to high art.

"We don't know why," he would add reflectively. "We don't know why some of Bobby Burns' four-liners are intrinsic poetry, but they are. We don't know why certain poems are done into music a thousand times, but they are."

Victor Herbert deliberately chose to be a Bobby Burns, not a Shakespeare. Whether he could have achieved the stature of the latter is debatable; perhaps not. But in his own sphere, he was, like Burns, a true artist. There was only good music and bad music, he had said. Well, Herbert wrote good music. The thousands who love it today bear witness to that.

Fame

1891-1894. This was the era of the "Gibson Girl," who wore a gored skirt, huge sleeves, lace fichus and berthas to exaggerate her shoulders, and a straw "sailor" hat. Nicholas II, last of the Russian Czars, ascended the throne. In England, elementary education was made compulsory and free for the first time. Ramsay was discovering helium. Nikolai Lenin was giving up his law practice in Russia to become a professional revolutionary. Sherlock Holmes and Dr. Watson appeared in the *Strand Magazine*. Boos and hisses greeted Debussy's *Afternoon of a Faun* in Paris. Popular songs in the United States were *You Can't Lose Me, Charlie; Danny By My Side; The Man Who Broke the Bank at Monte Carlo;* and *Ta-Ra-Ra-Boom-De-Ay.*

BY 1891, Victor Herbert was firmly entrenched in the artistic life of New York. His hearty laugh and generous nature would have won him a place in the affections of his fellow-artists, even if he had not had the outstanding knowledge of music and the performer's skill to command their respect.

He was very soon invited to become a member of the famous club known as the Lambs. This was a group composed of men of the theater primarily, but including also men of music and literature. Founded in 1875 "for the purpose of social recreation and the cultivation of musical, literary, and artistic talent," this club copied the Lambs of London. August Thomas, Shepherd of the New York Lambs in 1909, wrote a brief history of this famous organization for the Chicago *Record-Herald:*

In the years 1820-1834, he explained, in quaint chambers in Inner Temple Lane, London, lived Charles and Mary Lamb, who wrote the famous *Tales from Shakespeare* (Charles the tragic ones, Mary, the comic). These two were famous for their hospitality. Social gatherings in their house included such famous men as Coleridge, Lloyd, Southey, Wordsworth, Hazlitt, Leigh Hunt, Talford, George Dyer, and Tom Hood. When the coffee houses closed for the night, notables would say, "Let's go round to the Lambs'."

After their death, a group of actors formed a club in London. They called their club the Lambs, in memory of the genial little author of the *Essays of Elia* and his beloved sister, the "Cousin Bridget" of the essays. Members of this club migrating to New York established the Lambs in America.

"If there exists anywhere in America any suggestion of the fraternal and convivial and literary flavor that made the various coteries of London coffee houses famous, it is to be found in the Lambs," declared Shepherd Thomas. "The Lambs Club is a strong club because with its artistic and musical element there is united that of the dramatic writers."

Herbert belonged also to the Friars, a group recruited from the Lambs. Election to the Friars placed a man among the really popular and successful on Broadway. It was a badge of honor, this membership, a sort of informal election to a Hall of Fame.

The Friars did nothing more serious than have fun. For Herbert, the Lambs was always a business club, a place where he met business associates and talked shop. The Friars was an outlet for his boyish conviviality, and he was nearly always on hand for the weekly "gambols," to which he contributed generously with clever songs and sketches. The rousing club song, called simply *The Friars Song,* was given a brisk musical setting by Victor Herbert. The words are a hearty toast to the club:

THE FRIARS SONG

The Friars of old
Were a merry old fold;
Care and sadness to them were but folly.
With pipe and with glass,
And an eye for a lass,
And a quip, to defy melancholy;
Well-versed in the stars
And in musical bars,
Dispensers of fiction and fable;
And at friendship's command
They would pass the glad hand,
With a toast that would ring 'round the table.

Refrain:

Here's to the Friars!
Here's to them all!
Out on the road or here in the hall.
Raise high your glasses with cheer that inspires,
And drink a deep toast
To the boys we love most!
A toast to all other good Friars!

Herbert also contributed his composing talents for the famous Lambs' Gambol, an entertainment offered every year as a money-raising venture for the club. Featured with scenes from the best plays and musical comedies of the Broadway season are numerous skits specially written for the occasion. Herbert's *Songbirds* was such a skit. This operatic travesty in one act was a take-off on an absurd situation which developed in New York when impresario Oscar Hammerstein tried to produce opera as he liked it in competition with the directors of the Metropolitan Opera House. Hammerstein liked Italian opera; the Metropolitan favored German opera.

For his travesty, Herbert used the idea of opposing choruses, one dressed in German opera costumes, the other in Italian opera garb, each trying to sing the other down. The whole play was pure farce, as the names of some of the characters—Madame Yellba, Madame Emma Screams, and Peter Pantson—indicate. The music, in grand-opera style treated in a humorous way, requires good voices and makes a lighthearted, melodious setting for the funny dialogue.

When an exclusive little musical organization known as the Rubato Club welcomed the genial Victor to its "inner sanctum," a specially composed song was offered as a tribute to the new member's talents. Such men as Fritz Kreisler joined in the merriment, forgot for the moment that they were famous, and sang like mischievous schoolboys:

> "Tonight we initiate the first
> New member in the Club.
> O Victor Herbert! You're a brick,
> You're welcomed by this mob.
>
> Today he writes an opera,
> Tomorrow a symphonie;
> He plays the violoncello and
> He leads the Philharmonie."

One can guess how lustily the laughter rang out, and be sure that Herbert's sounded joyously above the rest. How he loved a good story, a good dinner, and good company!

Some people wondered how he found time for all this activity—writing music, playing in a large orchestra, giving solo performances on the side, traveling with concert groups in summer, and contributing freely all the while to the activities of these clubs. The fact is, Herbert liked both his work and his play, and he had learned early in his boyhood how to cram a good deal of both into twenty-four hours.

Though Victor Herbert could not endure the typical "practical joke," he sometimes indulged in a mild prank at the expense of his fellow-musicians. The Lotus Club was the scene of one of these sly jokes of his. Caruso was being honored at a club banquet. Herbert, who was to make the principal speech, rose and began what the discreetly bored members thought would be a conventional tribute to a great man and artist. Suddenly, those who were giving but half an ear sat up and took notice. Comical expressions of surprise and dismay came to their faces. Without the slightest indication, by tone or gesture, of a change, Herbert had slid into fluent Italian. He continued and finished his speech in the language which only he and Caruso at that table could understand. Caruso, hugely amused at this device of Herbert's for waking up bored banqueters, entered into the spirit of the thing and made his reply in Italian also.

About this time, Herbert's desire to write light music was taking very definite form. He actually tried his hand at an operetta score. It was never produced or published, so that even the subject matter of the libretto remains a mystery; but it was a start. When Steele MacKaye decided to present a huge pageant with music for the Chicago World's Fair, Herbert was delighted to be asked to contribute some original music. The pageant died a-borning, but Herbert's efforts were not wasted.

"I know now that I must write for the theater," he told his wife. "I simply *must* find a libretto."

It was not long afterward that Herbert met the man who was to play a fateful rôle in shaping the composer's future career. This man was William MacDonald, head of that famous light-opera troupe, the Bostonians. These two became fast friends.

At that time, the Bostonians were playing Reginald De Koven's *Robin Hood*, a tuneful, romantic light opera with excellent music and colorful libretto.

"Victor, you could do something of this sort for us. We need some additions to our repertoire. Why not try your hand?" suggested MacDonald.

Actor Henry Clay Barnabee, chief singing comedian and assistant manager of the troupe, added his persuasion. "We'll see that your piece is produced," he promised.

Someone else suggested that a writer by the name of Francis Neilsen might provide the libretto that Herbert needed.

Neilsen did provide a libretto—a satirical piece in the manner of the English Gilbert. Herbert set to work. The lamps burned late at night in his study as the composer wrote music for the characters of Neilsen's amusing story, which is mainly a take-off on the oddities and temperamental vagaries of theatrical folk. When the operetta was ready, the Bostonians began rehearsals immediately. It was produced at the Broadway Theatre, New York, on the night of November 20, 1894.

The first scene of *Prince Ananias* was laid in the Pyrenees Mountains of France. In the courtyard of a picturesque inn, a merry harvest festival was taking place. Ninette, the village belle, who, the librettist tells us, "has jilted swains of every size," was the center of interest. The villagers were agog over the announcement that she proposed to marry the village miser—the least agreeable man in town.

The merrymaking was at its height when Louis Biron, a vagabond poet and adventurer, arrived. Biron began to flirt with Ninette in the hope that she would give him some of the stew he smelled through an open window of the inn.

Before Biron could carry out his plans with the stew, an old friend of his arrived. This was George Le Grabbe, who made haste to confess that he was dying for love of a young lady named Mirabel, daughter of the King's Lord High Chamberlain. He revealed further that he was known to the villagers as an outlaw with a price on his head; that some weeks before he had held up the Lord High Chamberlain's coach; and that this circumstance had naturally prejudiced that dignitary against his daughter's suitor.

La Fontaine, head of a troupe of play-actors, joined the guests at the inn, and Biron promptly fell in love with the beautiful leading lady, Idalia. Forgotten was Ninette, but the little coquette was not to be easily discarded. She overheard Biron and Le Grabbe making plans to go to the court of the King of Navarre. Biron would pose as a prince, Le Grabbe, disguised to conceal his true outlaw identity, as his personal physician. By this ruse, they hoped to gain the confidence of the king and win Mirabel for Le Grabbe, a fortune for them both. They even persuaded La Fontaine and his troupe to go with them, promising that "the Prince" would present them at Court. Ninette decided to go along. She made a deal with the actors to become a member of their company.

Act Two was set in a glade near the palace of the King of Navarre. The monarch was too sad to raise his head. This condition had been brought about by the treacherous Lord High Chamberlain, who, for purposes of his own, had contrived to keep the king from laughing. The members of the Court had been induced to carry onions about with them; whenever a joke was told, they sniffed the onions and thus managed to weep "onion tears" instead of laugh as the king expected them to. This state of affairs was highly discouraging to any attempt at levity, and the king was actually dying of melancholy.

It did not take Biron and Le Grabbe long to learn the secret of the Lord High Chamberlain's plot against mirth. They looked on knowingly as La Fontaine and his troupe put on their funniest play for the king. No matter how they tried, the actors could not make the king smile; and pretty soon they were weeping too, from sheer dismay at the failure of their comedy.

Biron saved the day. He begged leave to relate the story of a play which the actors (so he said) had once presented for another king's pleasure. There was a king in the play, Biron said, whose court was a happy place until a wily Lord High Chamberlain hatched a plot. He persuaded everyone to carry onions, so that they should be eternally weeping. No one was to smile or laugh, and in this atmosphere of gloom the king died of grief.

Biron was merely telling the King of Navarre the story of his own trouble, and as a light broke over that perplexed monarch, a laugh—his first in many a long day—made him well. The scheming Lord High Chamberlain was immediately put in chains or boiled in oil or something of the sort, and the grateful king gave La Fontaine his job. Biron, who had accomplished all the good work, was made Inspector of Birdseed. Mirabel and Le Grabbe were united, and Biron and Idalia. Ninette, seeing that she could not win Biron, consoled herself with Eugene, playwright for the theatrical troupe.

The libretto was clever, and Herbert's music was good; but audiences did not leave the theater humming and singing the songs. In other words, the operetta was not a complete success. Barnabee insisted on including *Prince Ananias* in the repertoire when the company went on the road, alternating it with *Robin Hood*. However, it was soon dropped. The fact is, Neilsen's satire was not of the caliber of the English Gilbert's; and, in any case, Herbert's pen did not easily write the music for satire. What he needed was a romantic libretto, with emphasis on love and youth and beauty and lighthearted adventure.

Even though the Neilsen libretto was not the work of a Babs-ballad Gilbert, still it was clever—too clever, Herbert afterward decided. The composer once told a reporter from the *Christian Science Monitor* that the operetta's very cleverness was against it. America, he said, presented librettist and composer with the difficulty of combining simplicity with originality. You could not hope to write a "Pinafore" which would please the American public. That public, essentially sentimental, demanded musical comedy of sentiment, charm, and warmth. It would not grasp the satirical verse, the sarcastic dialogue of thrust and parry with the foibles and politics of the day. It was the country's loss, of course, musically; but melting sugar made the best musical comedy music; the piquant sauce of satire would be tasted but not relished.

Publisher Frederick Kraft, who had enough faith in this opera to publish it, recognized at once that Herbert's music excelled the libretto in audience appeal. "The book," he recalls, his eyes twinkling, "was written by an Englishman whose idol was Gilbert; it is not surprising that the humor was Gilbertian. Some of the humor was too subtle for the audiences of the day. For instance, there is the delightful line

'Under an oak *unostentatiously* was born.' It didn't make people laugh."

This first operetta of Herbert's is remembered chiefly for the graceful dances which the composer sprinkled through the score. They mirror the ballroom steps of the composer's own day, these schottisches, lancers, polkas, and sedate waltzes. Even the two-step seems an old-fashioned relative of the more modern dance.

Herbert was always loyal to the men of his profession. He did not blame the librettist for the moderate success of *Prince Ananias*. In fact, years later when someone stated that his music always surpassed the books of his operettas, Herbert spoke up in defense of librettists:

"It is very difficult to write a plot for a musical comedy," he said. "The musical numbers are constantly interfering with the action; every time a song is introduced, the plot is thrown down on the floor like a piece of old rope, and interest in the story is interrupted. Another thing that our librettists are up against is that they have to write clean stuff—thank God! In French musical plays the author can make vulgarity pass for entertainment."

This last statement is significant. Herbert detested the vulgar and the lewd in the theater and would never have any part in what was ugly or off-color. Once he told a producer who wanted him to write music for a salacious play, "I would not write music for that for less than a million dollars a note."

On the other hand, he delighted in writing for plays of youthful romance, with their innocent fun and simple, honest philosophy. He seemed positively to delight in writing music suitable for small children. In addition to the children's operettas—*Babes in Toyland* and *Little Nemo*—some of the "grown-up" operettas have tunes set to words surely written for children; in these melodies the composer caught something of the charm of childhood itself.

Victor Herbert's daughter, Ella Herbert Bartlett, writes in her recent book (*Victor Herbert: Songs for Children*):

"Father dearly loved children. He liked the bright, happy side of life which childhood represents. He liked to see children play and hear them sing. He liked their songs, and this may be the reason that he scattered through his operettas so many delightful songs which, both in melody and lyrics, are 'Songs for Children.' Of these, *Always Do As People Say You Should*, from 'The Fortune Teller,' and *Mother Goose*, from 'Sweethearts,' are typical examples. In neither score is there other music of this type. It would seem as though, in writing these operettas, Father felt that he could not forget his little friends and just had to include a song for them regardless of the character of the other music.

" 'Babes in Toyland,' however, is an opera for children, and it has always been a great favorite of their mothers and fathers as well. It is a nursery tale containing nearly all of the characters dear to children, and one of Father's most enchanting scores. From this I have included that sweet lullaby, *Go to Sleep, Slumber Deep*, sung by the Good Fairy who protects the babes in the woods throughout the night; the reassuring song that Bo-Peep will find her sheep; and the famous melody *Toyland*, with words that are far too true! There are other beautiful songs too, each selected because of its appeal to children and because it is 'characteristically Herbert.' "

The prettiest melodies which Victor Herbert wrote for children are included in Ella Herbert Bartlett's book, and she is glad to have a few measures from these dainty songs take their proper place in this book about her beloved father.

The lullaby from *Babes in Toyland* was sung by a fairy to the babes in the woods; but the composer must have had in mind fat, pink babies in old-fashioned cradles when he wrote it. It is a gentle, old-fashioned mother who sings, "Little one, oh sleep, while watch I keep!" Here are the opening measures of the soothing "hush-o" *Go to Sleep, Slumber Deep:*

The pert nonsense of *I Can't Do the Sum* from *Babes in Toyland* reminds one of a naughty child, pouting because the lesson is hard.

Story-telling time comes, and the children settle themselves on their little chairs in the candle-lit nursery to listen to the jingles out of Mother Goose. *Babes in Toyland* furnishes a nursery song that has charmed its hearers ever since it was first sung. Bo-Peep is crying because she has lost her sheep, but she is comforted with *Never Mind, Bo-Peep:*

And then the grown-up who has been reading the nursery tales looks at the eager faces of the children and sighs, for a reason that boys and girls cannot understand. Childhood. Happy, happy time! Happy land of Toyland. "Once you leave its borders, you can ne'er return again." Those were the composer's thoughts when he wrote *Toyland:*

Even in the operettas written for adults, Victor Herbert remembered the land of childhood. In *The Fortune Teller*, a saucy girl sings the coquettish *Always Do As People Say You Should:*

In the *Lady of the Slipper*, the composer takes us to a Hallowe'en party, where make-believe spooks and goblins mingle with the Jack-o'-lanterns, and the children play *Games of Hallowe'en:*

Little Nemo has some music in honor of St. Valentine. All

the fun of paper lace, red cardboard hearts, golden cupid darts, and romantic verses are recalled with *Be My Valentine:*

With *Won't You Be My Playmate?* we enter a special part of childhood's realm, the land of make-believe. There the magic of "Let's pretend" and "Let's play like" can turn a boy or girl in the twinkling of an eye into a king or princess or Mr. and Mrs. Smith all dressed up for the Easter parade:

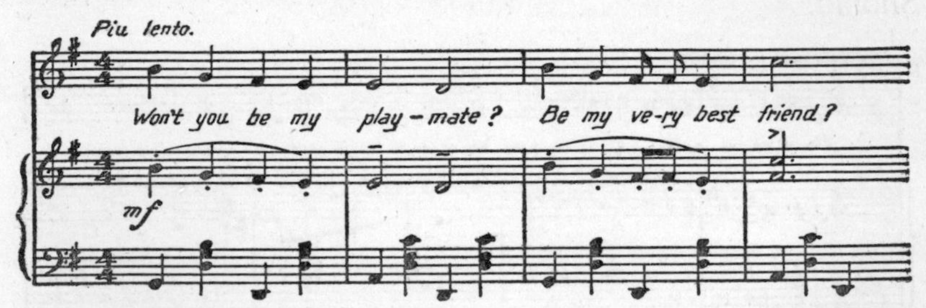

After a busy day, curly heads nod and bright eyes close in sleep. Then the dreams come thronging—all about Jack Horner and Bo-Peep and Jack and Jill, the children of "dear old, queer old, Mother Goose." In his romantic music for *Sweethearts,* Victor Herbert did not forget this good old lady of the nursery rhymes. He salutes her in *Mother Goose:*

In that same year of 1894, when Herbert turned from strictly serious music to the writing of operetta, he took another audacious step. He made a break with serious music in the realm of conducting, too, by accepting the leadership of the official band of the Twenty-second Regiment of the National Guard of the State of New York.

For a musician who had played 'cello in the orchestra at the Metropolitan Opera House, who had been assistant to the great Anton Seidl, who had made his bow to the critics as a solo 'cellist with the New York Philharmonic Society—for such a musician to take a position as leader of a band seemed to many of Herbert's friends more of a comedown than writing for musical comedy. They raised their eyebrows and shook their heads.

"I know what I am doing," said Herbert, smiling. "Why should a musician be ashamed of conducting a band? A band is popular, I know, and is it a crime to be popular?"

One of Herbert's chief reasons for undertaking to lead a band was to gain experience. He knew orchestral music and technique; he wanted to learn about bands and how to write good marches.

He would have been the first to admit, too, that money was another factor. He was frank in saying that serious music paid slow dividends in dollars, and he wanted and needed money. He was used to a good standard of living He liked a pleasant home, with good furnishings. He liked to have money for entertaining, for buying the luxuries of life. Even Anton Seidl had frequently lacked for these things; Herbert decided that he and his own family should not.

Herbert was, above all, a friendly, unaffected, democratic sort of man. He was happiest when he felt that his musical thoughts were being enjoyed by the masses of people. He himself expressed this point of view some years later in an interview with a representative of the *New York Sun:*

"In regard to music, we love only what we understand; we cannot love what we do not understand. I mean this superficial statement to refer to the great masses of people who have only time in their crowded lives to yield occasionally to their impulses to hear some good music and who cannot in those rare moments rise and fall to the heights and depths of emotion and understanding demanded by great compositions like those of Bach, Liszt, et al., but who really want good music and respond when you give it to them, with their patronage and applause.

"They don't want cheap music, but they want something delicate, pretty, graceful, sensuous, but not hyper-sensuous. . . .

"It is the easiest thing in the world to be serious, but to be nothing else—that is an anchor to inspiration, a deterioration instead of a progress in art. To take a serious subject and to so adorn it with the flower of fancy that you attract the most hidebound—is not that an achievement? I think so.

"Shakespeare never wrote a play into which he did not introduce a low-comedy rôle. 'Hamlet' is serious enough, that no one will dispute, and in no play is there any greater farce than in the famous graveyard scene of that tragedy.

"Even Beethoven had moments of musical comedy. If he lost a penny he would sit down and compose a rondo and call it, 'The Rage for a Lost Coin,' which, in German, sounds rather appalling.

"The popularity of my concerts has pleased me immensely, for it has proved that I have succeeded in doing what I have crudely outlined in this talk. . . .

"That time has passed when intelligent persons are content with any work, music or literature, of which they are forced to remark: 'Yes, it is very beautiful, indeed, although I do not understand all of it.'

"Personally, I hold that that which is not 'popular' is not of much benefit to the world."

The Twenty-second Regiment Band had achieved real fame under the leadership of the Irish-American Patrick Sarsfield Gilmore, a man of big ideas and prodigious energy in carrying them out. At the National Peace Jubilee in Boston in 1869, he had organized an orchestra of one thousand pieces and a chorus of ten thousand voices. In 1872, at the World's Peace Jubilee, he did not quite succeed in making his orchestra and chorus as much larger than the Boston aggregation as the world is larger than Boston; but he came close enough. His instruments numbered two thousand, his voices twenty thousand, and to this uproar he added cannons, a powerful organ, a drum eight feet high, anvils, and chimes of bells. If there was peace before this monster musical assemblage got under way, there surely was none afterward.

Gilmore was a popular composer of military marches, dance music, and songs. The men of the Twenty-second Regiment developed a celebrated band under his guidance, with smart uniforms and smarter playing. Naturally, when they had to look about for someone to fill Gilmore's shoes, they were very careful in their choice. Victor Herbert, who had his own ideas about doing things in a big way, felt flattered that they selected him to take Gilmore's place.

For the next four years, Herbert worked like a beaver on behalf of his band, taking it all over the country to play engagements at jubilees and expositions, and taking part in military parades with the regiment to which the band was attached. He wrote marches, made special band arrangements of orchestral music, rehearsed his men, and enjoyed every minute of his work.

The members of the band felt sincere appreciation for Herbert's efforts (though there once was a sort of in-the-family squabble about whose responsibility it was when the band lost money). On the whole, both the band and their leader profited by their association. Herbert's thorough musicianship whipped the band into an ardent desire for perfection. And Herbert learned the special requirements of martial music, which he used effectively in his later operettas.

Following Gilmore's custom, Herbert enriched the literature of his band with much original work. Many of the marches were composed at white heat, often for some particular occasion; and therefore show the traces of hasty or superficial writing. Nothing, however, that Herbert did was ever wholly trivial. A little-known march of the period—*The Belle of Pittsburg*—is one of these on the whole undistinguished pieces which has here and there a measure or two of unusual melody:

Minstrel for the Million

1894-1898. In these years, Freud introduced psychoanalysis. In the United States, Rural Free Delivery of mail brought the world to the farmer's door. The age of the horse and buggy was on its way out. In England, the law permitted automobiles to travel at the rate of twelve miles per hour. Roentgen discovered the X-ray. Stephen Crane's *Red Badge of Courage* was a fiction landmark for America. The Gold Rush to the Yukon was taking thousands of adventurers to the far north. The Olympic games were revived at Athens. Popular songs were *I Don't Want to Play in Your Yard, Just Tell Them That You Saw Me, Take Back the Ring.* The Spanish-American War began in April and ended in December, 1898.

BY 1894, Victor and Therese Herbert had been in the United States seven years. All this while, Herbert had been working hard at his routine duties as 'cellist, and in what might have been leisure hours, he worked even harder as composer.

Even though *Prince Ananias* had been something of a disappointment, Herbert began to cast about for another libretto. What he wanted was a light, romantic comedy. He needed a sympathetic librettist. Such a writer turned up about this time. He was Harry B. Smith, who wrote many of the books for the Herbert successes to come.

It was for the celebrated singing comedian of the day, Frank Daniels, that Herbert was engaged to write his second operetta. Kirke La Shelle, former business manager for the

Bostonians, was Daniels' new manager. Librettist Smith submitted the book of a comic opera to Daniels and La Shelle. It was called *The Wizard of the Nile*, and was an uproarious farce with a part tailor-made for Daniels' talent.

"But where can we find a composer?" Daniels asked glumly. The librettist was silent on that score. Good comic-opera composers were as scarce as hen's teeth.

"Why not Victor Herbert?" was La Shelle's suggestion.

"Herbert?" echoed Daniels. "Well, I don't know. He's a serious composer—suites and concertos are rather in his line, aren't they?"

"Don't forget *Prince Ananias*." La Shelle had been with the Bostonians when they were presenting this satirical piece, and he was convinced that the composer of "Ananias" showed great promise.

Like Daniels, Smith was somewhat dubious about engaging a theatrical newcomer to write music for his book. The two of them gave in to La Shelle's eloquence, however, and agreed to take a chance on Herbert's ability to catch the popular ear.

When Herbert read the libretto he was thoroughly pleased and agreed at once to do the music. "I shall write you a real 'standing room only' success this time," he promised La Shelle.

"You'd better!" was La Shelle's dry retort. "Smith and Daniels will scalp me if this thing doesn't click. I think you can do it, though, and I like to back my judgment."

The truth was that La Shelle, shrewd manager and judge of people that he was, had seen in the composer of *Prince Ananias* an invaluable combination—a composer with a classical background and training, and a musician who had the instincts of an actor and a genius for theatrical effects.

La Shelle's confidence was not misplaced. Herbert set to work with a will to redeem his "popular" reputation. Two weeks after he received Smith's manuscript, he had the first act set to music.

Smith, Daniels, and La Shelle went over to Herbert's home

to hear the composer play the melodies for them. There was no longer any doubt. Herbert had written the kind of music which the public would eat up.

The rest of the score for *The Wizard of the Nile* was written on the jump, so to speak; for Herbert was touring constantly with the Twenty-second Regiment Band. Much of the operetta was written in Atlanta, Georgia, where the band was filling an engagement at the Atlanta Exposition. One of the bandsmen, Otto Schreiber, told in later years how amazed everyone was at Herbert's capacity for hard work. After the evening concert, the composer would go to his room in the exposition building, where, sweltering in the excessive heat of a Georgia summer and fighting off mosquitoes, he worked on the score of his operetta.

"You'll kill yourself with work!" warned Schreiber. "It isn't possible to work like a beaver all day in this heat and half the night, too. It's burning the candle at both ends!"

Herbert laughed. "Don't worry. I can stand it. You see, nature really intended me to be a ship's stoker or something of the sort."

Schreiber, looking at Herbert's strong, well-built figure, his healthy color, his muscular hands and arms, was inclined to agree.

It was Schreiber who told of Herbert's working methods. The composer usually wrote his music away from 'cello and piano, for he had the true composer's ear and mind. Melodies sounded in his head without help of strings or keys.

It was Herbert's habit to carry with him at all times a notebook about the size of a billfold. This notebook contained paper ruled for music. Whenever a melody came to him—and melodies had a way of singing their way into his thoughts no matter what he was doing, walking, traveling with his band, or hiking in the Adirondacks—he jotted it down in this book. Later, at his leisure, he expanded the musical ideas into songs and instrumental music, working at a high desk before which he could stand or sit on a high stool. Both the famous notebook and the desk have been presented to the Library of Congress of the United States by Victor Herbert's daughter.

Once his musical thoughts were on paper, Herbert seldom altered a note. The original melody and any necessary revisions were worked out mentally, so that there was no need for erasures and scratches on paper. Completed scores, prepared by Herbert for music publishers and editors, were marvels of neatness and clarity.

When a composition was completed, the composer would play it through on his 'cello, if it were a simple melody for voice or solo instrument; on the piano, if the music was orchestral. A story grew up and found its way many times into print that Herbert was a wretched pianist—and all because it was frequently necessary for the composer to demonstrate to librettist or producer how a finished operetta score would sound. Indeed, some special magic would be required if a musician were to play simultaneously all the parts of an orchestral score, with but two hands and one piano keyboard at his command. An excellent pianist might give a sketchy idea of how the parts would sound. That is what Herbert did. He would run his fingers over the keys, indicating the melody given to this instrument or that, showing how the voice parts came in, frowning as he worked, and explaining apologetically to his listeners, "Of course, I can't give you *any* idea of this!"

The Wizard of the Nile was produced at the Casino Theatre in New York, November 4, 1895. The overture was hardly at an end when both librettist and composer knew that they had a success.

The story—one of Smith's best—was novel in setting. The audience was delighted with the Egyptian background. There were the huge columns of the temples of Alexandria, the pyramids, and glimpses of the Nile. The colorful costumes of the cast were faithful to the old pictures found on Egyptian tombs and palaces.

Herbert's music was pleasantly suggestive of the ancient East and yet never once lost its songlike quality understandable to the musical-comedy audience. The tunes were catchy, easy to remember. Where the story had a touch of romance to temper the farce, Herbert's music was at its best. Throughout the story, there was plenty of absurd comedy for Daniels' clowning talent. In short, *The Wizard of the Nile* was nearly perfect operetta material.

The story goes that Kibosh, a Persian magician, is making a professional tour of Egypt. He and his assistant, Abydos, learn that the land is suffering from famine because the Nile has failed to overflow as usual to fertilize the crops. Ptolemy, King of Egypt, has let the word go out that anyone able to conjure up a flood shall be given the hand of the Princess Cleopatra in marriage.

This idea is repugnant to Cleopatra and to Ptarmigan, her music teacher; for these two are in love. Kibosh, however, is entirely in favor of the idea, for Cleopatra is very beautiful. What is more, the magician thinks he may have a chance of winning her. He knows something about the seasons of the Nile's overflow, and feels sure that a flood is about due. He waves his arms in some amusing hocus-pocus, and sure enough the waters of the Nile begin to pour over the banks. Everyone gives Kibosh credit for the event, of course.

However, the matter gets out of hand. Instead of rising to a normal level, the Nile floods the district disastrously. Since Kibosh is supposed to have caused the flood in the first place, he is expected to make the waters subside. This he cannot do, and he finds it beyond even his powers of glib and persuasive speech to explain why. The King blames him for the damage and orders him to be punished in fifty-seven charming ancient Egyptian ways.

Other absurd characters wander through the story. There is Simoona, Ptolemy's second wife, who is a sort of Alice in Wonderland queen. Her obsession seems to be "Off with his head, whoever he is, whatever he's done!" There is Cheops, the Royal Weather Prophet, bitter rival of the Persian magician who has rather upset the King's faith in Cheops' prognostications. There are outrageous characters like Odelisk, Captain of the Amazons; and Merza, an Alexandrian barmaid.

The headsmen, Chop-chop and Chopum, and two policemen, McIbis and O'Pasht (whose reincarnated spirits, apparently, were on the New York police force, for they were typical "Micks" in brass buttons), mingle with the chorus. The chorus is not the least amazing part of the cast. There are Royal Guards, citizens of Egypt, dancing girls, galley slaves, and maids of honor.

Comedian Daniels romped through his part, taking eggs from the mouths of various characters, commenting on his own cleverness with the aside to the audience, "Am I a Wiz!" an expression which immediately became part of the American "slanguage."

Naturally, before the final curtain, Kibosh talks and tricks his way out of his fifty-seven varieties of punishment, and all ends happily. Cleopatra and Ptarmigan are united, and Kibosh is in great favor with the King.

Though Herbert's music is not uniformly of the standard he was to set with his later operettas like *Mlle. Modiste* and *Naughty Marietta*, some of the melodies are tuneful and genuinely charming. One of the prettiest of these is the waltz song *Star Light, Star Bright.*

The duet sung by Ptarmigan and Cleopatra is delicately plaintive:

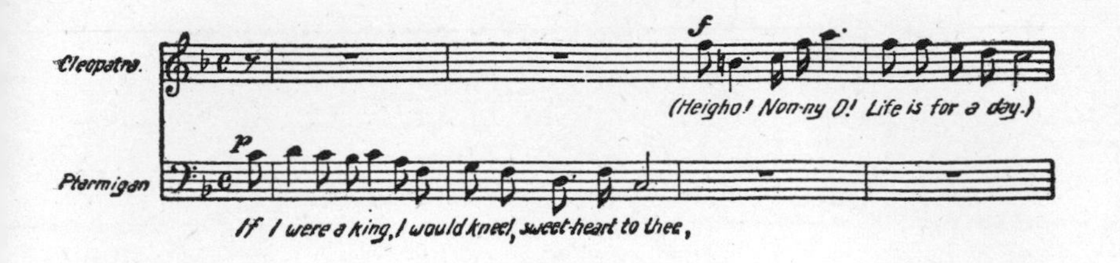

The *Oriental March,* less effective than most of Herbert's music for *The Wizard of the Nile,* illustrates an interesting fact. Though extremely simple, the musical thought of this march is actually made to seem complex and brilliant by the alchemy of Herbert's inspired orchestration. The composer himself recognized this ability of his to orchestrate even a prosaic melody into vivid poetic life, and frequently remarked of a doubtful tune, "Oh, it will come out all right in the orchestration!"

The Wizard of the Nile was destined for international fame. It was translated into German as *Der Zauberer vom Nil,* and published by the State Publishing House in Vienna. The operetta was performed in German both in Vienna and for German-speaking audiences in New York at the Terrace Garden in 1897.

The "Wizard" was followed by another operetta which had a moderate success. This was *The Gold Bug* of 1896, billed as "A Musical Farce." It was more farce than music, having but three numbers. It is remembered best for the stirring *Gold Bug March.*

Manager-comedian Barnabee of the Bostonians came to the composer with an offer about this time. Barnabee was eager to commission another work from the composer who had given his company *Prince Ananias.* A creative artist of Herbert's caliber would soon be in demand by the theatrical producers, now that he had three successful operettas to his credit. Both Herbert and Smith accepted Barnabee's offer eagerly. An operetta would never suffer hasty or cheap production at the hands of the Bostonians, who still held their own in the comic-opera field despite the fact that some of the singers were well past their prime.

Smith set to work and wrote his best libretto, *The Serenade*. Herbert, too, surpassed his first efforts and provided a truly delightful score.

The Serenade is one of those happy "accidents" among libretti, where the story itself revolves around a song—in this case the serenade "I love thee, I adore thee," sung by Alvarado to his fair Dolores. The principal theme recurs again and again throughout the score. It is first heard as a duet, sung romantically in the moonlight. Then it becomes a parody of itself in the lampoon of grand opera *The Singing Lesson*. Next it is heard in the monastery, sung in chant style by the monks. The girls of the convent make a chorus of it, and the parrot shricks a comical echo. The outlaws sing it, too, and in the *finale* everyone adapts the melody to his own purposes in the spirited debate on love.

Too often in opera and operetta, the plot of the story has to be left in the wings while the music of aria or lyric takes the center of the stage. And when the singing is at an end, the poor old plot is dragged in by the heels again. The audience, in the meantime, has forgotten the story. Just as they are about to get matters straightened out in their minds, off goes the plot again, and another song or chorus takes the spotlight. If the librettist and composer are not careful, the whole thing is likely to appear to be a sort of endurance contest between the action of the story and the tunes.

With *The Serenade*, Herbert had a plot which could be closely dovetailed with his music. The operetta attained a unity seldom achieved in this field.

The Serenade was the opera for which Therese "discovered" the celebrated Yvonne—Alice Nielsen. Therese heard the winsome young star singing at the old Murray Hill Theatre, and insisted that she be given the rôle of Yvonne.

Herbert protested. Hilda Clark had already been selected by the Bostonians to play this part. "I would bring a hornet's nest about my ears if I suggested that the prima donna should yield her place to a newcomer like this," said the composer, laughing.

Nevertheless, when he had heard Alice Nielsen sing, he was won over to his wife's point of view. Just as he expected, objections were raised by the Bostonians and their prima donna. But when Victor Herbert set his head to a thing, he was not one to accept defeat. It was finally arranged for the two singers to appear on alternate nights. Herbert, good showman that he was, knew that this "competitive singing" would help the show.

It was not long before Frank Daniels needed another show. Herbert and Smith set to work once more. Another exotic Eastern setting was chosen, this time Indian. Smith dug up the piece of information somewhere that in India a person who saves another's life is thereafter responsible for that person's keep, and liable for all his actions. Using this as the motif of his plot, he wrote *The Idol's Eye*, a tale of lighthearted nonsense.

Jamie McSnuffey, the last of the McSnuffeys of Castle McSnuffey, a kleptomaniac drummed out of a Highland regiment in India, steals one of the ruby eyes of a Brahmin idol. This eye is the "eye of love" and it has the power to cause everyone to fall in love with its possessor.

Running from the scene of his theft, McSnuffey has the ill fortune to fall into a river. He is rescued by an American balloonist, Abel Conn, who sings as he performs the rescue "I just dropped in." The balloonist, by virtue of this act of mercy, has acquired a dependent, whom he must feed and clothe, and try to keep on the straight and narrow path of honesty.

Before the difficulties into which McSnuffey gets himself and everyone associated with him are resolved, a motley crew sing their way through the story. There are Don Pablo Tabasco, a Cuban planter traveling in search of big game; Maraquita, his daughter, in love with an American novelist,

Ned Winner; and a wide assortment of officers, priests of the temple, priestesses, officers' daughters, and Nautch girls.

For all these people, Herbert wrote effective music. Don Pablo's *Cuban Song* is both humorous and musically good. The opening chorus of Act Two and the dance of the Nautch girls delight the ear with languorous melody.

The perennially popular comic song from this operetta is *The Tattooed Man*. Frank Daniels was long remembered for his description of the man who was "a human picture gallery."

During those years when Herbert was discovering his preference for composing music in the light popular vein, he did not by any means abandon his connections with serious music. He attended concerts and gave concerts, for a number of years, delighting audiences with his beautiful 'cello performances.

Even in serious music, though, it was evident that he leaned toward the lighthearted and gay moods of the composers. He liked Tchaikovsky's romantic themes, but the Russian's *Sixth Symphony*, called the *Pathétique*, depressed him. Librettist Smith went with Herbert to hear the Russian conductor Safonov direct the Philharmonic in Carnegie in a presentation of this famous symphony. Herbert's remark after the concert was, "It is magnificent music; all the same, I wish it had never been written!"

Herbert's preference was for color and gayety, and, if there must be sadness, the gentle melancholy of romance. He loved the songs and instrumental works of Franz Schubert, and often remarked, "Not one note of Schubert's songs can be changed!"

Herbert, true to his classical training, was extremely critical of contemporary composers, and often expressed himself bluntly.

"Rubbish!" he said unkindly of one of Reginald De Koven's scores, and it is reported that the composer of the sprightly *Robin Hood* never forgave his colleague in the comic-opera field for his frank criticism. The work in question (not *Robin Hood*, which Herbert admired) has long since been forgotten; so it seems that though Herbert may have been undiplomatic, he was right.

For musicians making a beginning with composition, Herbert was all sympathy and helpfulness. He recognized young George Gershwin's talent, advised him to keep on with his composing, and even offered to coach him in orchestration. At the time, Gershwin refused the offer. Later, he came to realize that Herbert's emphasis on technique was right, that it was not enough to have a gift of melody without the knowledge of how to expand and develop a tune effectively.

Herbert could be wickedly sarcastic, as a little episode related by librettist Smith shows: The story has gathered embellishments with the years, but the kernel of truth is still there and the trimmings merely make a dramatic setting of the sort that Herbert would have appreciated:

Old man Schirmer—if he had any other name, none of the composers who sent him songs or symphonies bothered to use it—raised his eyebrows and looked across a cluttered desk at his visitor, a stage comedian and singer of popular songs. He had taken to composing serious music, and haunted the offices of music publishers with his "masterpieces."

"What makes you boys do it?" the publisher inquired with the air of one who has no expectation of receiving an answer in this life where "we see as through a glass darkly."

"I have been studying serious music for some time," declared the actor with dignity.

The publisher continued to thumb through the expensively bound manuscript which the comedian had titled "Grand Mass in F."

"So you want to be a composer," mused Schirmer, and his tone was almost hopeful, suggesting that in some future and better life he would not be surprised if the whole thing were explained to him "face to face."

At that moment, the banging of the outer door and the commotion which followed in the reception room indicated that someone of importance had entered. The "Good mornings" of the clerks were greeted with some pleasant blarney in an educated Irishman's brogue, and Schirmer was no longer in doubt.

"Well, the question's answered," declared the music publisher. "All of you want to be Victor Herberts, of course. An operetta this week, a concerto next. Come in, Victor!" he called out.

Herbert's booming laugh preceded him into the office, to serve as advance advertising for the vigorous person in correct morning attire who entered with a jaunty walk. Twinkling eyes, ruddy cheeks, dark hair growing pleasingly gray at the temples—this was the great Victor Herbert whose current operetta was packing them in on Broadway.

Schirmer shook hands with Herbert and introduced the actor. "He's brought me a 'Grand Mass in F,'" explained the publisher. "Take a look at it, Vic, and see what you think."

There was a gleam in Herbert's eye which boded no good for the would-be composer of serious masses in F. Taking the manuscript, the big man turned a few pages at random, looked up in mock surprise, and commented dryly, "By golly, it *is* in F!"

How the incident ended is not recorded, but if Herbert acted in character, he probably erased the sting of his joke with a sympathetic smile and offered some practical advice.

No doubt he ended by inviting the amateur composer to have lunch with him, and in some favorite little Bohemian café, with a bottle of his favorite Moselle wine before him, offered to help him.

Herbert's was essentially a democratic and generous nature. There was never anything of the "stuffed shirt" about him. He was really a simple man. His humor, which endeared him to Broadway, was never subtle or involved, but as ready and honest as his candid Irish smile.

He was never a patient man, particularly where indolence or incompetence were concerned. He prided himself on a certain hardboiled, blunt manner with the singers and orchestral musicians of his musical plays whenever the artists showed signs of "letting down." His sharp tongue could be wielded like a scalpel, and his scoldings were fearsome things. Yet those who worked with him even for a short time discovered that he was never unfair or unreasonable, that he was essentially friendly and warmhearted, always good for a "touch" if you happened to be down on your luck. It did not take long to discover, too, that in his heart of hearts the big man who "knew his business" was as sentimental as a schoolgirl, and believed in romance with a capital R.

His colleagues were aware of the many little kindnesses he showed others. Herbert never boasted of these good deeds; in fact, he promptly forgot them. He liked to be comfortable himself, and it made him uncomfortable to see others even mildly unhappy.

The story is still told of an incident in the office of the American Society of Authors, Composers and Publishers, in the early days when, despite its long name and ambitious aims, it was a tender young sprout of an organization, struggling for existence. In the outer office was a switchboard. The operator was a thin, delicate girl, who was always complaining of the cold. One day Herbert overheard her. When he left the office, he went to the nearest store and bought her a heavy sweater. To make the gift seem less like "charity," which he hated, he added a whimsical touch by choosing an Irish green color.

An old friend at the publishing house of Witmark, George J. Trinkaus, commented on the mysterious quality which made Herbert at once so dynamic and so human and lovable:

"He electrified the whole office when he came in. He seemed to have the stamp of success on him. He was one of those rare persons who make their presence felt as soon as they enter a room. Everyone looks up, expectant. Who can say why? And Herbert was one of those even rarer souls whose very existence makes people feel better. Generous, genial, effervescent, always ready to tell or listen to a good story—he was a good friend to have!"

Herbert was not unaware of the effect he produced on others. He once spoke his thoughts on the meaning of personality:

"Humanity," he said, "can't be put on one dead level. A man is born with a light in his eye, with a song in his heart, with a gift for friendship, or with the power to stamp his personality on others. Nothing can take those gifts away and nothing can put them in a man but the power that made him. Some people without a penny to bless them are born aristocrats—and some aren't."

To Herbert, a man might be poor as Job's turkey and still qualify for the title "aristocrat" if he were decent, kindly, and openhearted; and no amount of money or family prestige could confer the title if the man's nature were otherwise.

Above all, Herbert was ardently Irish, full of Irish anecdotes, songs, stories, and emotional patriotism. He was a member of numerous clubs which fostered Irish culture and political aims, though it must be confessed that, for all his activity with the latter, he was not much of a "politician." Herbert was all for the underdog, and Ireland was that. Like his music, Herbert's political opinions came from his heart rather than his head. He wanted Ireland to be free of England, but he was against the Irish Free-State Rebellion.

The composer's emotional, "nationalistic" approach to the Irish question found outlet in writing songs and choruses for such organizations as the Friends of Irish Freedom, and the Irish Musical Society. The Society dearest to his heart was that known as the Friendly Sons of St. Patrick. This group dated from pre-Revolutionary days in Boston, and only those with Irish ancestry could belong. Herbert was president of the club for two years (the maximum term) and wrote a rousing choral piece for it—*The Hail of the Friendly Sons.*

A contemporary of the English light-opera team of Gilbert and Sullivan, Herbert has often been likened to Sullivan, the musical partner. In his ability to create light, tuneful music for the operetta stage, Herbert did partake of the genius of his fellow-Irishman. There, however, similarity ceases; for little of the Sullivan satire is to be found in Herbert's work.

In his playful moods, Herbert wrote in warm chuckling vein. Whereas Sullivan wrote wittily, Herbert wrote humorously. And when Herbert left off laughing in his music, he breathed nostalgic longing and delicate romance into his songs and ballads, asserting and reasserting his faith in love and sentiment through the more than forty productions for which he composed bewitching music.

Two children were born in the Herbert home—a daughter, Ella Victoria, and a son, Clifford Victor. As they grew up, they lived simple, normal lives, much as other children did whose parents were not so famous. Bedtime and mealtime hours were regular. A certain amount of work was required of them. Fun was homely and wholesome—parties on Hallowe'en, with bobbing for apples in a tub; the birthday parties, with cake and ice cream; Easter parties, with boiled eggs colored and hidden in odd corners for the "Easter-egg hunt."

On Christmas Eve, Victor Herbert always hired a professional Santa Claus, with beautiful white whiskers and real fur on his red suit. With sly winks and merry chuckles, this actor handed out gifts to the family gathered round the Christmas tree.

At bedtime, the children heard the old tales from Germany and from Ireland—tales of the dog with eyes as big as mill-wheels and Hänsel and Gretel in the witch's hut; tales of the "little folk" playing pranks on unwary mortals wandering too late at night near the Irish peat-bogs.

Only in the matter of schooling were the Herbert children treated differently from the children of the corner grocer or the postman. They attended private schools as day pupils, and music tutors came to the house to instruct Ella in piano and Clifford in violin.

At home, Herbert liked to be informal. He liked nothing better than to have his friends drop in for supper and an evening of impromptu playing. Then he would bring out his beloved 'cello. The music took him back over the years to Sevenoaks, when his mother had played graceful background music for the guests of his grandfather, and young Victor had listened to grand talk about his native Ireland, land of the harp.

About the year 1897, Victor Herbert's mother made the long trip from Germany to visit her son and his family. She is remembered as "a little old lady" of nearly seventy, with bright, birdlike eyes and a winning smile. This was the last time Herbert saw his mother. She returned, after this short visit, to her family in Germany.

In 1900, Herbert's half-brother paid his American relatives a visit. Then William Schmid, too, returned to Germany.

Friends who made a habit of dropping in for these evenings with the Herberts were many and famous. As the years rolled on, names like Antonin Dvořák, Madame Schumann-Heink, Joseph Hoffman, Fritz Kreisler, Marcella Sembrich, Pol Plançon, Enrico Caruso appeared in the guest book.

Victor Herbert was present when Hoffman, as a boy of ten, made his début. Herbert remarked, "I feel like giving up music after hearing that boy play!"

Enrico Caruso was one of Herbert's closest friends. Like

Babes In Toyland

Herbert, Caruso was a simple, laughter-loving man, democratic and sincere.

Joseph Redding sometimes blew in from California. This musical amateur, a lifelong friend of Herbert's, was a member of the unique Bohemian Club of San Francisco (where business and professional men indulged their artistic hobbies). Redding was, by profession, a lawyer. As a hobby, he wrote plays. Years later, he won a national prize-contest for the best American grand-opera book. For this libretto, Herbert provided the music. The result was the opera *Natoma*.

Beethoven and Ballads

1898-1909. At the turn of the century, England launched the conquest of the Boer Republics. The Commonwealth of Australia extended the suffrage to women. A young revolutionary, Stalin, was jailed in Russia. Caruso began his first season at the Metropolitan. Paris decreed "fin de siècle" fashions, with emphasis on the "morning glory" skirt. Plumes and wings for hats were modish, and for a time the "chanticleer" hat (a whole rooster perched on top of milady's head) was all the rage. Popular songs were *A Bird in a Gilded Cage; Go Way Back and Sit Down;* and *Wait Till the Sun Shines, Nellie.* In 1901, Theodore Roosevelt became President. Upton Sinclair's novel *The Jungle* horrified America into demanding pure-food legislation. In 1906, San Francisco was devastated by earthquake and fire. By 1909, women were turning from the fitted waists and full, heavy skirts to the old Greek tunic with graceful flowing lines.

THE usual thing for Herbert was to do the unusual. Just as his friends in serious music circles had reconciled themselves to his being a leader of a band, and to his devoting his composing talent entirely to light music for the stage, Victor Herbert accepted the position of conductor of the Pittsburgh Symphony Orchestra.

Andrew Carnegie had made the city of Pittsburgh a gift of a library and music hall. Charles W. Scovel immediately set to work to promote a symphony orchestra. Frederick Archer, an eminent organist and conductor, launched the enterprise in 1896.

Herbert accepted the post of conductor in 1898 and remained with the symphony for the next six years. Selection of Herbert to replace Archer may have seemed an odd choice to some who deplored Herbert's musical comedy connections; but it was pleasing to Andrew Carnegie, who was often heard to remark, "My idea of heaven is to listen to Victor Herbert conduct his own music."

And just as the old stand-patters in music felt that a classic talent had been "redeemed," Herbert startled them once more by continuing his labors on behalf of operetta.

"Beethoven and ballads!" The rigid classicists shook their heads. But to those thousands who had come to know and love the genial Irishman through his gay operettas, there was satisfaction in the thought that Victor Herbert was still the "minstrel for the million."

Herbert did much to take the "stuffiness" out of the symphony concerts. "Conductors organize their programs in the wrong way," he declared. "We shall do it differently here in Pittsburgh."

And so he did, building his programs in a manner that showed common sense as well as a knowledge of "good theater." He always placed the heavy meat course first on the menu, the hors d'oeuvres next, and a frothy dessert of whipped cream last. In other words, the difficult symphony of the evening came first, then a suite or light number with soloist, and finally a group of very light pieces, short and easily understood.

"The best should come first," he said, "while the audience is still fresh."

The serious works included on the Herbert programs were the best in music: Beethoven's *Sixth, Seventh,* and *Eighth* symphonies; Berlioz' *Symphony Fantastique;* Brahms' *Second Symphony;* Dvořák's *New World;* Glazounoff's *Sixth Symphony;* Hadley's *The Four Seasons;* Haydn's *Second* and *Seventh* symphonies; Mozart's *G Minor Symphony;* Rubinstein's *The Ocean;* Raff's *Lenore;* Saint-Saëns' *Third Sym-*

phony; Schubert's *C Major Symphony;* Tchaikovsky's *Fifth Symphony* and *Manfred.*

A good many years after this "Pittsburgh period" of Herbert's, a Cincinnati paper called attention to the composer's ability in orchestral work. At the time (January, 1918), Herbert was filling one of his numerous engagements as guest conductor for important symphony orchestras—the Cincinnati Symphony, in this case. The article gave a vivid picture of Herbert's method of conducting rehearsals. His was the happy achievement of putting his musicians at ease without for an instant relaxing his demand for a high artistic standard.

"Let no one imagine," the article reads, "that the composer of *Babes in Toyland, It Happened in Nordland,* and a score of other comic operas does not know the classics. He knows every line of them. He is a thoroughgoing musician, a man of deep musical learning who mastered all the symphonies before he himself developed into the master of comic opera. . . . He felt perfectly at home when he opened his Tchaikovsky No. 5 Monday—it was an old and intimate friend. . . .

"The rehearsal took on the form of a conference between conductor and players. Herbert has a genial way of leading that promptly wins the hearts of his men. He breaks out into song constantly, singing his interpretation of any passage that there is any question about—and it is a happy and effective voice, too. Herbert reasons with his men. He not only tells them how he wants a thing played, but tells them why."

The writer illustrated this point by telling of one place in the Tchaikovsky symphony where it is the usual thing for the musicians to put down their instruments for a brief pause at the end of the passage.

" 'Please do not take down your instruments,' said Herbert —for he does not overlook any points—and he gave the reason for his request. 'If you take down your instruments, the public often erroneously thinks the movement is over at this point and applauds. You see, the public does not know as well as you do that this is not the end of the movement. By holding up your instruments you will help us get into the next section without the untimely applause.' "

Herbert constantly injected humor into his demands. Once he halted the orchestra to say, "I know that is the way the passage is generally played, and they may finally make it a law to play it that way. But I don't like it, and we'll play it this way." And he sang out his conception of the tempo.

"We've got to have more A there," he insisted at another point. "Emphasize the A! That's better!" He laughed as the musicians bore down with fervor on that A.

Later he halted the playing to give instructions to the brass section. "Sustain that note," he urged. "Don't hit it on the head and let it go."

He gave his string section good advice: "Vibrate more with the left-hand fingers and don't press so hard on the bow with the right hand." For the second violins, he demonstrated just where they should bow. "You'll get more resistance there and won't have to saw so much," he explained with a merry smile. And "Higher F, higher F, finger nails down!" he called out at another time, commenting on how weather conditions affected the instruments.

Once he stopped the playing to speak impatiently to the second strings. "An A there, please! Give me an A!" It was explained that the score showed no A. Herbert's musical ear had detected the fault, the result of a printer's error.

Musicians of the orchestra were secretly amused, too, at the conductor's odd way of marking a passage which he wished them to notice particularly. He would move from desk to desk, indicating the place in the score under discussion. Where others would have circled the passage in question or indicated it with an arrow, Herbert made a drawing of a hand with pointing finger, a feat which he accomplished with lightning speed.

Herbert was noted for his generosity and kindness toward those who worked with him. Cecille Lorraine, a singer who appeared as guest artist with the Pittsburgh Symphony when

Herbert was the conductor, wrote in later years to the composer's daughter to tell her of an amusing incident which illustrated the sympathetic understanding of the man:

"Dear Miss Herbert:

In the year 1899 I sang two concerts with the Pittsburgh Symphony Orchestra. . . .

"When I arrived for rehearsal the morning of my first concert I was given a seat on the stage and when the orchestral number was terminated, your father came over to bid me welcome and repeated, 'Lorraine—Lorraine. French?'

" 'No,' I replied. 'Irish.' Whereupon he gave me a good hearty handshake and told me I was thrice welcome.

"When I stood up to sing, it was discovered that a mistake had been made in the orchestral score sent on from New York. Filina's Aria instead of Ophelia's 'Mad Scene from Hamlet.'

"I was terribly disappointed, because the latter aria was my 'cheval de bataille' but I said I would make the best of it. To my amazement, he volunteered to write the orchestral score for that evening. A tremendous task, there being at least fourteen pages. I don't think any other conductor in the world would have taken on such a task, and I would like the world to know, besides being a genius, what a wonderfully generous soul he was."

The Herberts adapted themselves easily to a pleasant social life in Pittsburgh. They lived in a comfortable residence on Aikins Avenue. Herbert had his billiard room, where he could relax and forget the nervous cares of a musician and composer. Billiards was the only game which could really occupy his mind to the exclusion of other matters.

In the Pittsburgh home many of the famous men and women of the day were guests. They included Richard Strauss, who came to Pittsburgh as a guest conductor, to lead the Symphony in some of his own work; Madame Schumann-Heink, who sang in 1899 with the Pittsburgh orchestra; and Fritz Kreisler, who appeared as soloist.

There is a story about Kreisler's appearance as soloist in Pittsburgh. Kreisler played for a particularly appreciative and enthusiastic audience, which became tumultuous in its demand for an encore. Victor Herbert urged Kreisler to grant their wish. Just as the violinist came out to give the encore, there was a mishap:

"A string broke on my violin. I did not have another violin on hand. I asked Herbert what I should do. He said to me, 'You can play the piano; play it.' And that was my encore, on the piano, even if I was violin soloist."

Henry Burck, the second concertmaster of the Pittsburgh Symphony Orchestra; Von Kunitz, the concertmaster; and Henry Merck, first 'cellist, were frequent dinner guests in the Herbert home. Many a celebrated musician-guest was to remember for years to come the high good humor, the witty conversation, and the good fellowship which prevailed in the Herbert household.

Nearly everyone who visited the Herberts were music enthusiasts. It is related that once when Fritz Kreisler was with them, the guests made up an impromptu string quintet. Kreisler took the violin part and Herbert the 'cello. They selected the Schubert Quintet for an appetizer before lunch. Kreisler was quite excited over the good music which resulted, and after the meal was over, he suggested that they play the Quintet again.

The enthusiasts took up their instruments and played the Quintet once more. Then they adjourned to the billiard room. But Kreisler was not to be diverted long.

"Before I return to the hotel, let us play it just once more!" he suggested.

Herbert and the rest agreed, but Therese called to them, "Supper first!"

After the evening meal, the group returned to the music room and began their third performance of the Schubert Quintet.

"When we parted late that evening," Burck related, "we

had spent one of the most completely happy days of our musical lives."

In this anecdote lies a significant comment on the reason for Herbert's success in his chosen work. He was wholeheartedly in it. It filled his whole life, his leisure moments as well as his working hours. He had no hobbies, in the accepted sense of that term, because he needed none. Music was his vocation and avocation.

During the Pittsburgh years, Herbert took the opportunity to introduce some of his own compositions. These included his *Suite for Strings, Suite Romantique, Woodland Fancies, Hero and Leander*, and the *Columbus Suite*. It pleased and consoled him when men like Richard Strauss expressed their admiration of his work.

The old-fashioned musicians of the Pittsburgh Symphony, knowing their conductor's love of melody, sometimes could not understand his tolerant attitude toward the ultra-modern in music. These men shook their heads over the weird effects which they were expected to produce in their rehearsals of Strauss' *Death and Transfiguration, Till Eulenspiegel*, and the love scene from the opera *Feursnot*. Herbert, who himself did not care for extreme modernism, took a never-failing delight in hearing the remarks of these oldtimers.

"It just isn't music!" one of the older men would say sadly, and Herbert would laugh that hearty laugh of his.

"That's what always has been said about 'new' music," said Herbert. "Only time will tell. If it *is* music, people will accept it. If it isn't, the years will bury it."

When Strauss conducted in Pittsburgh, he proved to be quite as ready for fun and play as Victor Herbert. Herbert had arranged to have a photographer take a picture of the orchestra and its famous guest conductor. For a joke, Herbert took up the "bull fiddle" and posed with his men. The bass viol, it seems, always had been and always will be a subject for jest among musicians. For the second picture, Strauss insisted that Herbert pose on the conductor's podium, and the composer of

Till Eulenspiegel took up the big fiddle. These souvenir pictures were autographed and exchanged between the two composers.

Herbert was not one to make life all play and no work, however. He always expected a high standard of artistry from his men, and if they fell into indifferent playing, he let them have the full fury of his Irish tongue. But when the storm was over, he was the same smiling, comradely Victor. His men were always his friends, and frequently showed their affection for him by a bit of good-natured chaffing. Once a group of the Pittsburgh musicians serenaded the conductor on his birthday, an event which gave rise to the later fiction that Herbert's men always followed this custom.

Herbert was a great man. Legends were beginning to fasten on him like mistletoe on an Irish oak. The story got around that the men of his orchestra appeared every birthday morning at dawn and played in the February snow until Therese invited them in for breakfast. The actual custom was a stag dinner at home, with as many as eighteen close friends invited.

The Pittsburgh musicians were not slow to discover how proud Victor Herbert was of his Irish ancestry. On every St. Patrick's Day, they appeared for rehearsal wearing bright green ties. The idea amused and pleased Victor.

On nights following rehearsals, and between tours with the orchestra, Herbert somehow found time to write his operettas. For six years—between 1898 and 1904—he "commuted" between Pittsburgh and New York, seeing to the details of production, publication, dress rehearsals and first-night conducting.

Herbert, who never knew what it meant to spare himself when there was a call for his services, traveled to New York for various benefit concerts, too. In 1900, he came specially from Pittsburgh to conduct at Madison Square Garden an orchestra of four hundred twenty performers. Proceeds of the concert went to the sufferers of the Galveston, Texas, flood. In 1906, he directed a similar concert at the Hippodrome to help the victims of the San Francisco earthquake and fire.

The Fortune Teller belongs to the Pittsburgh years. It is one of the best of the Herbert operettas, ranking with *The Serenade, The Singing Girl, Naughty Marietta, Mlle. Modiste, The Red Mill, Babes in Toyland, Eileen,* and *Sweethearts.*

By this time, the Alice Nielsen Opera Company had been organized. Frank Perley, former manager for the Bostonians, acted as business head. From the Bostonians, also, came Eugene Cowles, one of the most popular men singers of the day.

At the "première" of *The Fortune Teller*, at Wallack's Theatre, September 26, 1898, an artist who, like Miss Nielsen, was to become a grand opera singer in future was included in the cast. This was Marguerita Sylva, later one of the celebrated Carmens. Harry B. Smith's libretto and Victor Herbert's music were not handicapped by inferior talent, that is certain.

Herbert harked back to the golden days of his youthful wanderings when he wrote the music for *The Fortune Teller*. The story is set in Budapest in Hungary. The scenes and peoples of the Danube were familiar to the composer; so was the music of Hungarian folk dances, played with such fiery abandon by native gypsy orchestras.

The story of this operetta opens with Count Berezowski, a Polish nobleman and amateur musician, visiting the ballet kept by Fresco, ballet master at the Grand Opera of Budapest. The Count wishes to meet one of the ballet pupils, Irma, a beautiful young girl, who (all unknown to herself) has just become an heiress of considerable fortune.

Thinking to get hold of this legacy, the Count offers the unscrupulous Fresco a reward of five thousand florins if he will arrange a marriage for him with Irma. Meanwhile, of course, the girl is to be kept in ignorance of her fortune.

When Fresco suggests the idea of marriage, Irma objects. She does not care for the old Count, and besides, she is in love with handsome Captain Ladislaus, an Hungarian Hussar. Irma's twin brother, Fedor, is also a member of this regiment.

When the Count becomes too attentive, Irma decides to run away from the ballet school. She is concerned not only for herself but also for her twin, who is supposed to have deserted his regiment to elope with Mlle. Pompon, opera singer and member of the ballet school.

When the Hussars enter the school in search of Fedor and Mlle. Pompon, Captain Ladislaus contrives to give Irma a uniform. The soldiers naturally suppose that she is her twin brother. By this stratagem, she leaves the school without the ballet master's knowledge, and also saves her brother from disgrace.

When Fresco discovers that Irma has gone, he is furious; he has a mental picture of his five thousand florins taking wing. At this point a band of Gypsies arrives. Boris, their leader, his daughter, Musette, and Musette's sweetheart, Sandor, enter the garden of the ballet school. They have come to sing and dance and tell fortunes. Fresco notices that Musette closely resembles Irma, and he persuades the Gypsy girl to help him deceive the Count. Musette has dreams of being a countess, and Fresco thinks he sees a way to collect his reward even with Irma missing.

In the second act, preparations for the marriage between the Count and Musette, whom he believes to be Irma, are going forward at the Count's château on the Danube. Irma, disguised as Fedor, arrives with a group of Hussars. The Gypsy Sandor puts in an appearance, too. He pleads with Musette to give up her dream of being a countess, and finally persuades her to return with him to the wild, free life of the Romany folk.

In the third act, the Count goes to the neighboring camp of the Hussars, to plead with the brother of his vanished bride-to-be for help in finding her. It is Irma, of course, in her boy's disguise, whom he interviews. The whole thing ends in an argument, and Irma is challenged to fight a duel. This is a pretty kettle of fish, for Irma knows nothing about dueling, and yet she dares not reveal her identity until she knows where her brother is. Fedor's prolonged absence is serious.

The situation is saved when word comes that the real Fedor has not absented himself from his regiment to run away with an opera singer, but is fighting valiantly at the front. Irma tells the Count who she really is, and Ladislaus claims her for his sweetheart. The Count is only momentarily downcast; for Mlle. Pompon turns up and he decides to court her instead.

It has good music, Victor Herbert melody at its sparkling best. Irma's song *Always do as people say you should* is piquant and tuneful. The Hussar Chorus is vigorous, stirring music. The Gypsy airs, *Romany Life* and *Gypsy Jan*, are full of the fire and romance of the Romany folk. *Romany Life* is particularly effective. The second melody of this song à la czardas suggests madly whirling skirts and rhythmic stamping boots.

The world of music-lovers has set its seal of approval on *Slumber on, my little Gypsy sweetheart*. This song has tenderness and longing, and a gentle lullaby quality that touches the heart:

The charming waltz song, *The Lily and the Nightingale*, is in Herbert's happiest style, the style he absorbed in gay Vienna where dancers whirled in graceful spirals to the music of the Strauss orchestras:

In 1899, Herbert turned out two operettas to which neither public nor critics took kindly. One, *The Ameer*, written for Frank Daniels, had a libretto by Kirke La Shelle and Frederick Rancken. It was immediately panned off the boards by critics like the one who remarked caustically:

"The libretto . . . is a trivial and infantile affair, without wit or point or grace or anything else that is of the slightest moment."

Harry B. Smith furnished the libretto for the second. This was *Cyrano de Bergerac*, a burlesque of Rostand's famous play. It was written for comedian Francis Wilson.

Three weeks later, a third Herbert operetta opened on Broadway. "Three operettas in one year!" people marveled. "How does the man do it?"

The libretto of this third operetta, *The Singing Girl*, was written by Stanislaus Stange, the lyrics by Harry B. Smith. Alice Nielsen created the title rôle, at the Casino Theatre on October 23, 1899. Rupert Hughes, writing reviews for *The Criterion* in those days, echoed the feeling of the first-night audience when he acclaimed the production a success:

"The most fetching thing this town has seen since Cissy Fitzgerald's wink brought a new sensation to a worn old heart, is the mischievous eyelid Alice Nielsen interpolated into her song 'Beware,' in her new opera 'The Singing Girl.' And she sings it in the most stunning suit of white silk and silvered doublet ever worn by a girlish boy. And the song itself is one that the whole country will be infected with soon—a lyric as graceful artistically as it is popular.

"When you have said that the company is so fine that it reaches the standard of stock company, that the music of Victor Herbert is at his best and that the costumes are gorgeous, you have said all you can say. . . . The music by Mr. Herbert dignifies the American Stage. It reaches the highest level of European comic opera, particularly in the very elaborate entrance song for Miss Nielsen. Then, too, it is learnedly humorous. He sprinkles his scores with Attic salt."

Critic Hughes, like the first-night audience, was possibly a trifle too enthusiastic. The test of time has not been as kind to this operetta as to the other Herbert "hits." It was "good theater," however, and contained a number of tunes of lasting merit.

The Singing Girl has an Austrian setting and an absurd law for its motivation. Duke Rudolf of Linz has made a decree that two people caught whispering romantic vows of love to each other must immediately be married or suffer severe punishment. What is more, if they are alone together and merely appear to be making love, the law applies.

Greta and her twin brother are singers who make a living by traveling from town to town. They warble ballads for those who care to listen a while and toss a few coppers to them. When the troubadours arrive in Linz, two people hear Greta sing—Baron Aufpassen (the minister of police) and Count Otto—and both men fall in love with her.

Greta finds herself attracted to Count Otto, but cannot endure Aufpassen. In order to escape the unwelcome attentions of the minister of police, Greta changes clothes with her brother, and much of the comedy which follows is the *Charley's Aunt* sort; for the foolish Aufpassen pursues Greta's brother.

Matters begin to take a serious turn when Greta is found whispering to Marie, sister of Duke Rudolf. Since everyone supposes her to be a boy, she is ordered to marry Marie at once in accordance with the Duke's law. Then Greta in her own character is found alone with Prince Pumpernickle, who is in love with Marie. Greta and the Prince are ordered to marry, and all is hopeless confusion.

Matters are straightened out when the Duke decides to repeal his silly law. Then Greta marries her beloved Count Otto, Marie is united with Prince Pumpernickle, and everyone is happy.

Herbert's next work was the enormously popular *Babes in Toyland*. This was not an operetta in the true sense, but rather a musical extravaganza, brilliantly staged and provided by the composer with some bright and charming music.

The fanciful nursery tale by Glen MacDonough was filled with such quaint people out of the old Mother Goose rhymes and fairy tales, and staged with such elaborate costumes and settings that it was immediately devoured by a public hungry for a chance to return to that happy land "Toyland! Toyland! Little girl and boy land."

For children, the various scenes of the story were like pages from a book of fairy tales. Imagine their delight at being taken to a country fête in Contrary Mary's garden, to the Spider's Forest, the Palace of the Moth Queen, and the Christmas Tree Grove in Toyland. Best of all, for here the composer seemed to become a child himself and play the game of "Let's pretend!", was the Master Toymaker's Workshop.

The characters of the fantasy matched the settings: The Widow Piper, "a lonely widow with fourteen children"; the Brown Bear; the Master Toymaker, "who designs the toys of the world"; Bobby Shaftoe, with silver buckles at his knee; Bo-Peep, the careless shepherdess; and many others.

For this odd assemblage, Herbert wrote some delicate and winsome music. *The Country Dance,* which opens the extravaganza, is a piece suggestive of brisk autumn weather and harvests garnered in before the frost, of rosy-cheeked lasses and gawky country lads.

Never Mind, Bo-Peep, We Will Find Your Sheep might be the music for a pleasant singing game, danced and acted out on a daisy-pied meadow.

The Birth of the Butterfly is a delightful salute to the spring.

Hail to Christmas recalls the joyous anticipation of children waiting for Kris Kringle.

Fairy tales are not forgotten, either, and *A Legend* evokes the mood of a pleasant story hour before the crackling fire, when sleepy heads are beginning to nod.

In the Toymaker's Workshop roosters crow, ducks quack,

cows moo—all to the most exciting music imaginable; and the dolls keep saying *Mamma, Mamma, Mamma*. The cuckoo and the dog add their voices, and the toy whistle pipes a shrill tune.

Best known of all the songs from *Babes in Toyland* is the saucy *I Can't Do That Sum*. And best-remembered music of the instrumental score is the lively *March of the Toys*. The opening measures of this march, a fanfare of toy trumpets, has become familiar to millions:

Many years later, *Babes in Toyland* found its way into a motion picture. The story was altered somewhat, but the joyous music was just the same, and the fairy-tale scenes more fascinating than they had been on the stage. Comedians Laurel and Hardy entered into the spirit of fun and fantasy as the "Babes" who went adventuring in Mother Goose Land.

In the same year that the delightful score of *Babes in Toyland* was written, Herbert turned out an operetta called *Babette*. The tunes from this work have almost been forgotten, but *Babette* is important because it was the first of the Herbert operettas in which Fritzi Scheff sang.

The Alice Nielsen Opera Company had gone to England for a tour, and Alice herself remained in Europe to take up serious study for grand opera. The problem of finding an excellent voice and attractive stage personality to take Miss Nielsen's place worried Herbert and the companies for whom he wrote. And then someone thought of Viennese Fritzi Scheff, "the little devil of the Metropolitan," as Paderewski once called her.

It took a high salary to persuade Fritzi that she could afford to leave the dignity of grand opera to sing in comic opera. A thousand dollars a week did the trick, and another vivacious star with a magic voice assured artistic interpretation of Herbert's music.

In 1905, this singer appeared in *Mlle. Modiste,* the operetta which, with *Naughty Marietta,* stands out as the most inspired of the composer's works for the stage. Herbert himself regarded *Mlle. Modiste* as something above the average operetta, and even feared that he had flown too high. For a New York musical magazine *Tone* (April, 1906) he wrote:

"I confess that when I wrote *Mlle. Modiste* it was with a dull dread in my heart that the public would reject it and cast it into ignominious seclusion from which it would never return. On the opening night I felt like a man going to the gallows. . . .

"I cannot express the gratification I felt on the following morning when I awoke and found that I had been deceived in my friends, the public; that after all they had welcomed with outstretched hands the musical play. . . ."

Henry Blossom's book and Victor Herbert's music for *Mlle. Modiste* were written with Fritzi Scheff in mind. As a matter of fact, Herbert never wrote an operetta unless he had a contract, and usually he knew in advance what cast was to present the work.

With the knowledge that Fritzi Scheff's wonderful voice and piquant acting were "under contract," Herbert was free to write a soprano part of brilliance and difficulty. From the very beginning Fritzi Scheff *was* Fifi, the little milliner who was destined to delight audiences for an amazing first run of 252 performances.

Act One takes place in Paris and St. Mar. It opens in a Parisian millinery shop, where pert Fifi models hats for the customers of Mme. Cécile's, with a chorus sung by the milliners—*Furs and feathers, buckles, bows.* This song, in the saucy tradition of Offenbach, is followed by the trio *When the cat's away.*

Captain Étienne de Bouvray, handsome nephew of the

Count de Bouvray, comes into the shop and flirts with Fifi. With the chorus of milliners he sings the wryly humorous *The time and the place and the girl.* Following close on the heels of these hits comes the song which is undoubtedly Herbert's best known song: *If I were on the stage,* known more generally by the words of the refrain, *Kiss me again.*

This is the song which will be forever linked with the name of Fritzi Scheff.

Gaston, the amiably stupid son of Mme. Cécile, contributes *Love me, love my dog,* as a prelude to his attentions to Fifi. And Fifi closes the story of the first act with the coquettish *Hats make the woman.*

The story is the conventional one. Étienne and Fifi are in love, but neither has enough money for marriage. Étienne is under the thumb of a wealthy, aristocratic uncle, Count de Bouvray, who turns thumbs down on Fifi as a wife for his nephew. Fifi has no intentions of marrying, anyway, until she has realized her ambition to become a singer. Trouble for both Étienne and Fifi appears in the person of Gaston. Then an American, Hiram Bent, comes on the scene. He solves Fifi's problem, temporarily at least, by financing her vocal lessons.

Act Two takes place in the Count de Bouvray's castle. A charity fête is in progress, and the celebrated prima donna Mme. Bellini has been engaged to sing. This Mme. Bellini is none other than Fifi. Angry at first when he discovers her identity, the Count finally relents. Fifi's singing so charms gouty old Count de Bouvray that he decides to give his blessing to her marriage to his nephew.

This act contains many songs and choruses which were to win America's heart. There is a comic chorus of footmen, followed by the Count's song, *I want what I want when I want it.* Then comes Gaston's witty comments (in song) on the oddities of the English language. Fifi and the male chorus contribute *The Mascot and the Troop.* Mrs. Bent's hilarious *The Keokuk Culture Club* anticipated Sinclair Lewis' satire in *Main Street.* Fifi's *The Nightingale and the Star* and the finale *Hark, the Drum* concluded the score of a truly great musical show.

Most operettas are fortunate if one tune of the score is remembered years afterward by the public. *Mlle. Modiste* provided at least six hit tunes which are as popular today as they were on the opening night.

"It was mainly the encouragement which Mr. Blossom and I received in the reception of our little French milliner that spurred us on to write *The Red Mill,*" Herbert once said.

The Red Mill was produced in 1905, a year after Herbert had given up his post with the Pittsburgh Symphony and returned to New York to devote himself almost exclusively to composing. This operetta is memorable for two important circumstances: It was a starring vehicle for the famous team of Montgomery and Stone, who came to the cast of *The Red Mill* fresh from their triumphs in the Frank Hamlin production of *The Wizard of Oz.* And for *The Red Mill,* the Knickerbocker Theatre was provided with a moving sign in lights, the first of its kind on the "great white way." Wings of a windmill, studded with red lamps, were turned by an electric motor.

The Red Mill was one of the most successful of the operettas. Montgomery and Stone romped through the gay Herbert-Blossom show for 274 performances in New York.

Act One is laid in a little Dutch town, in an inn at the Sign of the Red Mill, where two Americans, "Con" Kidder and "Kid" Conner, find themselves stranded and unable to pay their bill. They try to get away without their landlord knowing it, but they are caught climbing from a window. The innkeeper is inclined to be lenient. He tells Kidder and Conner that they may work out their board. "Con" is to be an interpreter; "Kid" is to be a waiter.

"Con" and "Kid" do not let their duties interfere with their interest in the affairs of the people at the inn. Gretchen, pretty daughter of Jan, the innkeeper, becomes their particular concern. Her father wishes her to marry the Governor of Zeeland, but she is in love with young Captain Van Damm. The two Americans tell her that they will help her elope, but Jan overhears the plot and informs the Burgomaster. Gretchen is promptly locked up in the mill.

Montgomery and Stone made the most of the acrobatics required of them in rescuing Gretchen. They went round and round, clinging to the sails of the huge mill, keeping the audience gasping and laughing at their antics. They finally reached Gretchen's window and brought her safely to the ground.

Before this spectacular "escape" is effected in the operetta, a number of charming songs and choruses are sung: *By the Side of the Mill, Mignonette, You Can Never Tell About A Woman, Whistle It, The Isle of Our Dreams, Go While the Going is Good,* and *Moonbeams.*

Of these, the tender and yearning *The Isle of Our Dreams* is Herbert at his Romantic best:

Act Two takes place in the great hall of the Burgomaster's house. All is in readiness for the marriage of Gretchen and the Governor, but Gretchen cannot be found. Her father storms and rants, and finally offers a reward for her capture.

"Con" and "Kid" in disguise mingle boldly with the guests. First they appear as organ grinders, and in this guise they sing their popular *Good-a-bye, John.* Later, they change their "disguise" and appear as Sherlock Holmes and Dr. Watson, pretending to make a scientific search, magnifying glass and all, for the missing Gretchen. There is fun in plenty and a festival of gay music before the Governor arrives and clears up matters so that Gretchen may marry her Captain.

The Legend of the Mill, I Want You to Marry Me, Every Day Is Lady's Day With Me, Because You're You are four of the best tunes of the second act. *The Streets of New York* with its well-known melody and the words "In old New York, in old New York" caught the tender, sentimental spirit which is one side of the great city Victor Herbert loved:

From 1903 on the Herbert family began to spend their vacations on Lake Placid. They played and rested at this beautiful lake resort in the Adirondack Mountains from the end of May to the first of October.

The composer often had to take his work along, and business associates kept in touch with him. But work was confined to morning hours when the air blew fresh and clean from the lake into the composer's study and the birds made music which was actually written into the scores.

Pointing out a certain accompaniment to an aria in *Natoma*, Herbert once told George Trinkaus: "Those are my birds!" Then with a twinkle, he went on, "You know, a couple of robins have returned year after year to make a nest in the tree outside my studio window. Papa Robin and I are what you might call old cronies. He's been coming back so many years! And do you know, the old fellow is getting positively gray!"

In 1905, Herbert built a home at Lake Placid—a Swiss chalet-type dwelling with half-timber walls, carved wooden balconies, and blinds decorated with peasant designs. The house nestled in the cool woodland right beside the lake. The composer could look up from his work on a hot summer morning to watch the little boats skimming on the blue water, or to wave to neighbors taking a dip near the piers which jettied out from boathouses below other cabin-homes.

Herbert had a boathouse and a boat, too. In the twenty years he stayed at Placid during vacations he owned many boats, in fact. His very first one was called the *Handy Andy*, after the droll character of Samuel Lover's book of that name. It was a launch type, similar to the old naphtha launches, and its top speed of twelve miles per hour was very good for those days. This boat was sold to another of the "lake dwellers" when Herbert decided to buy a larger and faster boat. The new owner learned to his dismay, after the deal had been made, that he had bought the boat but not the name.

"But the name *Handy Andy* is the main reason I want the boat!" he protested.

"And the name's the main reason I want another boat," laughed Herbert. "It's a good name!"

So the new owner had to agree to re-christen his craft. As the *Sarah Jane*, this old "Handy Andy I" is still on the lake.

Handy Andy II was followed by other and larger boats. Two were called *Rory* after Lover's witty Irish boy of *Rory O'More*, and the last one was named *Natoma* for the heroine of Herbert's opera. The *Natoma* was an open powerboat, the largest on the lake when it was first put there. Its one-hundred-twenty-horsepower engine made so much noise that Herbert finally had to bow to the verdict of his neighbors and remove the engine. In 1942, the *Natoma* was sold and taken to Lake Champlain. In 1944 it performs its war duty by ferrying soldiers to and from Canada.

Henry Blossom, one of Herbert's most successful librettists, and a close personal friend, often came to Lake Placid to work out plans for a new operetta. It was Blossom's habit to cut out comic stories, jokes, anecdotes, and cartoons from newspapers and magazines; these furnished him with inspiration for novel situations and amusing dialogue for his comic-opera books. He was very fussy about keeping his clippings in order, and treasured unused ideas for years.

One day, he went out to the boathouse to work. He took with him all his precious scraps and spread them about on a bench just below a window overlooking the water. He moved the clippings this way and that, sorting and resorting them and pondering deeply. Without warning, a gust of wind puffed through the screenless window, caught up Blossom's papers, and scattered them all in merry abandon on the lake below. Blossom was such a picture of amazement and impotent rage that Herbert, who had just entered the boathouse, roared with laughter. Therese came out to ask what the joke was. The composer explained:

"Blossom's jokes—they're all wet—every last idea he had just blew into Lake Placid!"

Blossom made a rueful face, then added to the merriment by singing some lines from an old sailors' chanty:

> "He sank them in the low, in the lonesome low—
> He sank them in the lonesome sea!"

Herbert always relished an absurd situation. He was forever coming home with funny stories about his own adventures and misadventures on the road. If he had cut a comic figure in the course of these adventures, he was the first to see the joke.

There was a story about the time he tried to buy white kid gloves on a Sunday in a town in Tennessee. These gloves had seemed important to him at the time, and with the aid of several acquaintances and friends he succeeded in routing out nearly every haberdasher in town. During the search, a group of curious citizens joined them. Others joined them from time to time, so that Herbert and his fellow-searchers moved with a veritable retinue from store to store. An enthusiastic cheer went up when the composer emerged victorious from one of the stores with the gleaming white gloves.

One of Herbert's favorite stories was an anecdote about Sam Bernard, the comedian. The actor had accepted an invitation to dinner at the home of the Witmarks, the music publishers, but on the scheduled evening he became interested in a game of cards at the Friars and lost track of time. Mrs. Witmark's dinner was getting cold and her other guests impatient. She knew the actor's habit of dropping in at the Friars; so she sent a messenger to remind him of his engagement.

The comedian was appalled at his thoughtlessness. He rushed into the club cloak room, grabbed his overcoat, and called a cab. As he settled back into the seat, he put a hand into one of the coat pockets. To his amazement and disgust, he found that some member of the club had placed a set of false teeth in the pocket.

"Some idiot's idea of a joke!" he muttered angrily and forthwith tossed the teeth through the cab window.

When he arrived at the Witmark home, he was profuse with apologies, and to make amends explained with what haste he had rushed into his coat and into a cab.

Mrs. Witmark, who knew the actor well, looked closely at his coat.

"And is that your own coat you grabbed?" she asked.

No one was prepared for the startling change that came over the comedian's face. He stared at the coat. It was not his! And those teeth!

"Come on!" he yelled to the astonished dinner party. "Call some cabs and help me find those teeth!"

The whole party accompanied the distracted actor back to the point on Broadway where he had thrown a fellow Friar's teeth to the four winds. Passers-by, New Yorkers who were seldom surprised at anything, stopped to stare at the group of men and women, all dressed for dinner, who were making a methodical search of street and gutters.

Friends who visited Herbert at the Lake Placid home, which Mrs. Herbert christened "Camp Joyland," recall the bronzed giant that Herbert was in those years. He was over six feet tall, and weighed two hundred ten pounds, a big-chested, muscular man who swam, rowed, played ball, and hiked up Mt. Cobble and Mt. Whitney in the Adirondacks with the vigor and enthusiasm of youth. Herbert was an excellent swimmer. On hot summer days he went into the water two or three times a day.

The villagers at Placid remember him for another and more "professional" reason. The little resort town had organized a band. The butcher played the flute, the blacksmith the cornet, and other tradesmen the various horns and trumpets. Herbert delighted in their performances, perhaps because they were a reminder of the absurd *ump-pah-pah* German bands he remembered hearing in village squares in his schooldays. The composer did not make fun of the amateur efforts of the Lake Placid band, however. He was genuinely interested in helping them.

Many years later, when the band was no more, the flute-playing butcher reminisced about Victor Herbert:

"Herbert would spend all kinds of time helping us," he said. "And do you know"—here he leaned forward as if to impart a really exciting secret—"do you know, I never even knew how to *hold* a flute until Victor Herbert showed me how!"

The scent of pine needles on woodland trails, the lapping of Lake Placid's water on the beaches, the songs of the Adirondack birds, the cool of wind and water spray as the *Handy Andy* or the *Natoma* skimmed across the lake—all these things inspired the composer to write some of his beautiful compositions. These included titles like the *Woodland Fancies* suite (*Morning in the Mountains, Forest Sylphs, Twilight, Autumn Frolics*), *Sunset*, and *Whispering Willows*.

His suite of six piano pieces, published by Witmark, were melody-pictures of Lake Placid. This work, somewhat on the plan of Ethelbert Nevin's *Water Scenes Suite*, Opus 13, which contains *Narcissus*, has interest-provoking titles: *Ghazel, La Coquette, Yesterthoughts, The Mountain Brook, On the Promenade, Punchinello.*

Yesterthoughts is a little piece which Debussy might have woven out of his gossamer fancies. Originally written and published as a piano number, and later orchestrated by the composer, it has been a favorite with several generations of music lovers. We can imagine the composer sitting on the veranda of his lake home in the soft evening dusk, playing this nostalgic melody on his 'cello. That is why a 'cello arrangement of the work, made in recent years, brings us close to the spirit of Victor Herbert when he composed and played this gently melancholy little piece:

Many years later, *Indian Summer* was written for Herbert's own orchestra, and later arranged for piano by the composer. For thousands of hearers, this music called up all the lazy warmth and smoky haze, the golden color, and the strangely sad hush of an Adirondacks autumn.

The popularity of *Indian Summer* will not diminish. As late as 1936—twelve years after the composer's death—the theme melody of the piece was adapted to words written by Gus Kahn. This song, *Indian Summer*, was featured for fourteen weeks on the *Hit Parade*, and for two weeks of that time was the top song.

As with *Yesterthoughts*, a 'cello arrangement brings out the softly singing quality of the beautiful melody:

Besides these instrumental compositions, Herbert wrote music for his best operetta scores at Lake Placid. Among those which mirror the happiness of those days are *Babes in Toyland, Mlle. Modiste, The Red Mill, Naughty Marietta, Eileen,* and *The Only Girl. The Only Girl* was actually composed in ten days. Only a composer with buoyant health and happiness as an added boon could have done that.

Victor Herbert's friends realized that the Lake Placid environment was good for the composer. Frederick Kraft voiced the general opinion:

"Herbert was too busy in New York. If he would have retired to his home on Lake Placid for a couple of years, there is no doubt he would have composed a great symphonic work."

It Happened in Nordland was produced in 1906. From this work, *Absinth Frappé* is known best. In this same year, *Dream City,* a dramatic "pipe in two puffs" offered the public a clever satire on the speculative real estate craze. This piece was followed by *The Magic Knight,* a travesty on grand opera.

The Rose of Algeria, brought out in 1909, was the next of

the Herbert operettas. The score contained a number of good songs, which deserve to be better known.

The story of the operetta harks back to *The Serenade*, for the action centers about the songs and poems of a mysterious "El Mokani," who has so entranced the Sultana, Zoradie, that she has declared that she will marry none but this singer of sweet songs. In a walled oasis of the Sahara, and later outside the Sultana's palace in Algeria, the characters of the play search for the elusive El Mokani, until at last he is discovered to be dashing Captain de Lome. All ends well for the poet and the princess—that is to be expected.

The song *I've Been Decorated* is one of Herbert's virile march tunes. The words, too, are spirited and funny.

My Life, I Love Thee is a romantic serenade which has become a general favorite.

Zoradie's song *Rose of the World* has a husky, oriental passion that makes it a happy choice for the 'cello transcription made in recent years:

The Rose of Algeria was followed shortly by a whimsical fantasy based on Winsor MacCay's cartoons (originally published in the *New York Herald*) of the little boy Nemo, who was always having dreams filled with weird adventure.

As he had done for *Babes in Toyland*, Herbert composed fanciful and charming music for *Little Nemo*, where the boy hero visits the "Land of the Fairies of St. Valentine," the "Office of the Weather Factory," the "Deck of a Pirate

Ship," "Slumberland," and other strange places built on suppers of mince pies, ice cream, and pickles.

Old Dutch, written as a starring vehicle for Lew Fields, and two operettas for Fritzi Scheff—*The Prima Donna* and *Mlle. Rosita* (later called *The Duchess*)—showed plainly the haste with which Herbert was writing his music at the time. These pieces were "good theater," but that special magic which makes certain music live on in memory was lacking. *The Duchess,* in fact, was not well received even by contemporary audiences; and its partial failure so discouraged Fritzi Scheff that she bowed out of the Herbert productions for good.

There were those who shook their heads and declared that Herbert was "washed up." The composer made no answer to these critics. He merely rolled up his sleeves and worked harder than ever.

The Crest of the Wave

1909-1912. The liner *Lusitania* made its maiden voyage to New York in five days, one and one-half hours. The first Ziegfeld Follies were a smash hit. In 1909, Peary reached the North Pole. The famous "Tin Lizzie" Model-T Ford rolled off the assembly line. Suffragettes were chaining themselves to statues in the British Parliament. Mount Etna erupted. Halley's Comet convinced many hysterical people that the end of the world was at hand. George V of England came to the throne. Popular songs were *Yama Yama Man, Shine On, Harvest Moon, Schooldays, Put on Your Old Gray Bonnet, Red Wing,* and *Casey Jones* until Irving Berlin's *Alexander's Ragtime Band* ushered in a new era of ragtime and jazz. The so-called "hobble skirt" was the chief fashion note after 1910. 1912 was the year of the *Titanic* disaster.

UPON his return to New York in 1909, Herbert became a veritable music mill. Operetta followed on the heels of operetta. The lights burned late at night in his studio. When he was pressed for time—and when was there a time that he was not?—the composer orchestrated his melodies as he set them down, a feat possible only to those for whom the technique of their art has become second nature.

Fourteen full-length operettas in five years represented a tremendous amount of hard work; yet Herbert was able to undertake even more. He had his own orchestra, known as Victor Herbert's Orchestra. Their concert tours during the winter season always included one or two appearances in

Carnegie Hall or Aeolian Hall in New York City, and their summer itinerary included summer resorts like Saratoga Springs, New York, and the outdoor shell at Willow Grove Park in Philadelphia, Pennsylvania.

Even in this whirlwind of activity, Herbert continued to compose, writing with his usual care and charm. There were many who marveled that a man with so much routine concert work to attend to could find the necessary inspiration and energy to turn out such an excellent score as that provided for *Naughty Marietta*, a piquant, saucy, tuneful work which continues to delight millions of music lovers. With this operetta in 1910, Herbert reached the zenith of his fame. *Natoma*, the composer's grand opera, which was produced the following year, brought him prestige and the satisfaction of having achieved something fine in the field of serious music; but it did not make his name known to millions of people as *Naughty Marietta* did.

Naughty Marietta marked the advent of a new librettist for Herbert—Rida Johnson Young—and the début in comic opera of the third of the trio of really great sopranos whose names are linked with the composer's best operettas. This new star was Emma Trentini, an Italian girl with a marvelous voice. Like Fritzi Scheff, she was recruited from grand opera —not the Metropolitan, however, but Oscar Hammerstein's rival venture, the Manhattan Opera House.

Oscar Hammerstein was quite as colorful as any of the operas or operettas which he produced. It had become a habit with him to make and lose fortunes, and, like some temperamental prima donna, he always aired his troubles before the world. Among his unfortunate financial ventures was the Olympia Theater, which he had built twelve years before and lost through mortgage foreclosure. When his theater was taken from him, Hammerstein had to be removed from the auditorium by force. Once evicted, he vowed he would never enter the building again, never even walk by it in the street.

He broke that vow when he and his son produced *Naughty Marietta* in this very theater, renamed the New York.

The story goes that on the night of the dress rehearsal, the famous figure known by his top hats and expensive cigars came alone to the stage door. When Hammerstein entered his old theater, he walked to the edge of the stage and peered silently into the auditorium. The actors interrupted their rehearsal and waited for him to speak.

"All right," Hammerstein said at last. "Go ahead with the show. You see," he added dramatically, "I, too, needed a dress rehearsal for tomorrow."

The story of *Naughty Marietta* is set in old New Orleans, in the days when Louisiana was owned by the French. The plot revolves around the fact that girls who wanted to go to the new world from France as brides of the men settlers were sent at government expense to New Orleans. These brides-to-be were called "casquette" girls, because of the little trunks of that name which held their few belongings. The rough pioneer men of New Orleans lined up at the wharf whenever a shipload of these girls came in. When a man and girl had looked each other over and decided that they liked each other well enough, the man would pay the girl's passage money to a French official. A simple ceremony, and the new bride went off with her husband to live in a frontier cabin.

Beautiful young Countess Marietta, daughter of a noble Italian family living in France, is unhappy at home and decides to run away. Learning of a ship about to sail with a cargo of casquette girls, she dresses herself in humble clothing and joins the company of peasant lasses. It is no part of her plan to marry a rough frontiersman in New Orleans. She has an idea that she will be able to find a way to get off the boat without letting anyone pay her passage money. Something will turn up to take care of this part of the bargain, she feels sure.

Naughty Marietta

When the boat docks and Marietta sees the bearded trappers and hunters lined up to select their future wives, she realizes to the full what she has let herself in for. Her extreme fright is noticed by Captain Richard Warrington, an American frontiersman. When Étienne Grandet, unpleasant son of the Governor of the colony, makes it clear that he intends to pay Marietta's passage money, Captain Dick takes pity on the girl. Pretending that he wishes to marry Marietta himself, he pays her passage and thus frees her from Étienne's unwelcome attentions.

Étienne becomes a real threat to Marietta's plans, even so; for he recognizes her as the Countess for whose return to her family a large reward has been offered. Angered at the girl's flaunting of his attentions, he decides to be revenged by exposing her identity. However, an old love of his, the quadroon Adah, turns up to bother him, and meanwhile, Captain Dick persuades Rudolfo, the keeper of a marionette theater, to pass Marietta off as his son and helper. Dressed in boy's clothing, the girl is safe from detection.

Matters become complicated when Marietta falls in love with Captain Dick, who apparently does not return her affection. He goes off on a scouting expedition as soon as he has arranged matters with Rudolfo.

While the captain is away, Étienne persuades Marietta to attend a masked ball with him. He has almost succeeded in convincing the lonely girl to marry him when Captain Dick returns with word to the colony that Étienne is the hated Bras Piqué, a notorious pirate, leader of a band of desperate criminals who prey upon the colonists.

Then Captain Dick tells Marietta that he loves her, and all ends happily.

The score of this operetta is fresh and sparkling, and the story has a good deal more solid worth than most operetta plots. The play opens with an interesting morning scene in the Creole city. The market square is bustling with activity, with the melodious calls of the flower girls, the fruit vendors, and the sugar-cane vendors making a charming background. The street cleaners enter, singing:

"Clear the way! Clear out!"

Captain Dick and his men make their appearance with the hearty *Tramp! Tramp! Tramp!*:

"We're planters and Canucks,
Virginians and Kaintucks,
Captain Dick's own infantry."

When the casquette girls arrive in the square, crowds of men line up to beg:

"Maiden fair, oh, maiden fair,
Won't you marry me?"

But the girls, not to be hurried, tease with:

"Taisez-vous! Taisez-vous! Taisez-vous! Taisez-vous!"

At this point, Marietta is given a merry melody by the composer. In her first song, she says that within her are two girls, one very mischievous, one very proper.

"Naughty Marietta, come be good," says the proper one; but the mischievous one answers, *Mais non!* (No, indeed!)

'Neath the Southern Moon, sung by Adah, is a languorous melody suggestive of summer evenings under the crêpe myrtles and magnolias, and lazy afternoons in gardens sweet with honeysuckle. It is a melody meant for Creole lovers drifting with the leisurely current of the bayou, in an old pirogue close to the moss-draped trees shading the water.

The *Italian Street Song*, for Marietta and the chorus, is lighthearted and melodious. Everyone knows its sprightly "Zing, zing, zizzy, zizzy, zing, zing," where the solo voice soars and dips, coquets and teases:

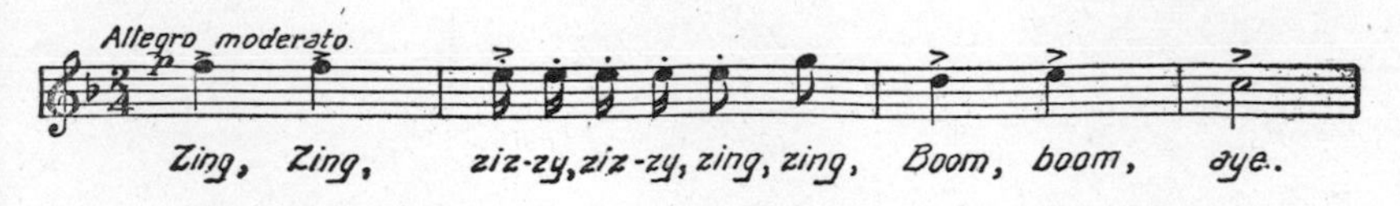

In the *Dance of the Marionettes*, Herbert caught the spirit of these little wooden people, their stiff movements, their awkward gestures, their impish fixed expressions:

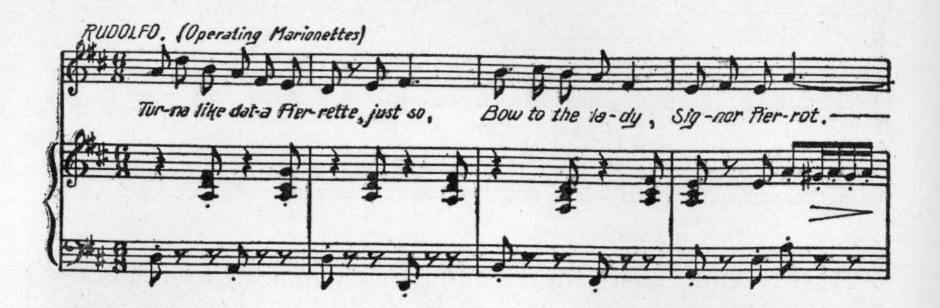

In this connection, it is of interest to know that the composer remembered the puppet folk in a work composed fourteen years after this marionette dance for *Naughty Marietta*. A *Chinese Shadowgraph*, one of Tony Sarg's famous marionette plays, inspired Herbert's *The Willow Plate*, for piano.

The intermezzo of *Naughty Marietta*, the "Dream Melody," contains phrases of haunting and memorable beauty. Orville Harold, the famous tenor of the show, liked the melody so well that he suggested that words be written to fit it. Herbert agreed, and asked Rida Johnson Young to write the lyric. The resultant song was called *Ah! Sweet Mystery of Life* and was published by the house of Witmark. The song was never a part of the operetta *Naughty Marietta*, though the melody was always part of the "Finale Ultimo." A 'cello arrangement of the original dream-melody theme has been made in recent years. It brings out to the full the poignant, romantic quality of this music, which, like much that Herbert wrote, sings softly and sweetly on the deep-toned 'cello strings.

There is an amusing story about the publication of the song *Ah! Sweet Mystery of Life.* Just before Witmark published it, the firm was very shaky financially, having issued a string of songs which did not "catch on." The employees were so despondent that they had about given the old firm up for lost; some were actually looking for new jobs. Then the new song of Herbert's came out, and the publishing house made so much money on it that instead of closing up shop they gave the help a bonus at Christmas time.

Victor Herbert would not have been himself if he had not inserted a waltz. The instrumental *Prelude* and Marietta's *Live for Today* are in the romantic three-four time dear to the composer's heart.

Captain Dick's *I'm Falling in Love With Some One* is one of the world's most appealing love songs:

Modern audiences probably know this story and music best from the motion picture *Naughty Marietta*, starring Jeannette MacDonald and Nelson Eddy. The picture score, arranged by Herbert Stothart, and the glorious singing of the stars made a hit with the public. The film brought the operetta to thousands who might otherwise never have seen and heard it.

Joseph D. Redding provided the libretto for *Natoma*, a story of California in 1820, the time of the Spanish régime. Redding, a San Francisco lawyer, was the veriest tyro at writing libretti for opera, but in spite of his inexperience, he did a workmanlike job and provided an acceptable story. Herbert rather liked the story of the Indian girl Natoma, who resembled Aïda, and the colorful Spanish background reminiscent of Bizet's *Carmen*.

The Indian characters of Redding's story call to mind an amusing anecdote. Herbert had expressed himself shortly before he read the libretto of *Natoma* as thoroughly opposed to anything Indian in opera.

"If the subject be an American one," he had said when he signed the contract with Hammerstein, agreeing to write music for a book not yet decided upon, "it is not necessary that the *dramatis personae* be either Indians or Puritans. Indians are not a suitable subject for an opera. The state of the Indians is pathetic, it is true, but in an opera they would not strike audiences seriously. You will see what I mean:

"Suppose an Indian tenor, taking a high C and then trilling on a high D in order to touch the emotions of a sopranofied prima donna squaw! The taste balks at such things!"

It is particularly to the credit of librettist Redding that he succeeded in producing in the character of Natoma, the Indian girl, a tragic figure that did not become absurd when translated into grand opera. Herbert hastily reversed his opinion about the possibilities of Indian themes for opera as he read Redding's story of the girl who maintains her dignity and pride of race to the end.

Hammerstein's periodic runs of bad luck had not deserted him. After Herbert wrote the music for the Redding score, financial reverses made it impossible for the impresario to undertake the production of the opera. Was all that work to be wasted? Unthinkable! With his usual energy, Herbert set out to sell the opera to another company. The management of the Metropolitan Opera House in New York refused it, but the opera was finally accepted by Andreas Dippel, Director of the newly formed Chicago-Philadelphia Opera Company. This was a venture underwritten by Mr. and Mrs. Harold McCormick, of Rockefeller oil and McCormick farm implements. The company was recruited largely from Hammerstein's Manhattan Opera Company, when that organization disbanded in 1910.

The "première" of *Natoma* took place in Philadelphia at the Metropolitan Opera House on February 25, 1911. Three nights later, the opera was given in New York's Metropolitan Opera House. The cast was notable:

Don Francisco de la Guerra.................... Gustave Huberdau
Father Peralta.................................... Hector Dufranne
Juan Bautista Alvarado........................ Mario Sammarco
José Castro.. Frank Preisch
Kagama.. Constantin Nicolay
Pico .... Armand Crabbé
Paul Merrill....................................... John McCormack
Barbara de la Guerra........................... Lillian Grenville
Natoma.. Mary Garden

There is some excellent music in this work, which has the distinction of having been produced more times than any other American opera. With considerable skill, the composer conveyed, in his "Indian themes," the impression of genuineness and naturalness.

In Act One, Natoma's impassioned "Oh, the wonder of his speaking, Like the wind upon the mountain" has the eerie minor quality of true Indian music. Natoma's earnest prayer to Manitou has the authentic dignity of a tribal rite:

The story of *Natoma* involves three sets of characters—Indian, Spanish, and American. The plot is motivated to some extent by the cross-currents of racial and national feeling, the loyalties and hatreds and conflicts of the various peoples living in California in the days of Spanish rule. The Indians' distrust and dislike of the Spaniards, the Spaniards' fear of the encroaching Americans, and the personal likes and dislikes, loves and hatreds of individuals cutting diagonals across all these furnish a situation charged with emotion.

The first act is laid on the Island of Santa Cruz, one of the Santa Barbara Channel Islands, at the *hacienda* (ranch) of Spanish Don Francisco de la Guerra, wealthy landowner. The curtain opens on a peaceful scene—a garden, with the blue waters of the channel beyond, and in the distance, the dim outlines of the mainland. It is a warm summer's day. Nearly everyone at the ranch house is taking his *siesta* (nap). Only Don Francisco remains in the garden. He looks out over the water, hoping to catch a glimpse of a boat. He expects his daughter Barbara, who is returning home from the convent school of the mission of Santa Barbara. Her return is of special significance, for the girl has reached her majority and so will inherit the vast estates of her dead mother.

Don Francisco's musings on the flight of time and the new life ahead for his daughter are interrupted by the arrival of four dashing young bloods—Juan Bautista Alvarado, Barbara's cousin, and his three comrades, José Castro (a half-breed Indian) and the *vaqueros* (cowboys), Pico and Kagama. They tell Don Francisco that they have come to his island for a wild-boar hunt. The truth of the matter is that Alvarado intends to be on hand when Barbara arrives. It is his intention to win the hand of his beautiful cousin and her estates into the bargain. Don Francisco, seeing nothing beyond their polite phrases of greeting, makes them welcome.

To keep up the pretense that hunting alone is the reason for their visit, Alvarado rises and urges his companions to follow him:

"Come, we must away. The shadows deepen early in the mountains. Our sport awaits us."

And Don Francisco, in courtly Spanish fashion, declares: "Good luck attend you! I beg on your return to come this way. My house, my cellar, my boats are at your command!" Then he retires for his siesta, and the young men start on their hunt.

When everyone has gone, Natoma, a handsome Indian girl enters. She walks hand in hand with Lieutenant Paul Merrill, an American naval officer from one of the warships anchored in the bay of Santa Barbara. Natoma in all her simplicity and directness has fallen in love with the American, who is merely amused by the girl's exotic beauty and childish ways, calling her "little witch" and "little wild flower."

Natoma begs that Paul tell her something of his people, but Paul insists that she tell him of her own people instead. In poetry which has the *Hiawatha* rhythm (which Longfellow borrowed from the Finnish national epic, the *Kalevala*), Natoma speaks:

"From the clouds came my first father;
Out he stepped upon the mountain."

She goes on to tell how famine came to her people, until they sickened and died one by one. Natoma remains the last of her race, mourning:

"Vanished are my father's people.
Now the stranger comes as chieftain."

Pointing to the hacienda, Natoma tells Paul about Barbara. These two had been playmates as children, and Natoma loves the Spanish girl, even though for the Spanish race in general there is a fierce resentment in her heart. She blames the conquering Spaniards for the misfortunes of her people.

Distant music from the water heralds the coming of Barbara and the convent girls. Don Francisco comes from the house to watch their boat put in. Natoma introduces him to Lieutenant Merrill, and the three of them are standing together on the terrace when Barbara reaches the garden. The eyes of the lieutenant and Barbara meet, and it is at once clear to any who have eyes to see that these two have fallen in love.

Alvarado and his boon companions arrive, and Don Francisco invites everyone to stay and join the household in the happy celebration of Barbara's return. Only Natoma and Castro do not go into the house with the others. Natoma's tragic eycs tell of her knowledge of Paul's love for Barbara and the hopelessness of her own love. Castro has observed the true state of affairs, and proceeds to upbraid Natoma for wasting her affections on an American. Natoma turns from him in distaste. She has only hatred for the Indians with Spanish blood.

There is a gay celebration, which lasts till evening. Finally Don Alvarado and his guests retire. When the garden is lighted only by the moon, Barbara comes out to the terrace. Alvarado steps from the shadows, and serenades his cousin in Spanish style. His song is one of considerable poetry, the music sighing with Latin passion. To Alvarado's amazement and anger, Barbara coldly rejects his advances. The Spaniard's expressions of love turn to scorn. He accuses her of being in love with someone in the Mission town on the mainland, and insults her by saying that she is an immodest girl, unworthy of her convent training.

Alvarado leaves, and Paul comes into the garden. In a charming duet, he and Barbara declare their love for each other. Natoma watches from the shadows. When the lovers go inside the house, she voices her hopeless longing in a theme which recurs as Natoma's love theme.

Meanwhile, Castro has revealed to Alvarado the growing love between Barbara and the American lieutenant. Alvarado is all for killing Paul on the spot, but his friends persuade him to wait. They suggest the plan of abducting Barbara during the *fiesta* (festival) which is to be held in her honor on the mainland next day. Natoma overhears the plot, but says nothing to Paul or Barbara or Don Francisco. Only the suffering eyes in the Indian girl's impassive face betray her tragic thoughts.

The second act of the opera takes place in the *plaza* (public square or marketplace) of Santa Barbara. At one side of the plaza is the church, and beyond rise the mountains of Santa Inez. There is an early-morning stir of life. A milk boy and his donkey bring a pigskin of milk to the mission. Market women appear, and Spanish soldiers. Booths are decorated with *sarapes* (blankets worn as cloaks), water jars, fruits, and flowers. Mandolin and guitar players stroll about the walks, flirting with the girls who are drawing water from the public fountain.

Alvarado is among the strollers. He flirts with Chiquita, the dancing girl, and joins her in one of the most popular Spanish dances ever written, the *Habañera:*

A grandstand has been erected for Barbara and her father, their friends and the Spanish Alcalde (mayor) and other dignitaries of the town. From this vantage point, these wealthier citizens of the town will watch the dancers and other entertainers of the fiesta. The *pobres* (poor people) will stand at the sides of the square, wherever they can find room.

A colorful procession of the merrymakers is heralded by Pico's wild boasting *Song of the Vaqueros*. Dancers, rope-swinging cowboys, singers and guitar players—all who are to furnish entertainment—enter singing and shouting. Barbara and her friends ride in on mettlesome horses. They dismount and allow their horses to be led away by Indian servants. When they have taken their places in the grandstand, Barbara expresses her joy and appreciation of this celebration in her honor in a gay song:

"Awake, my love, the spring is here!"

Natoma stands in the square, quietly, with folded arms, taking no part in the festivities.

Spirited dances open the festival. Then Barbara steps down from the grandstand to be Alvarado's partner in a stately minuet. Their dance is interrupted by a cannon salute from the American warship offshore. A group of American sailors come into the square with a lusty chorus with a smack of the sea about it. Paul and two brother officers follow, and are invited to sit with Don Francisco's party in the grandstand.

Alvarado, burning with jealousy, demands that Barbara continue the dance with him. The musicians play with more and more spirit until the stately minuet has turned into the lively "hat dance." This is a courting dance. In the last figure, each gallant places his *sombrero* (hat) on his lady love's head. If he has found favor in her eyes, she removes the hat, places it on the ground, and dances about it—sometimes, if she is skillful enough and the hat brim is wide, on the brim itself.

Barbara spurns Alvarado's hat when it is offered her in the time-honored ceremony. The crowd standing in the square mutters angrily. It is clear that their sympathies are with handsome Alvarado, rather than with the daughter of the landowner, in this affair.

Castro creates a diversion by throwing his dagger quivering into the earth as a challenge for someone to dance the dagger dance with him. The crowd falls silent. None will accept the challenge; for the dance of the dagger is a primitive dance, and make-believe has been known to become reality in the intoxication of its frenzied rhythm.

The silence grows deeper. Then Natoma moves forward dramatically and casts her dagger into the earth beside Castro's. Natoma's ominous "fate motif" in the orchestra gives way to the music of the *Dagger Dance*.

The *Dagger Dance* is wild and barbaric in the extreme. The opening phrases suggest the primitive beat of Indian drums:

While this dance holds the spectators fascinated, Alvarado and his men throw a serape over Barbara's head and drag her from the grandstand. No one notices except Natoma. With one swift lunge, she hurls herself, dagger in hand, beyond the weaving and leaping figure of Castro and buries her dagger in Alvarado's heart.

When the crowd sees Alvarado fall dead at Natoma's feet, it surges forward as if to tear the Indian girl to pieces. Paul leaps into the square and holds the angry people at bay with his sword. Natoma seeks the sanctuary of the church.

The last scene of the opera is within the church. After escaping the enraged crowd, she falls in a heap at the foot of the altar. Dazed by the situation, she tries to comfort herself with an Indian lullaby, the infinitely sad *Beware of the Hawk, My Baby:*

The mission *padre* (priest) is compassionate. He tells her that the church will give her permanent sanctuary if she will renounce her Indian creed and enter the convent forever. Natoma will not listen until the padre adds that this plan will save Barbara and Paul much grief. For her beloved Barbara's sake, the Indian girl agrees.

In the last scene, Natoma is being prepared for the convent. The music is solemn and impressive. A choir of monks sings an old Gregorian chant, and the nuns welcome Natoma with a chorale. Through the church music, Natoma's love theme develops in the orchestra, its tenderness enhancing the tragedy of the girl's broken life.

At the end of the ceremony, beautiful church harmonies soar exultantly. They sink to quiet as the Indian girl walks slowly and sadly into the convent garden and the doors close behind her. There is a brief pause. Then the orchestra breaks into thunderous sound, reaching an impassioned climax in the fate theme of Natoma, music somber, inexorable, and terrible in its finality.

The rehearsals for *Natoma* had not been without incident. The arduous task of teaching four non-English-speaking singers how to pronounce the words of the libretto was entrusted to Irish John McCormack, noted for his beautiful diction. McCormack drilled his pupils—Sammarco, Dufranne, Huberdeau, and Crabbé—with utmost care.

Of the four, Sammarco had the greatest difficulty. One day the excitable Italian came rushing to McCormack, shouting, "Giovanni! Nobody can sing this phrase! Listen!" And he proceeded to sing words that sounded like "Wee bag the preeveeleedge of a oont upon the raaanges of your heels."

Careful research revealed that he was trying to sing Alvarado's request in the first scene:

"We beg the privilege of a hunt upon the ranges of your hills."

McCormack sang the line back to the famous baritone in his own accent. Sammarco collapsed with laughter at the sound of it.

McCormack had some complaining of his own to do. He spoke to librettist Redding about a line that defied his best efforts at phrasing:

"How in the name of music," demanded the Irish tenor, "am I to phrase the strange sentence, 'Tell me, gentle maiden, have I seen you in my dreams, I wonder?' How can Natoma tell him if he saw her in his dreams?"

This was not a complaint against librettist Redding alone. McCormack often remarked on the unreality of opera books, but if the music was good, he would shrug this objection away with "Queer things happen in opera libretti!"

McCormack also felt that the music which Herbert had provided for the tenor part was too high to be effective. He was generous in his praise of Natoma's part, however, saying it "had some beautiful phrases with the American Indian flavor. . . ."

The first performance of Natoma was a great occasion. Nearly every newspaper and musical journal in the country sent a representative to report the success or failure of the great Victor Herbert's first grand opera.

Mary Garden sang the rôle of Natoma, acting her part as she sang it, with flawless ease. John McCormack's voice, sweet and clear as a bell, gave beauty and meaning even to the less poetic passages of his part. Cleofonte Campanini was the conductor; his interpretation of the score was colorful and effective. Both composer and librettist were present—Herbert flushed with excitement, Redding pale with apprehension.

The performance went well. The entire company was keyed up over the opera. They sang with an enthusiastic determination to make a go of it. A delighted audience greeted their efforts with hearty applause. When the final curtain was rung down, the critics went to their offices and hotels, to make their reports. They were not too kind in their reviews, some of them, but none could truthfully say that, as far as the audience was concerned, *Natoma* was anything short of a success.

Victor Herbert congratulated all the singers, and was particularly flattering to John McCormack. The Irish composer had brought the Irish singer a little gift—a photograph of Herbert with all the motifs of the opera written on it.

There were undoubtedly many flaws in *Natoma*. The libretto leaves much to be desired. It was written by a man with an aptitude for the dramatic, but he was not a poet, with a poet's fine ear for the beautiful sound of words. As for the music, it is sometimes thin and stagey. The Indian themes are likely to ring false, just when they should be most sincere and authentic; and the Spanish idiom is not always characteristic. There is something artificial, for instance, in the *Habañera*, which for all its blood-stirring rhythm in Spanish style is still an alien speaking in foreign accents.

John McCormack himself said frankly, "Victor Herbert was a great master of operetta, and I always feel that *Natoma* was an overgrown operetta, one that had grown bigger . . . and more bombastic."

This was an extreme view, though not meant unkindly. It was not an accurate appraisal, either. At least five solos and dances from *Natoma* are known to thousands of people today. Of how many other operas may this be said?

Judged by the standard of Victor Herbert's operettas (which often played a first-run of nearly a year), *Natoma* does not bear favorable comparison. But that is no fairer than to compare the total annual number of performances of Beethoven's *Fifth Symphony* with the number of times *Old Black Joe* is sung in a year.

Victor Herbert had not escaped his composer's fate. He was not able to rest content until he had proved, both to himself and to the world, that he could write serious music for a successful grand opera. Having done so, he discovered that victory was tempered with disappointment. John McCormack once spoke of the heartaches in store for the composer of such a work:

"I have often wondered," he said, "if there is any greater speculation than writing a grand opera. The poor composer, bitten by the fatal bug, gets the libretto. He studies it, he restudies it, he digests it, he visualizes it on the stage, he considers its possible dramatic material, and then he calls upon his muse to inspire him. After two or three years of heartbreaking work and brain fag—not to mention eye fag—he shows it to some impresario. The impresario decides to take a chance and produce it—with no remuneration to the poor musical slave, of course, till most of the expenses are paid. Then come tedious rehearsals with orchestra, conductor, singers, stage managers, and the whole pack of them.

"At last, the first performance! Everything goes well. The public seems pleased, and the impresario is enthusiastic. The poor composer says to himself: 'It was a hard tussle and a terrible grind, but it was worth it.'

"He is awake at cock-crow to read the notices. He seizes the papers with trembling hands, and, as often as not, a mist of tears fills his weary eyes, as he sees his four or five years' hard work dismissed with supercilious reference to the Wagner influence in the first act, the Debussy atmosphere in the second, and the want of individual idiom in the third. Bah!

"To me, the whole thing is unspeakably cruel. I don't for one moment question the good faith of the men who write these criticisms, but I think, and I always will think, that it is grossly unfair to damn a musician's hard work on one or two hearings. After all, it is infinitely easier to criticize than to create. . . ."

Victor Herbert was heartily in accord with such sentiments. There was always a "friendly warfare" on between him and the critics. An amusing caricature of Victor Herbert once appeared in *Musical America* (No. 6 in the journal's *Gallery of Celebrities*). The caption read:

"VICTOR HERBERT, DISTINGUISHED AS CONDUCTOR AND COMPOSER. ENJOYS A NATIONAL POPULARITY. NEVER LOSES AN OPPORTUNITY TO BERATE THE CRITICS, WHICH DOESN'T HURT THEM BUT MAKES HIM FEEL BETTER."

There are many friends of those old days who know how hard and earnestly Herbert worked at the music for his opera. It was written in that wonderful New York studio of his, on the fifth floor of his home. On the wall above the high desk were pictures of Herbert's mother, father, grandparents, and wife. On the other walls hung pictures of Wagner, Beethoven, Liszt, Haydn, Bach, Mozart, Richard Strauss, Anton Seidl, and many others. There were bookshelves with a large musical library and many volumes of United States history. Next to musical literature—biographies and critical essays—history was Herbert's favorite reading.

In a special case, Herbert had many autographed scores—presents from the great composers he had known. And because he was a man of the theater, he included among his treasures photographs of the scenes and principal singers in costume of all his comic operas. Some of these pictures hung on the walls; others lay in theatrical scrapbooks.

Near the studio piano stood a 'cello. This was the little workaday 'cello which Victor Herbert used when he wanted to try out his musical ideas or to illustrate a point in discussion with musicians who dropped in for a visit. The concert 'cello in its case was cared for lovingly, as if it had been a child. It was much too precious to be exposed to a room's variations of dust and damp, heat and cold.

The composer worked out the musical sketches for *Natoma* with greatest care. With meticulous attention to the smallest detail, he expanded his thematic material and wrote the voice parts and the orchestral score.

A musical friend who came up one day when Herbert was hard at work on his opera, looked with interest at a page of the score where an unusual suspension caught his eye. (*Suspension* is the term applied to retaining in any chord some note, or notes, of the preceding chord, resulting in a dissonance which is finally resolved in the harmony of the chord.)

"Isn't this suspension slightly unorthodox?" the musical visitor asked Herbert.

"Not unless you call Schumann unorthodox," said Herbert. "Wait. I'll find the song where he used a similar device."

Herbert's library of the works of famous composers was extensive, and the particular song he had in mind that day had buried itself in a mass of material.

"Never mind!" protested his visitor. "You're busy. I'll take your word on it that you remember that suspension."

Herbert sensed good-natured doubt and was more determined than ever to prove his point. Once the composer had made up his mind to do a thing, it was characteristic of him not to give up until it was accomplished. Book after book was pulled out and examined until the very song he wanted was found at last.

"See? Look at that!" Triumphantly the composer pointed out the Schumann suspension, which was his authority for using a similar device in *Natoma*.

His visitor smiled to himself. He might have known! Victor's wonderful memory was an accepted fact in musical circles.

End of an Era

1912-1924. In 1913, Peace Palace at The Hague was dedicated. In 1914, the first World War began. Woodrow Wilson was re-elected President of the United States in 1916. In 1917, the Soviets seized power in Russia. In 1921, Warren G. Harding became President of the United States. Mussolini marched on Rome and proclaimed the Fascist state in 1922. In 1923, an earthquake in Japan killed half a million persons. Calvin Coolidge was elected President. In 1924, the speakeasy period of Prohibition was at its peak. Lenin died in Russia, Wilson in the United States. Hitler's *Mein Kampf* was published in Germany but created very little stir at the time. The most important fashion note of this period was the incredibly short skirt of 1920. Rolled stockings and bobbed hair ceased to shock. Songs of the twelve-year period were a strange hodge-podge which included *Japanese Sandman, K-K-K-Katy, Over There,* and the *Sheik of Araby.*

IN 1913, the world was rapidly coming to the end of one volume of history and getting ready to open the next. The first World War was to be the terrible opening chapter of the new volume, and, as if the war set the mood for the whole volume, the chapters following were by turns grim and hectic. For a time it seemed that the innocent pleasures of a calmer day would be forgotten.

The change was abrupt. Just the year before war broke out, life in New York and in other capitals of the world was deceptively "normal." Vienna was gay, Paris was gay, London was sober, New York was bustling, busy, devil-may-care.

Victor Herbert's sprightly contribution to the spring of 1913 was his operetta *Sweethearts.* The first performance was given in the Academy of Music at Baltimore, where its success was prophetic of the stir this tuneful piece was to make in New York.

Sweethearts has a story and music in the gay Viennese tradition. The action takes place in Belgium and a mythical kingdom called Zilania. Act One is set in the courtyard of the Laundry of the White Geese, Bruges, Belgium. Act Two takes place in the picturesque Royal Hunting Lodge of Zilania.

The fragile plot revolves around Sylvia, Princess of Zilania, and Prince Franz, Heir Presumptive to the throne of Zilania. As a baby, Sylvia had been abducted and left with Dame Paula, proprietress of the Laundry of the White Geese. Sylvia knows nothing of her claim to the throne, however. With Dame Paula's numerous daughters—Jeannette, Clairette, Babette, Lisette, Toinette, and Nanette—she works in the laundry and complains how stupid it is to "Iron! Iron! Iron!"

Prince Franz meets Sylvia, whom he believes to be merely a village girl, and falls in love with her. Sylvia is also in love with Franz, but feels that a simple village girl would never be accepted as queen. Besides, she has previously become engaged to Lieutenant Karl.

Eventually it is disclosed that Sylvia is entitled to be Queen of Zilania. Prince Franz finds that he is just one of her subjects. The tables are turned, but Sylvia's and Franz' love is not affected. Sylvia assures her prince, "Tho' queen I may be, still my love is yours!"

Before this happy ending is effected, there are several songs that make a bid for operatic fame:

The *Sweethearts* waltz, sung by Sylvia and the chorus, is one of Herbert's most charming melodies.

Mother Goose is one of those delicate little fancies written with the composer's very young friends in mind.

The Prince and the chorus remind us tunefully that *Every Lover Must Meet His Fate:*

The supporting characters of the play—Liane, a milliner of Bruges; Hon. Percival Slingsby; Petrus Van Tromp; and Aristide Caniche—sing the blithe *Jeannette and Her Little Wooden Shoes.* The music for Jeannette's sabot dance is a gay *characteristique:*

Pretty as a Picture, sung by Van Tromp and chorus, has taken its place in the list of Herbert romantic favorites:

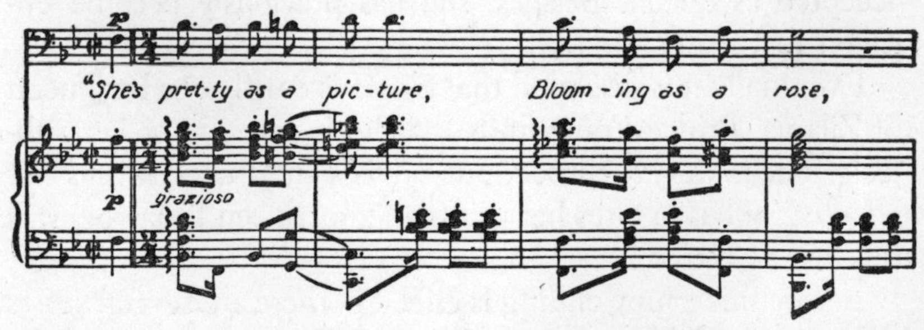

Sweethearts was the immediate cause of Herbert's organizing the composers and librettists of America to protect the performing rights of their works. United States copyright law was vague; more important, it was seldom invoked, and restaurant and theater owners felt free to let their orchestras play whatever music they chose, without pay to the copyright owners. Herbert had always resented this "pirating" of his work, and reached the limit of his patience one night when he walked into a large New York restaurant, where an orchestra was merrily playing the hit tunes from *Sweethearts*, showing just around the corner.

Next day, Herbert rounded up a few of "the boys"—Gene Buck, formerly a Detroit newspaperman, working as publicity director for Florenz Ziegfeld and the Follies; bandmaster John Philip Sousa; and attorney Nathan Burkan; and others. They talked the problem over in the quiet half-gloom of Lüchow's. Herbert proposed an organization modeled on the successful French society of Authors, Composers, and Editors of Music. The rest agreed, and the foundation was laid for the American Society of Composers, Authors, and Publishers.

The purpose of the organization was to see that theatrical and restaurant men observed the copyright laws. This involved an enormous amount of "research" as to where music was being illegally performed. A sort of gigantic "police force" was necessary, and a legal staff capable of prosecuting the music pirates. All this required more than any one individual could accomplish. With resources pooled, however, artists might accomplish the gigantic task.

For years the founders of ASCAP dug up their hard-earned dollars to support the Society, and received little return in money. But the dogged members, led by Victor Herbert, whose tenacity was a kind of stubbornness, clung to their purpose. Gene Buck was actually thrown into jail in Arizona, when the theater interests in that state tried to break the composers' organization there with the same tactics the copper interests had employed against the trade unions.

Victor Herbert worked unselfishly on behalf of ASCAP. His daughter states: "Father probably profited little in actual dollars and cents."

But others have since reaped important benefits. Time and

time again, author, composer, and publisher members have discovered that in union there is strength.

Herbert's rôle in fostering this protective organization was an inevitable one. He was one of the most canny and business-like artists of his day. He was careful to safeguard his earnings by never selling a copyright. His songs belonged to him and might be played for a price, but never purchased outright. Even today, the rights to perform Herbert's music are always leased, not sold.

When the composer undertook a lengthy work, he was careful not to run the risk of having it remain on his hands. He signed contracts in advance. This protection by contract did not mean that he wrote "to order" as some have suggested. Herbert was as uncompromising in maintaining his independence as a composer, free to write the kind of music he wanted, as he was insistent on pay for his time and effort.

Victor Herbert had an exclusive "artist's recording contract" with the Victor Record Company. Most of the record companies paid him a regular "retainer fee." His orchestrations of the works of other composers were always in demand, and still hold their own. When the Boston Pops Orchestra made a record of Anton Rubinstein's *Kamenoi Ostrow,* they used Herbert's orchestration; 60,000 of these records were sold the first two years the recording was out.

Herbert's own New York Orchestra played for recordings, too, using their conductor's arrangements. The Victor Company still lists one of these records in their catalogue—the two well-known wedding marches of Mendelssohn and Wagner.

Herbert had iron-clad contracts with all these companies. They were required to pay royalties on all his compositions and arrangements.

Many of Herbert's orchestrations have been published. Among these are the delightful *The Cat and the Mice* and *The Donkey and the Driver,* composed by Hubert Leonard, then head of the Paris Conservatory. In these two works, Herbert displayed his mastery of instrumental effects. The various "voices" of the orchestra are made to speak humorously, each in its own character, yet blending harmoniously to produce a charming effect of playfulness and fantasy.

Victor Herbert knew the value of his name, and made it pay dividends; but he did not like to think that his fame alone might account for the success of his later works. The story goes that he once had an urge to make a test to determine if his music sold on its own merits.

He decided to introduce one of his new compositions under a *nom-de-plume* (pen-name) at a Sunday night concert played by his orchestra at the New York Theatre. On the program, the name *Nobel MacClure* was printed as composer of the piece.

The work of the "unknown" was received with tremendous applause—for it was *Al Fresco*, which has gained in popularity with the years. The composer was left with no doubts as to the ability of his work to speak for itself.

Next morning, Herbert called on his publishers, who were making haste to issue *Al Fresco* in sheet-music form. He had satisfied himself that his name was not essential to a composition's popularity, but he saw no good reason to continue the masquerade.

"Take that nom-de-plume off and put mine on," he commanded.

It was good business to take credit for his work.

Some doubt has been cast on the authenticity of this amusing story, and, indeed, it may be another of the many "legends" which have grown up around the name of Victor Herbert. It is a fact that the music of *Al Fresco* is that of the opening chorus of the second act of Herbert's operetta *It Happened in Nordland*, rewritten by the composer as a purely orchestral number. The name Nobel MacClure, however, was one used in copyrighting other Herbert compositions: the piano numbers *Get Together* (Fox Trot); *On Your Way* (One Step); and *Valse à la Mode*.

In spite of all his protestations that comic opera satisfied him, artistically as well as financially, the composer secretly yearned to write another serious work. He tried his hand at one more grand opera. This was *Madeleine*, the book of which was written by Grant Stewart. Stewart based his libretto on a French story about a successful opera singer, a beautiful woman with a host of admirers who shower jewelry and flowers upon her. Success, wealth, adulation—these, she thinks, represent complete happiness. Then one New Year's Day, she discovers that not one friend or admirer, not even her maid, will have dinner with her. Each one makes polite excuses. Each of her beaux is so sorry, but he is planning to dine with his mother. Left alone, the singer is overwhelmed by the knowledge that she is poor indeed. Jewels do not take the place of family ties. In her loneliness, Madeleine takes a picture of her own mother, long since dead, and props the likeness up on the table with the pathetic words:

"I, too, dine with my mother."

Madeleine was produced at the Metropolitan Opera House of New York on January 24, 1914, with Frances Alda in the leading rôle. Though the score contained some of the best music Herbert had ever written, it was considered too "abstract" by many. Herbert had made a conscious effort to discard his gift of ingenuous melody in favor of subtle themes, and he wrote into *Madeleine* ephemeral fancies which vanished into thin air before they could be grasped. He was trying to do something in the manner of Debussy, but neither critics nor public would accept Herbert as an impressionist. *Madeleine* was not a real success. Today the opera is remembered chiefly for one moment of exquisite melody, *A Perfect Day*.

The composer continued to busy himself with his New York orchestra, which in summer he took on tour. The open-air shell at Willow Grove Park in Philadelphia, Pennsylvania, brought him back for two or three weeks year after year. On August 3, 1914, he played his fifteenth engagement there. It was during this engagement in 1914 that he caused a considerable stir by playing a Turkish march by the Russian

Moussorgsky, "a composer entirely new to Willow Grove audiences," one reviewer said uncomfortably.

Ragtime was turning into jazz, and the bewildering new idiom was as foreign to Herbert's temperament as impressionism. With jazz he felt as uncomfortable as the Willow Grove audiences had with Moussorgsky's wild, exotic music. Herbert knew and liked George Gershwin and admired his *Rhapsody in Blue*, it is true; but he often remarked that he found much of the "new music" discordant, and he always became eloquent when he told how he disliked the saxophone, that star of the jazz orchestra.

Herbert became almost wistful whenever he advanced his pet idea of a home for operetta, such as London's Savoy had provided for the works of Gilbert and Sullivan. Speaking of musical comedy to a reporter from the *Christian Science Monitor* in 1915, he called operetta a branch of art without a home. There was no Savoy, he said, to develop a Gilbert and Sullivan. And why not? It could be done in New York, surely. An adequate house, well equipped; one production running while another was in preparation; older productions on tour under the label of their New York producing house. A sort of setting up of a standard for musical comedy was the idea. Just look at the hundreds of good singers idle in New York. They had sung in Paris, Berlin, London, Vienna. They couldn't sing in America. The Metropolitan Opera standard was too high. If a singer not up to this standard sang there, the press would say, "He was not as good as Caruso." But why should he be? argued Herbert. Why compare good singers with a man in a class by himself? Yet to be heard in opera in America your singer nearly always must belong to that class. To those who did not so belong, a New York Savoy would be a shelter. And the public would not lose its talent.

It is America's loss that Victor Herbert's dream of a permanent home for comic opera has not yet been realized. A whole generation now exists which has been denied the pleasure of seeing a Herbert operetta and which knows the music only through random pieces broadcast by radio. Motion pictures have offered several "adapted" versions of the originals, and have made use of the music of the operettas—but until an American Savoy comes into existence, much of the charming music of the great Victor Herbert will remain between the covers of printed scores.

In 1915, Herbert went to San Francisco to fulfill a conducting engagement for the Panama-Pacific Exposition, which celebrated the completion of the Panama Canal. An amusing tale is told of the adventure. The orchestra was playing in Festival Hall. The month was November—and November means fog in San Francisco. On Alcatraz Island, the doleful wail of the fog signal was repeating the warning to the ships and boats of the bay. This weird warning signal penetrated the hall where Herbert and the orchestra were about to perform the delicate opening measures of Cadman's *Land of the Sky-Blue Waters*. They were using Herbert's arrangement, which is noted for the beautiful voice of the oboes.

Three times the composer raised his baton, and the opening measures breathed softly. And three times the mournful cry of the foghorn ruined the opening.

Three times Herbert pulled his men up short with a peremptory click of his baton. A sort of contest ensued between the brasses, reeds, and strings of the orchestra and the banshee wailing of the foghorn.

Deciding that surrender was the only recourse, Herbert shifted to Dvořák's *Humoresque*. A reporter commented next day:

"*Humoresque* is said by musical folk to portray laughter. Herbert wouldn't say whether he considered the laugh on him or the foghorn."

In 1917, Herbert completed the operetta which must have been a long-cherished wish. This was an operetta with an Irish background, a story set in the rebellious Ireland of 1798. The Blossom book, called at first *Hearts of Erin* became, with Herbert's music, the operetta *Eileen*.

Eileen is a work which deserves to be better known. The plot has the dash and verve of a Charles Lever novel, and the wit and gayety with which it is leavened are infectiously "Irish." Herbert's music throughout is effective. His thorough understanding of the Gaelic quality in music is shown in the nostalgic *When Shall I Again See Ireland?*, which breathes a Celtic melancholy and mystic longing reminiscent of the Irish folk music.

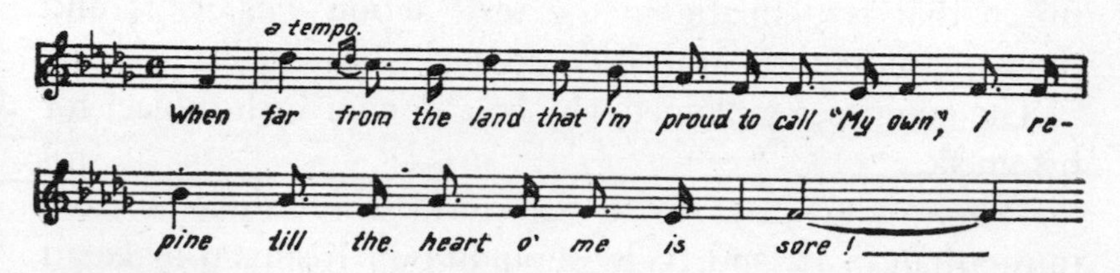

Eileen was presented first in Boston. The *Boston Transcript* printed a brilliant review of this last great operetta by America's grand man of music.

Insisting that readers of the article should go to see the show, the reviewer promised them that they should "hear a composer of operetta who knows that violins can shimmer and bite, that 'cellos can sing darkly, plaintively, that flutes can set phrases dancing in air, that clarinets are the voices of sentiment when it does not fall to the horns, that brass may be mellow-throated, that drums may snap out a rhythm and not thump it into lifelessness; who knows how to set his melodies against rich and deep harmonic background until his orchestra glows, to warm or prick the ear with his instrumental color, to sharpen his rhythms, to give his climaxes musical roundness and nervous thrill."

And of the skilled adaptation of music to the moods of the story, the reviewer said: "His rhythmic verve is fertile and tireless in his dances; his humorous melodies are light, pithy, pungent. He dapples a duet like that between the colonel and the lady of the manor with courtly fancies or makes a serenade sound like an Irish melody with Tom Moore rhyming it and Stevenson setting it on the spot. He invents eighteenth-century music, as in the 'round' at the beginning of the second act quite as well as do some of the 'serious' Italians; he is ready with the churchly modes of the intermezzo of the passing acolytes. His songs of sentiment, whether Captain O'Day or the ladies sing them, are full-bodied, warm-hearted, romantic, glamorous, without a simper or a trick. His patter tickles the ear and his declamation stirs it. At the end of the first act and at the end of the second—each a long finale—he is writing music that is dramatic to the text, action, characters and dramatic in its thrill and stride upon the hearers."

The composer explained why he chose an Irish subject for his music:

"There is no place in all the world where there is more music than in Ireland. Why shouldn't an Irishman make an opera of it? . . . The Irish sing when they work, and they sing when they suffer—unluckily, they've never known much but work and suffering."

It is an interesting fact that the great music-buying public has placed the seal of approval on this tuneful *Eileen* music. Sheet-music sales for *Thine Alone* from *Eileen* have for the past three years been second only to *Ah! Sweet Mystery of Life (Naughty Marietta)*, which has long held first place. As for the operetta as a whole, there has been but one year (1942) that it has not been done many times by amateur groups, and the entire work was broadcast twice in 1943.

In 1917, the United States entered the war against Germany. The general fanatical hatred of the "Hun" annoyed the composer, who had spent so much of his life among the German people. Prussian militarism he condemned, but he could not believe that the simple, everyday people of Stuttgart, for example, had become ravening beasts.

Herbert was indignant when anti-German feeling rose so high in America that educators were removing the German language from the curricula and musicians were refusing to play the music of German-speaking composers—even those who had lived and died a century or more before the days of German imperialism. It struck him as utter nonsense, this refusal even to understand the enemy. Burning books, outlawing languages, proscribing music—these were not the way to enlightenment, or to winning a war, he thought.

The July following the entrance of the United States into the war, Herbert and his New York Orchestra were scheduled to play at Willow Grove as usual. The management of the park concerts informed Herbert by letter that no German music could be played.

Shortly after this communication arrived, a friend visited the composer in his studio. Herbert was complaining that he had to make new selections for his orchestra. He was pulling one album after another from his well-stocked shelves.

Mozart! Haydn! Händel! Weber; Beethoven; Wagner! Schubert! Schumann! Mendelssohn! Strauss! Every one of them had spoken German. Their music was taboo.

Victor Herbert exploded. "You can't get along without German music. Anyway, what have Beethoven and Wagner to do with this war?"

No matter what his disturbed thoughts, Herbert kept right on working. In these years, he added another activity to his crowded schedule—the writing of overtures for a motion-picture theater in New York. Motion pictures in Herbert's day were silent. Dialogue, which today is spoken by the film characters, had to be written on the picture as "sub-titles." The picture industry soon realized that music would be a tremendous help in setting the mood of these silent plays. Orchestras were employed in the larger theaters, and special scores were provided for them to play during the showing of the film. Usually there was an overture, too.

In 1923-24 the Cosmopolitan Theatre, New York, was given over to International Pictures, Inc., for the feature showing of pictures starring Marion Davies. Victor Herbert and his orchestra were engaged for the whole season, and he was conducting there at the time of his death.

Herbert's contract called for the writing of an original overture for each picture scheduled. To identify the overtures, the composer named them for the picture playing at the time the music was performed. Otherwise, the music had no connection with the films; it was not a part of the films in the way that background music for motion pictures today is thematic "mood material" for the action of the story. Five such overtures in all were written by Victor Herbert. These include *Dramatic Overture,* written for use at the time the picture *Under the Red Robe* was shown.

Though the overtures were not intended to be descriptive music for the films which they introduced, Victor Herbert did actually write music of this kind, as early as 1916. For the film *The Fall of a Nation,* a silent motion picture produced by National Films, shown for the first time at the Liberty Theatre in New York, June 6, 1916, Victor Herbert wrote a descriptive score closely following the action of the picture. This is said to be the first original musical score ever written for a motion picture.

Herbert's score for *The Fall of a Nation* contains some excellent music. Many of the "themes" are actually complete compositions and as such have been published separately: *Entrance of the Heroes, Forebodings, Karma, Little Italy, Love Theme,* etc.

Because Herbert knew motion pictures in the old silent days, he did not hold them of much value for serious drama. Only operas and plays which were essentially records of action and not thought could be made into motion pictures, he declared. He could not imagine Hamlet's soliloquy screened. Would they, he asked humorously, attempt to picturize the "slings and arrows of outrageous fortune"? And how about showing the "native hue of resolution, sicklied o'er with the pale cast of thought"? No, pictures, he decided, were not for plays like these. How could he know that before long, pictures would speak? That even Hamlet's soliloquy would not seem out of place on the screen? He granted that pictures would be useful as records of historical events, and suggested that, as such, they might play an important rôle in the history classes of the future.

The number and variety of Herbert's activities, which he

The Fortune Teller

carried on to the day of his death indicate how he was driving himself. The *New York Tribune* of May 27, 1924, mentioned that "Among the tasks which Mr. Herbert was trying to complete at the time of his death was the musical score for the coming Ziegfeld 'Follies.' For several years he has been a big factor in these productions, doing much of the ballet and incidental music. . . . He had been engaged to prepare six overtures for the Cosmopolitan Motion Picture Productions. . . .

"Mr. Herbert had been at the Cosmopolitan Theatre Saturday working on the overture, and on Sunday had stayed up until after midnight at a rehearsal of the 'Follies.' He was to go to Philadelphia for concerts. . . ."

Before these plans could be carried out, however, America's great composer died on May 26, in 1924.

Victor Herbert's death was mourned by none more sincerely than by the men with whom he worked. Members of his New York Orchestra were to have gathered for rehearsal on May 27. When news came that their leader had died, the men were stunned. It was a touching tribute to a beloved figure in their world of music when the orchestra assembled as scheduled. On the music stands were two compositions. The musicians took up their instruments and played the first of these—Chopin's poignant funeral march. And then they burst forth with Victor Herbert's own composition *Little Old New York*, playing it joyously, gayly, as the composer would have wished, thus saluting that mirthful, ever-youthful part of the man who had loved life well, who had worked hard, who had achieved fame, and who, above all, had won a special place in the hearts of the everyday people of his beloved Manhattan and of the world.

Funeral services for Victor Herbert were held in St. Thomas' Episcopal Church. An impressive funeral cortège included members of the Lambs, the Friars, the Irish societies, and musicians from nearly every orchestra in the city.

Rev. Dr. Ernest M. Stires spoke the eulogy. "We shall never be able to think of Victor Herbert without thinking of melody," he said. "He is not dead. His work lives and is permanent and eternal."

Herbert's memory has been honored many times and in many ways by a people grateful for his music. In recent years, a Victor Herbert postage stamp was issued by the United States Postal Department. This is the three-cent stamp in the "musicians' group" of the *Famous Americans* series. It was first sold in New York City on May 13, 1940. In 1943, a victory ship was launched and christened the *Victor Herbert*. This ship, a birthday present to Major General Jonathan M. Wainwright, taken at Corregidor, carries the spirit of Victor Herbert's Irish wrath against those who would destroy human life and happiness, burn books, close schools, and kill music.

On November 29, 1927, New York City—the city Victor Herbert loved so well—paid its own tribute to America's music master. On that day, on the Mall in Central Park, Sculptor Edmund T. Quinn's bronze bust of the composer was unveiled by the composer's daughter. The bust, an excellent likeness, bringing out Herbert's handsome profile and something of his geniality and warm humanity, was a gift from the American Society of Composers, Authors, and Publishers. Mayor "Jimmy" Walker accepted it on behalf of the city of New York. Gene Buck, Herbert's good friend, and president at that time of ASCAP, made the presentation speech.

Buck spoke of the bust as "a symbol of affection and esteem for a man whom we consider America's greatest composer. His music had distinction because Victor Herbert fundamentally had technique and taste. No greater, better, more lovable or admirable composer has graced our generation. His music had originality, force, simplicity, and charm, and that is why his music lives.

"Music is the universal language. His monument shall serve as an inspiration to those who have a song or a melody in their heart."

American Society of Composers, Authors and Publishers

A MEMORIAL

VICTOR HERBERT'S memorial is built on more than his music. The composer will long be remembered for his part in the formation of an organization which has been of material help to thousands of artists, the American Society of Composers, Authors and Publishers. Based on the principle that in unity there is strength, this organization through its collective action has secured its members and their estates against the pathetic fate of a Stephen Foster. When the Foster songs like *Swanee River*, *My Old Kentucky Home*, *Old Black Joe*, and *Old Folks at Home* were being sung across the continent and in the farthest corners of the world, their composer lay on a charity cot in Bellevue Hospital, New York City. When he died, he had but thirty-eight cents to show for his lifetime of creative work.

Victor Herbert and a group of nine, which included John Philip Sousa, Nathan Burkan, copyright lawyer, and Gene Buck (President of ASCAP from 1924 to 1942, when Deems Taylor succeeded him) formed the association that undertook to put an end to musical piracy in the United States. Lüchow's restaurant was the meeting place of the founders when, in 1914, they laid the cornerstone of the organization which now has a membership of one thousand five hundred and seventy-five American and forty-five thousand foreign writer members and one hundred and ninety-six publisher members. A letter from Daniel I. McNamara, of the American Society of Composers, Authors and Publishers, is a fitting tribute to the achievement which stands as a living memorial to Victor Herbert:

"You will have learned long before this that Herbert was a thoroughly established musician and composer in the Old World before Frank Damrosch, on a talent scouting trip for the Metropolitan Opera Company, discovered Therese Foerster, a diva of the Wagnerian type, in the grand opera house at Stuttgart, and tried to engage her for the Metropolitan, found her reluctant to leave Germany because of her sweetheart, Victor Herbert, 'cellist in an orchestra in Stuttgart—and that Damrosch solved the problem by engaging both of them for the Met.—that they were married and came to the United States. He was then 28.

"Because Herbert had composed extensively in Europe, he knew not only the art, but also the commerce, of musical composition—that a valuable part of the music copyright was that which controlled the public performance of the copyright music. This so-called 'performing right' belongs to the creator of the music, the extent of this right varying in different countries. In the United States for instance, the public performance of a copyrighted work must be FOR PROFIT in order to constitute an infringement. In some of the foreign countries, it is immaterial whether such performance is for profit or not—any public performance must be 'by permission of the copyright owner,' otherwise it is an infringement, and subject to the penalties, civil and criminal, fixed by the laws of the various countries.

"Herbert found all this changed when he came to America. While the United States copyright law specifically recognized this performing right, it was NEVER enforced, and commercial enterprises quite generally made whatever use of copyright music they wished. The general disregard for copyrights was a matter of considerable discussion shortly after the turn of the century when Puccini came to New York in connection with the performance at the Met. of some of his works. He was astonished on visiting various hotels, restaurants, and other commercial enterprises, to hear his music used frequently when he knew he was receiving nothing for it. Puccini's American visits were largely with George Maxwell, the American representative of the vast interests of the great Italian publishing house of Ricordi, of Milan. Maxwell, an Englishman long resident in the United States, was a close friend of Herbert, and the three discussed the injustices of the American music customs at length.

"Herbert carried these discussions into the Lambs Club, historic rendezvous of theatrical folks, and many an informal gathering of the men of music at this club discussed what ought to be done.

"One evening there was a spirited discussion at the Lambs of this topic and the meeting adjourned to the famous German restaurant, Lüchow's, in Fourteenth Street, for a continuation of the talk at a dinner table. Here, plans were perfected for the organization of ASCAP, and on February 13, 1914, a meeting was held of some one hundred composers, authors, and publishers, at the Claridge Hotel, where formal organization was effected. Herbert never would be president—Maxwell served until 1924, when he was succeeded by Gene Buck, who himself was succeeded in 1942 by Deems Taylor as president.

"You no doubt have the story of the actual 'straw that broke the camel's back'—Herbert's visit to the Shanley restaurant (on the site of the present Paramount Theatre and building at Forty-fourth Street and Broadway, Times Square), late one night after he had left a performance of his operetta 'Sweethearts,' then current at the New Amsterdam Theatre, just a few minutes away, around in Forty-second Street. As he entered the cabaret, he found the entertainers singing 'Sweethearts' from his show and he remonstrated with Shanley about such commercialization of his copyright music without paying him for the privilege.

"The actual legal question was whether, since no admission was charged at the door, this use was a 'public performance for profit' within the meaning of the copyright law. It remained for the United States Supreme Court to pass on the question. In a decision written by Chief Justice Oliver Wendell Holmes (unanimously concurred in) the court upheld Herbert's contention that the music was being used to promote business, and its use therefore was an infringement. ASCAP, meantime, had gotten behind this infringement suit.

"Holmes succinctly sized up the question thus: 'If the music didn't pay, it would not be there.'

"It took three years for the Supreme Court to reach the question, however, and meanwhile the one hundred-odd men who had organized ASCAP kept paying dues, meeting at various spots usually given free by someone interested, and striving to expand and solidify their movement. It was not until 1921, however, that the Society—then having a membership of some three hundred, was able to return anything to its members from collection of royalties.

"As of March 1 [1943], ASCAP now has exactly one thousand five hundred and seventy-five writer members, one hundred and ninety-six publisher members. (Writer means either composer or author of musical works, sometimes both.) In this roster, one hundred and twenty-eight are women. Of the total one thousand five hundred and seventy-five members, two hundred and eight (including thirteen women) are deceased, the death of a member not stopping the Society's activities in behalf of the member's heirs. Often a deceased composer who was not a member of ASCAP in life is represented through the estate's becoming a member—e.g., Edward MacDowell, who died before ASCAP was formed, or Ethelbert Nevin, whose widow for many years until her recent death, received large performing rights royalties from ASCAP, and whose son continues to receive them.

"Your work on the life of Herbert probably already has disabused your mind of the belief entertained in many places that ASCAP is exclusively popular music, or Tin Pan Alley. While it is true that virtually all the successful creators of popular music are members of ASCAP, it is equally true that the outstanding men of the more serious branches of music are also included.

"Here is an alphabetical list of men and women distinguished in arts and letters in American life who are members of ASCAP:

Maxwell Anderson
Samuel Barber
Ernest Block
Charles Wakefield Cadman
John Alden Carpenter
Frederick S. Converse (dec.)
Walter Damrosch
Eric De Lamarter
Henry Hadley (dec.)
Howard Hanson
Victor Herbert (dec.)
DuBose Heyward (dec.)
Brian Hooker
Philip James
Edgar Stillman Kelley
Edward MacDowell (dec.)
Archibald MacLeish
Daniel Gregory Mason
Edna St. Vincent Millay
Douglas Moore
Robert Nathan
Ethelbert Nevin (dec.)
Horatio Parker (dec.)
John Powell
Roger Sessions
Harry Rowe Shelley
Arthur Shepherd
Leo Sowerby
Albert Spaulding
Albert Stoessel
Deems Taylor
Randall Thompson

"This particular list contains a name that in each case is found in the roster of the National Institute of Arts and Letters. You will recall that this aristocracy of American creative artists is limited to two hundred and fifty in number—and you will find that virtually all of the members of the department of music in the National Institute of Arts and Letters are members also of ASCAP.

"And this is not to be regarded, by any means, as the only representative list of ASCAP membership. There are many brilliant names whose talent is both creative and interpretative who are in ASCAP—Rachmaninoff, Kreisler, Heifetz, Elman, Zimbalist, Geraldine Farrar, Edwin Franko Goldman, Sousa, etc.

"It is more generally recognized that ASCAP's membership is representative of the creators of operettas, musical comedies, film music, etc.—and popular music in general. Kern, Friml, Romberg, Harbach, Hammerstein, Berlin, Schwartz are only a few names from this category. Within the last few years many Europeans who had connections with the foreign societies have come to America and ASCAP is opening its doors to them—Korngold, Stravinsky, Weill, Gruenberg, for example.

"Now, as to the actual operation of ASCAP: It is concerned chiefly and almost exclusively in the protection of its members' copyright music from unauthorized exploitation in the field of public performance. It is not concerned with the publishing of music, the sale of music, or the royalties that accrue in those fields.

"It is obvious that any single composer of music would be entirely helpless to protect his works from infringement, the use of music being so ephemeral that an infringement of today would be forgotten by tomorrow unless a well-organized method of checking these infringements was in effect.

"So, upon becoming a member of ASCAP, the member assigns to ASCAP for a limited period (and then renews from time to time the assignment) his particular right under the copyright to the public performance of all his works. Thus the ASCAP repertoire contains a vast number of entries. Then, through affiliation with foreign societies, the repertoire includes the works of these societies as well, so that ASCAP is part of a world-wide movement in all the civilized nations for the mutual protection of copyrights.

"ASCAP is conducted by a board of directors of twenty-four members, eight elected for terms of three years every year. The directors serve without pay, and supervise the operation of the Society through its general office in the RCA Building, New York City, and in branch offices throughout the country.

"ASCAP's entire distributable revenue is divided equally

between the publisher group and the writer group. Members of these two groups are classified for participation in proportion to the value of their contributions to the Society's repertoire. Each member of a class receives the same as every other member of his class. There is a constant reclassification to reflect the fluctuation of the members' contributions. Income is distributed quarterly. Operating expenses run about twenty per cent. The current quarterly distribution is about one million dollars. There are some thirty-five thousand licensees.

"Radio is the chief source of ASCAP revenue, although theaters, hotels, dance halls, cabarets, night clubs, fairs, carnivals, circuses, and many miscellaneous activities also contribute to its income. Because of the great number of usages that any business makes of musical works, no attempt is made to collect for the use of an individual piece of music, but the simpler method of issuing a blanket license to users is the practice.

"Copyright law in America antedates the Constitution. The original colonies had copyright laws. But ASCAP has found it difficult to get American acceptance of the widely accepted principle (in other countries) that the copyright owner also owns the right to perform publicly for profit.

"To do so, ASCAP has had to litigate many types of public performances, latterly in the radio field. The courts have uniformly gone along with the Society in the acceptance of the broad principle that the copyright owner has exclusive and particular property rights in his creations, especially in the field of public performance.

"ASCAP often has been handicapped by hostile legislation in the various states, this antagonism being fostered and financed by groups of music users who sought to evade payment for the use of copyright music. However, this situation is greatly improved, largely due to the consent decree the Society signed at the instance of the Federal government during the height of the ASCAP-radio impasse of 1941. ASCAP's operations now are within the limits of a governmental blueprint, and within the limits of this, the Society may 'go the limit' in enforcing its members' rights. This situation has done much to dispel former threats of legislative retaliation on ASCAP.

"Several years ago, in the height of plans in advance of the struggle between the radio networks and ASCAP, *Harper's Magazine* (October, 1940) carried an extensive story about ASCAP and its operation. This is an impartial story which reveals in better perspective than anything else now available the story of ASCAP."

In the New York offices of ASCAP, Rockefeller Plaza, the staff will proudly show a visitor the old-fashioned piano which Victor Herbert used in his studio. On this piano, some of the most famous melodies from the operas, operettas, and instrumental works were played for the first time by the composer. The visitor to the Directors' room, where this old instrument holds the place of honor, is asked to try it out, to play a chord on the yellowed ivory keys. It is still a good piano, after all these years, just as Herbert's music is good. Fads and fancies come and go. But when the tumult and the shouting dies, and the latest "hit" is already forgotten, it is found that Victor Herbert's romantic tunes have been singing sweetly all the while. Like romance and laughter, Herbert cannot grow old, or die. He lives, this joyous, beauty-loving man, in every song which lifts us for a moment out of the ugliness and uncertainties of a workaday world to give us a glimpse of the "isle of our dreams."

Acknowledgments

A NUMBER of people have been most helpful in furnishing information about Victor Herbert and his works. The author takes pleasure in expressing appreciation of their generous assistance. Sincerest thanks are extended to:

Mrs. Ella Herbert Bartlett, who, in addition to sharing her memories of her father with the author, was good enough to read the biography in manuscript and make many invaluable suggestions for its improvement. The author is indebted also for the permission to include excerpts from *Victor Herbert Songs for Children,* selected and edited by Ella Herbert Bartlett, (1943) published by Whittlesey House, and for Mrs. Bartlett's gracious permission to quote from her delightful preface to this work.

Mr. Robert S. Bartlett, who checked the opus list against the Herbert family records of contracts and copyrights; the completeness and correctness of the catalog of music are due in large measure to Mr. Bartlett's corrections, additions and suggestions.

Mr. Daniel I. McNamara, of the executive staff of the American Society of Composers, Authors and Publishers, whose letter describing the beginnings and the present organization of this Society founded by Victor Herbert has been quoted in its entirety in the chapter called *A Memorial.* To the courtesy and thoughtfulness of Mr. McNamara and other members of the executive staff of ASCAP, the author is indebted for the names of several friends and business associates of Victor Herbert's; from these sources much valuable anecdotic material has been obtained.

Mr. George John Trinkaus, who knew Victor Herbert and who furnished many of the most attractive stories of the biography.

Mr. Frederick Kraft, of Edward Schuberth & Co., Music Publishers and Importers, for his charming reminiscences of "old New York" and for his generous help in tracing titles and copyright dates of some of the older Victor Herbert compositions.

Mrs. Elizabeth C. Moore, who took the author on a sight-seeing tour of the "music neighborhoods" of Victor Herbert's day, pointing out the locations of the historic old music halls, music academies and colleges, *pensions*, and restaurants which lined the quaint streets between Gramercy Park and Fourteenth Street and Irving Place in the '80's and '90's.

Mr. August Kleinecke, fellow-member with Victor Herbert of the Lambs, whose recent death has written a sad *finis* indeed to his pleasant correspondence with the author.

Mr. Gustave Reese and Mr. William D. Shaw, of G. Schirmer, Inc.; Mr. William Wiemann, of Music Publishers Holding Corporation; and Mr. Eric von der Goltz and Mr. Marion Breck, of Carl Fischer, Inc., for their carefully prepared catalogs of music titles and copyright dates, which helped materially in the preparation of the opus list.

Mr. Milton Gabler, of Decca Records, Inc.; Mr. E. C. Forman, of the RCA Victor Division of Radio Corporation of America; and the research staff of Columbia Recording Corporation for their courtesy in preparing up-to-date lists of all the recorded music of Victor Herbert.

Musical excerpts from the publications of Music Publishers Holding Corporation are reprinted by permission of M. Witmark & Sons:

Romany Life (Czardas) (1901), Gypsy Love Song (1898), The Lily and the Nightingale (1898) from *The Fortune Teller;* Tramp, Tramp, Tramp (1910), Taisez-vous (1910), 'Neath the Southern Moon (1910), Italian Street Song (1910), Dance of the Marionettes (1910), I'm Falling in Love with Someone (1910) from *Naughty Marietta;* Yesterthoughts (1940), Rose of the World (1942), The Little Red Lark (Old Irish) (1917), Sweet Mystery of Life (1910), Moonbeams (1942) from *Living Melodies—Victor Herbert* (for 'cello and piano); When Shall I Again See Ireland? (1917) from *Album of Songs;* If I Were on the Stage (1905) from *Mlle. Modiste;* The Isle of Our Dreams (1906), The Streets of New York (1906) from *The Red Mill;* March of the Toys (1903) from *Babes in Toyland.*

The musical excerpt Indian Summer (1940) from *Living Melodies —Victor Herbert* (for 'cello and piano) from the publications of Music Publishers Holding Corporation, reprinted by permission of Harms, Inc.

Musical excerpts from *Victor Herbert Songs for Children,* Selected and Edited by Ella Herbert Bartlett (1943) reprinted by permission of Ella Herbert Bartlett and Whittlesey House:

Go to Sleep, Slumber Deep; Never Mind Bo-Peep; Toyland; I Can't Do the Sum from *Babes in Toyland;* Always Do as People Say You Should from *The Fortune Teller;* Games of Hallowe'en from *The Lady of the Slipper;* Be My Valentine; Won't You Be My Playmate? from *Little Nemo;* Mother Goose from *Sweethearts.*

Musical excerpts from the publications of Carl Fischer, Inc., are reprinted by permission of the publisher:

Serenade, from Suite, Opus 3 (1903); Overture; Opening chorus; Song of the Carbine; Peering left and peering right; I love thee, I adore thee; The Singing Lesson; In Fair Andalusia; The Monk and the Maid; Cupid and I (Cadenza); The Serenade from *The Serenade* (operetta).

Bibliography

Biographical Sketches, by John Tasker Howard, for Decca Album No. 38; by Nicolas Slonimsky, for Columbia Masterworks Set M-415; for Victor Musical Masterpieces Album C-33.

Album of Songs by Victor Herbert, biographical preface. New York, M. Witmark & Sons, 1927.

Victor Herbert Songs for Children, Selected and Edited by Ella Herbert Bartlett. New York. London, Whittlesey House, McGraw-Hill Book Company, Inc., 1943.

Modern Music and Musicians, edited by Louis C. Elson. Vol. 4, part 2, New York, The University Society, 1918.

John McCormack, The Story of a Singer, by L. A. G. Strong. New York, The Macmillan Company, 1941.

The Book of Modern Composers, edited by David Ewen. New York, Alfred A. Knopf, 1942.

Our Contemporary Composers, by John Tasker Howard. New York, Thomas Y. Crowell Company, 1942.

The National Music of America, by Louis C. Elson. Boston, L. C. Page & Company, Inc., 1924.

Our American Music, by John Tasker Howard. New York, Thomas Y. Crowell Company, 1931.

Steeplejack, by James Gibbons Huneker. New York, Charles Scribner's Sons, 1921.

Letters of James Gibbons Huneker, collected and edited by Josephine Huneker. New York, Charles Scribner's Sons, 1922.

Tin Pan Alley, by Isaac Goldberg. New York, The John Day Company, 1930.

From Ragtime to Swingtime, The Story of the House of Witmark, by Isidore Witmark and Isaac Goldberg. New York, Lee Furman, Inc., 1939.

Victor Herbert, by Joseph Kaye. New York, G. Howard Watt, 1931.

Reminiscences of Henry Clay Barnabee, edited by George Leon Varney. Boston, Chapple Publishing Company, Ltd., 1913.

After the Ball, Forty Years of Melody, an Autobiography, by Charles K. Harris. New York, Frank-Maurice, Inc., 1926.

Ethelbert Nevin, by John Tasker Howard. New York, Thomas Y. Crowell Company, 1935. (Copyright Law of 1909.)

Samuel Lover, by Andrew James Symington, F.R.S.N.A. New York, Harper & Brothers, Franklin Square, 1880.

Handy Andy, by Samuel Lover. Boston, Little, Brown and Company, 1927.

Rory O'More, by Samuel Lover. New York, A. L. Burt Company.

Ireland, by Harrison Dale. London, A. & C. Black, Ltd., 1927.

The Reciter's Treasury of Irish Verse and Prose, compiled by Alfred Percival Graves and Guy Pertwe. London, Routledge & Sons, Ltd.; New York, E. P. Dutton & Company, Inc.

Library of the World's Best Literature, Vol. 16, edited by Charles Dudley Warner. New York, J. A. Hill & Company, 1902.

More Chapters of Opera, by Henry Edward Krehbiel. New York, Henry Holt and Company, 1919.

The Opera: A History of Its Creation and Performance, 1600-1941, by Wallace Brockway & Herbert Weinstock. New York, Simon and Schuster, 1941.

American Opera and Its Composers, by Edward Ellsworth Hipsher. Philadelphia, Theodore Presser Co.

The Book of the Opera and the Ballet, by Frederick H. Martens. New York, Carl Fischer, Inc., 1925.

Famous Stars of Light Opera, by Lewis C. Strang. Boston, L. C. Page & Company, 1906.

The Story of a Hundred Operas, by Felix Mendelsohn. New York, Grosset & Dunlap, Inc., 1940.

Prima Donnas and Soubrettes of Light Opera and Musical Comedy in America, by Lewis C. Strang. Boston, L. C. Page and Company, 1900.

Light Opera and Musical Comedy, by J. Walker McSpadden. New York, Thomas Y. Crowell Company, 1936.

Celebrated Comedians of Light Opera and Musical Comedy in America, by Lewis C. Strang. Boston, L. C. Page and Company, 1900.

The Story of One Hundred Symphonic Favorites, by Paul Grabbe. New York, Grosset & Dunlap, Inc., 1940.

Origin and Development of Light Opera, by Sterling Mackinlay. London, Hutchinson & Co., Ltd., 1927.

Operetta Synopses from the Witmark Catalogue of Royalty Productions. New York, M. Witmark & Sons.

A History of the Theatre, by George Freedley and John A. Reeves. New York, Crown Publishers, 1941.

The Story of Gilbert and Sullivan, by Isaac Goldberg. New York, Crown Publishers, 1935.

American Vaudeville, by Douglas Gilbert. New York, Whittlesey House, 1940.

They All Sang, by Edward B. Marks. New York, The Viking Press, 1935.

Old Time Song Hits, by Treasure Chest Publications, Inc., New York, 1935.

Our Familiar Songs and Those Who Made Them, by Helen Kendrick Johnson. New York, Henry Holt and Company, 1909.

Deutsches Liederbuch, by Wisconsin University Germanistischen Gesellschaft. Boston, D. C. Heath & Co., 1906.

Musical Vienna, by David and Frederic Ewen. New York, Whittlesey House, 1939.

In the Golden Nineties, by Henry Collins Brown. Hastings-on-Hudson, New York, Valentine's Manual, Inc., 1928.

The Real New York, by Helen Worden. Indianapolis, The Bobbs-Merrill Company, 1933.

Historic Costume, by Katherine Morris Lester. Peoria, The Manual Arts Press, 1933.

English Dress from Victoria to George V, by Dion Clayton Calthrop. London, Chapman & Hall, Ltd., 1934.

Dictionary of Phrase and Fable, by the Rev. E. Cobham Brewer, LL.D. Philadelphia, J. B. Lippincott Company, 1926.

The Story of Orchestral Music and Its Times, by Paul Grabbe. New York, Grosset & Dunlap, Inc., 1942.

Who's Who in Music, 1941 Edition. Chicago, New York, Lee Stern Press.

The American History and Encyclopedia of Music, edited by W. L. Hubbard. New York, Irving Squire, 1908.

An Almanac for Music-Lovers, by Elizabeth C. Moore. New York, Henry Holt & Company, 1940.

Baker's Biographical Dictionary of Musicians, Third Edition, by Theodore Baker, revised by Alfred Remy. New York, G. Schirmer, Inc., 1919.

Grove's Dictionary of Music and Musicians, edited by J. A. Fuller Maitland. New York, The Macmillan Company, 1911.

International Who's Who in Music, edited by César Saerchinger. New York, Current Literature Publishing Company.

The Oxford Companion to Music, edited by Percy A. Scholes. New York, Oxford University Press, 1938.

The International Cyclopedia of Music and Musicians, edited by Oscar Thompson. New York, Dodd, Mead & Company, 1939.

The Catholic Encyclopedia. New York, The Encyclopedia Press, Inc., 1913.

Encyclopedia Britannica, 14th Edition. Samuel Lover, Sevenoaks.

National Symphony Orchestra Magazine (Washington, D. C.), XIV, March 14, 17, 1943: Notes on Concerto in B minor for violoncello and orchestra, Op. 104, Antonin Dvořák, written by Edward N. Waters, Assistant Chief, Division of Music, Library of Congress.

Letter from Samuel Lover to Mr. Stetson in 1851, in *Music Library Association Notes*, March, 1944 (Publication of Music Division, Library of Congress).

Locke, Robinson (1856-1920). The Robinson Locke Collection of dramatic scrapbooks, New York Public Library.

Chicago Symphony Program Notes, January 20, 1911. Re. Concerto for Violoncello No. 2, in E minor, Opus 30.

The Battle of Tin Pan Alley, by Leonard Allen, in *Harper's Magazine*, Oct., 1940. Harper and Brothers, Publishers.

Ageless Tunes, by Gustav Klemm, in *Étude*, Feb., 1940.

Victor Herbert as I Knew Him, by Gustav Klemm, in *Étude*, March, May, 1939.

Biographical Sketch, in *Étude*, March, 1939.

Unknown Victor Herbert, by W. Emmett, in *Étude*, March, 1939.

Victor Herbert and ASCAP; portrait, in *Étude*, Nov., 1937.

Variety Weekly, March 29, 1944.

Series on "Modern Composers," by Abbot Eames, in *Entertaining*.

The Century Illustrated Monthly Magazine, Feb., 1897, Vol. LIII, No. 4, The Century Co., Union Square, New York.

Musical America. Vol. 13, No. 1, 1910; Vol. 13, March 4, 1911; Vol. 18, Oct. 11, 1913; Vol. 19, Nos. 3, 12 & 13, 1914; May 13, 1916; April 3, 1920.

Metronome, New York, 1921, Vol. 37, No. 19; 1914-15, Vol. 30, No. 12, Vol. 31, No. 1.

America, Jan. 2, 1909.

Musical Courier, Jan. 3, 1918.

Musical Observer, Vol. 5, No. 3, 1911.

Music Trade Review, Vol. 37, No. 23.

Opera Magazine, Nov., 1915.

New York Times, Aug. 1, 1920; May 27, 1924; May 29, 1924.

New York World, May 8, 1916; June 1, 1924.

New York Herald Tribune, May 27, 1924.
New York Telegram and Mail, May 30, 1924.
The Morning Telegraph (New York), Dec. 13, 1914.
Philadelphia North American, Aug. 3, 1914.
Philadelphia Record, July 9, 1916.
Chicago Post, June 28, 1916.
Chicago Record-Herald, May 23, 1909.
San Francisco Call, Oct. 22, 1915.
Los Angeles Herald, June 17, 1916.
Toledo Blade, May 5, 1916.
Cleveland Plain Dealer, Jan. 3, 1917.
Christian Science Monitor, Dec. 4, 1915.

Victor Herbert's Compositions

Note: In the following list, the forms in which the compositions were originally written and published determine the classification under which they are listed. There have been numerous arrangements and adaptations of Herbert's original compositions. No attempt has been made to list all of these. As far as possible, however, the composer's own transcriptions have been given, and the more important or popular transcriptions made by others.

For the operas and operettas, the librettist and the publisher of the score have been indicated, and the date and place of first performance, the producer, and stars, insofar as this information has been obtainable.

OPERAS

Madeleine. (One act.) G. Schirmer, Inc., New York, 1914.
Libretto by Grant Stewart. Adapted from the French play of A. Decourcelles and L. Thibaut. First produced at the Metropolitan Opera House, New York, Jan. 24, 1914, starring Mme. Frances Alda.

Natoma. (Three acts.) G. Schirmer, Inc., New York, 1911.
Libretto by Joseph D. Redding. First produced at the Metropolitan Opera House, Philadelphia, Feb. 25, 1911, and at the Metropolitan Opera House, New York, Feb. 28, 1911, by the Philadelphia-Chicago Opera Company, starring Mary Garden and John McCormack.

OPERETTAS

Angel Face. (Three acts.) Harms, Inc., New York, 1919.
Libretto by Harry B. Smith; lyrics by Robert B. Smith. First produced at the Knickerbocker Theatre, New York, Dec. 29, 1919, by George W. Lederer, starring Jack Donahue.

Babes in Toyland. (Three acts.) M. Witmark & Sons, New York, 1903.
A musical extravaganza. Libretto by Glen MacDonough; lyrics

of the song *Don't Be a Villain*, by Vincent Bryan; lyrics of the song *He Won't Be Happy Till He Gets It*, by Charles Noel Douglas. First produced at the Grand Opera House, Chicago, June 17, 1903, by Hamlin & Mitchell, and at the Majestic Theatre, New York, Oct. 13, 1903.

Babbette. (Three acts.) M. Witmark & Sons, New York, 1903.
Libretto by Harry B. Smith. First produced in Washington in 1903, by Charles Dillingham, starring Fritzi Scheff, and at the Broadway Theatre, New York, Nov. 16, 1903.

Cyrano de Bergerac. (Three acts.) M. Witmark & Sons, New York, 1899.
Libretto by Stuart Reed; lyrics by Harry B. Smith. First produced in Montreal in 1899, by Francis Wilson & Company, starring Francis Wilson and Lulu Glaser, and at the Knickerbocker Theatre, New York, Sept. 18, 1899.

Dream City. (Two acts.) Chas. K. Harris, New York, 1906.
Libretto by Edgar Smith. Always presented in combination with *The Magic Knight*. First produced at Weber's Theatre, New York, Deç. 25, 1907, by Joe Weber, starring Joe Weber and Cecilia Loftus. Now published by M. Witmark & Sons, New York.

Dream Girl. Harms, Inc., New York, 1924.
Libretto by Rida Johnson Young. Adapted from *The Road to Yesterday*. First produced in New Haven, Conn., in April, 1924, by Shubert, Inc., and at the Ambassador Theatre, New York, Aug. 20, 1924.

Eileen. (Three acts.) M. Witmark & Sons, New York, 1917.
First called *Hearts of Erin*. Libretto by Henry Blossom. First produced at the Shubert Theatre, New York, March 19, 1917, by Joe Weber.

Her Regiment. (Three acts.) Harms, Inc., New York, 1917.
Libretto by William LeBaron. First produced at the Broadhurst Theatre, New York, Nov. 12, 1917, by Joe Weber, starring Donald Brian.

It Happened in Nordland. (Prologue and two acts.) M. Witmark & Sons, New York, 1905.
Libretto by Glen MacDonough. First produced at the New Lew Fields' Theatre, New York, Dec. 5, 1904, by Lew Fields' Theatre Co., starring Lew Fields, Bessie Clayton, Marie Cahill, Pauline Fredericks and Harry Davenport.

Little Nemo. (Three acts.) M. Witmark & Sons, New York, 1908.
Libretto by Harry B. Smith. Founded on the cartoons by Winsor MacCay. First produced in Philadelphia in 1908, by Klaw & Er-

langer, and at the New Amsterdam Theatre, New York, Oct. 20, 1908, starring Joseph Cawthorn, Billy B. Van, Harry Kelly and Florence Tempest.

Miss Dolly Dollars. (Two acts.) M. Witmark & Sons, New York, 1905.

Libretto by Harry B. Smith. First produced in Rochester, N. Y., in 1905, by Charles Dillingham, starring Lulu Glaser and Elsie Ferguson, and at the Knickerbocker Theatre, New York, Sept. 4, 1905.

Mlle. Modiste. (Two acts.) M. Witmark & Sons, New York, 1905.

Libretto by Henry Blossom. First produced at the Knickerbocker Theatre, New York, Dec. 25, 1905, by Charles Dillingham, starring Fritzi Scheff. First Broadway run, 252 performances.

My Golden Girl. (Two acts.) Harms, Inc., New York.

Libretto by Frederic Arnold Kummer. First produced in 1919, by Harry Wardell, and at the Nora Bayes Theatre, New York, Feb. 2, 1920.

Naughty Marietta. (Two acts.) M. Witmark & Sons, New York, 1910.

Libretto by Rida Johnson Young. First produced in Buffalo, N. Y., in 1910, and at the New York Theatre, New York, Nov. 7, 1910, by Oscar Hammerstein, starring Emma Trentini and Orville Harold.

Old Dutch. M. Witmark & Sons, New York, 1909.

Libretto adapted from the German by Edgar Smith; lyrics by George V. Hobart. First produced in Wilkes-Barre, Penna., in 1909, by the Lew Fields Opera Company, starring Lew Fields, Eva Davenport, Ada Lewis, Vernon Castle, John Bunny and Helen Hayes, and at the Herald Square Theatre, New York, Nov. 22, 1909.

Orange Blossoms. Harms, Inc., New York, 1922.

Libretto by Fred de Gresac; lyrics by B. G. (Buddy) DeSylva. Based on de Gresac's play *The Marriage of Kitty*. First produced at the Fulton Theatre, New York, Sept. 19, 1922, by Edward Royce.

Oui Madame. Harms, Inc., New York, 1920.

Libretto by G. M. Wright and Robert B. Smith; lyrics by Robert B. Smith. First produced at the Philadelphia Theatre, Philadelphia, Penna., March 22, 1920, by Alfred Aarons, starring Georgia O'Ramey and William Kent. Lyrics for the song *My Day Has Come*, by Irving Caesar.

Prince Ananias. (Two acts.) Edward Schuberth & Co., New York, 1894.

Libretto by Francis Neilsen. Lyrics for the song *The Time Will Come*, by Fred Dixon. First produced at the Broadway Theatre, New York, Nov. 20, 1894, by the Bostonians.

Sweethearts. (Two acts.) G. Schirmer, Inc., New York, 1913.
Libretto by Harry B. Smith and Fred de Gresac; lyrics by Robert B. Smith. First produced at the Academy of Music, Baltimore, Md., March 24, 1913, by Weber and Luescher, starring Christie MacDonald, Tom McNaughton, Lionel Walsh and Thomas Conkey, and at the New Amsterdam Theatre, New York, Sept. 8, 1913.

The Ameer. (Three acts.) M. Witmark & Sons, New York, 1899.
Libretto by Frederick Ranken and Kirke La Shelle. First produced in Scranton, Penna., in 1899, by the Frank Daniels' Opera Company, starring Frank Daniels, and at Wallack's Theatre, New York, Dec. 4, 1899.

The Débutante. (Two acts.) G. Schirmer, Inc., New York, 1914.
Libretto by Harry B. Smith; lyrics by Robert B. Smith. First produced at the New Nixon Theatre, Atlantic City, N. J., Sept. 21, 1914, by John C. Fisher, starring Hazel Dawn, and at the Knickerbocker Theatre, New York, Dec. 7, 1914.

The Duchess. (Three acts.) M. Witmark & Sons, New York.
First called *Mlle. Rosita*. Libretto by Joseph Herbert and Harry B. Smith. First produced at the Lyric Theatre, New York, Oct. 16, 1911, by Sam S. & Lee Shubert, Inc., starring Fritzi Scheff.

The Enchantress. (Two acts.) M. Witmark & Sons, New York, 1911.
Libretto by Fred de Gresac and Harry B. Smith. First produced at the New York Theatre, New York, Oct. 19, 1911, by Joseph M. Gaites.

The Fortune Teller. (Three acts.) M. Witmark & Sons, New York, 1898.
Libretto by Harry B. Smith. First produced at Wallack's Theatre, New York, Sept. 26, 1898, by the Alice Nielsen Opera Company, starring Alice Nielsen, Marguerite Sylva, Eugene Cowles, Joseph Cawthorn and Joseph Herbert. Also played by the original cast at the Shaftsbury Theatre, London, England.

The Girl in the Spotlight. (Two acts.) Harms, Inc., New York, 1920.
Libretto by Richard Bruce. Lyrics of the song *I'll Be There*, by Robert B. Smith. First produced at the Knickerbocker Theatre, New York, July 12, 1920, by the George W. Lederer Producing Company.

The Gold Bug. Edward Schuberth & Co., New York, 1896.
Libretto by Glen MacDonough. First produced at the Casino Theatre, New York, Sept. 14, 1896.

The Idol's Eye. (Three acts.) Edward Schuberth & Co., New York, 1897.
Libretto by Harry B. Smith. First produced at the Broadway Theatre, New York, Oct. 25, 1897, by Frank Daniels & Company.

The Lady of the Slipper. (Three acts.) M. Witmark & Sons, New York, 1912.
Libretto by Ann Caldwell and Laurence McCarty; lyrics by James O'Dea. First produced at the Globe Theatre, New York, Oct. 28, 1912, by Charles Dillingham, starring Montgomery & Stone, Elsie Janis and Vernon Castle.

The Madcap Duchess. (Two acts.) G. Schirmer, Inc., New York, 1913.
Libretto by David Stevens and Justin H. McCarthy. First produced at the Lyceum Theatre, Rochester, N. Y., Oct. 13, 1913, by H. H. Frazee, starring Ann Swinburne, and at the Globe Theatre, New York, Nov. 11, 1913.

The Magic Knight. (One act.) Chas K. Harris, New York.
Libretto by Edgar Smith. First produced at Weber's Theatre, New York, Dec. 25, 1907, by Joe Weber. (See *Dream City*.) Now published by M. Witmark & Sons, New York.

The Only Girl. (Three acts.) M. Witmark & Sons, New York, 1914.
Libretto by Henry Blossom. Adapted from Frank Mandel's play *Our Wives* (a comedy). First produced at the 39th Street Theatre, New York, Nov. 2, 1914, by Joe Weber.

The Prima Donna. (Two acts.) M. Witmark & Sons, New York, 1908.
Libretto by Henry Blossom. First produced in Chicago, in 1908, by Charles Dillingham, starring Fritzi Scheff, and at the Knickerbocker Theatre, New York, Nov. 30, 1908.

The Princess Pat. (Three acts.) M. Witmark & Sons, New York, 1915.
Libretto by Henry Blossom. First produced at the Cort Theatre, New York, Sept. 29, 1915, by John Cort, starring Eleanor Painter.

The Red Mill. (Two acts.) M. Witmark & Sons, New York, 1906.
Libretto by Henry Blossom. First produced at the Knickerbocker Theatre, New York, Sept. 24, 1906, by Charles Dillingham, starring Dave Montgomery and Fred Stone. First Broadway run, 274 performances.

The Rose of Algeria. (Two acts.) Chas. K. Harris, New York, 1909.
Libretto by Glen MacDonough. First produced at the Herald Square Theatre, New York, Sept. 20, 1909, by Lew Fields, starring William Pruette and Florence Nash. Now published by M. Witmark & Sons. New York.

The Serenade. (Three acts.) Edward Schuberth & Co., New York, 1897.

Libretto by Harry B. Smith. First produced in Chicago, in March, 1897, by the Bostonians, starring Alice Nielsen, and at the Knickerbocker Theatre, New York, March 16, 1897. Now published by Carl Fischer, Inc., New York.

The Singing Girl. (Three acts.) M. Witmark & Sons, New York, 1899.

Libretto by Stanislaus Stange; lyrics by Harry B. Smith. First produced at the Casino Theatre, New York, Oct. 23, 1899, by the Alice Nielsen Opera Company, starring Alice Nielsen.

The Tattooed Man. (Two acts.) M. Witmark & Sons, New York, 1907.

Libretto by Harry B. Smith and A. N. C. Fowler. First produced in Baltimore, Md., in 1907, by Charles Dillingham, starring Frank Daniels, and at the Criterion Theatre, New York, Feb. 18, 1907.

The Velvet Lady. (Three acts.) M. Witmark & Sons, New York, 1919.

Libretto by Henry Blossom. Adapted from *A Full House*, a farce by Fred Jackson. First produced at the New Amsterdam Theatre, New York, Feb. 3, 1919, by Klaw & Erlanger, starring Georgia O'Ramey, Ernest Torrance, and Jed Prouty.

The Viceroy. (Three acts.) M. Witmark & Sons, New York, 1900.

Libretto by Harry B. Smith. First produced at the Columbia Theatre, San Francisco, Calif., Feb. 12, 1900, by The Bostonians, and at the Knickerbocker Theatre, New York, April 13, 1900.

The Wizard of the Nile. (Three acts.) Edward Schuberth & Co., New York, 1895.

Libretto by Harry B. Smith. First produced at the Casino Theatre, New York, Nov. 4, 1895, by the Frank Daniels Opera Co. Later produced in England, Germany and Mexico.

When Sweet Sixteen. (Two acts.) M. Witmark & Sons, New York, 1910.

Libretto by George V. Hobart. First produced in Springfield, Mass., in 1910, by Ever-Wall Co., Inc., and at Daly's Theatre, New York, Sept. 14, 1911.

Wonderland. (Three acts.) M. Witmark & Sons, New York, 1905.

A musical extravaganza. Libretto by Glen MacDonough. Based on *Alice in Wonderland* and *Through the Looking Glass*, by Lewis Carroll, and *The Dancing Princesses*, by the Brothers Grimm. First produced in Buffalo, N. Y., in Jan. or Feb.,1905, as *Alice and the Eight Princesses*, by Julian Mitchell, starring Eva Davenport, Lotta

Faust, Bessie Wynn and Sam Chip. Presented in New York, Oct. 24, 1905, as *Wonderland*. Lyrics of the song *I, Myself and Me*, by Vincent Bryan.

SKETCHES

Miss Camille. M. Witmark & Sons, New York.
Written for the Lambs. Libretto by George V. Hobart. First produced in 1908.

Songbirds. M. Witmark & Sons, New York.
Written for the Lambs. Libretto by George V. Hobart.

INCIDENTAL MUSIC TO STAGE PRODUCTIONS OF OTHERS

Cinderella Man. (A play.) One number only, *Out of His Heart He Builds a Home*. Lyrics by Edward Childs Carpenter. M. Witmark & Sons, New York, 1905.

Sally. (Musical comedy.)
Butterfly Ballet.

The Century Girl. Harms, Inc., New York, 1916.
Lyrics by Henry Blossom. *Humpty Dumpty; When Uncle Sam is Ruler of the Sea; The Romping Redheads; You Belong to Me; The Century Girl*.

The Dream Song. (A play.) Harms, Inc., New York, 1919.
Lyrics by Edward Locke. *Farewell; Lovelight*.

The Willow Plate. Harms, Inc., New York, 1924.
Five numbers from *A Chinese Shadowgraph*, marionette play by Tony Sarg. For piano.

Ziegfeld Follies of 1917. Harms, Inc., New York, 1917.
Lyrics by Gene Buck. *Can't You Hear Your Country Calling?*

Ziegfeld Follies of 1920. Harms, Inc., New York, 1920.
Lyrics by Gene Buck. *When the Right One Comes Along; Love Boat*.

Ziegfeld Follies of 1921. Harms, Inc., New York, 1921.
Lyrics by Gene Buck. *In Khorassan; Legend of the Golden Tree; The Princess of My Dreams*.

Ziegfeld Follies of 1922. Harms, Inc., New York, 1922.
Lyrics by Gene Buck. *Weaving My Dreams*.

Ziegfeld Follies of 1923. Harms, Inc., New York, 1923.
Lyrics by Gene Buck. *I'd Love to Waltz Through Life With You; Lady of the Lantern; That Old Fashioned Garden of Mine*.

COMPOSITIONS FOR ORCHESTRA

The Fall of a Nation.

A silent motion picture produced by National Films. Book by Thomas Dixon. Shown for the first time at the Liberty Theatre, New York, June 6, 1916. This is the first original musical score ever written for a motion picture. It is a descriptive score following closely the action of the picture. The separate themes of the score are now published as orchestral numbers and are:

The Love Theme	M. Witmark & Sons, New York, 1916.
Devastation	Carl Fischer, Inc., New York, 1925.
Entrance of the Heroes	Carl Fischer, Inc., New York, 1925.
Forebodings (Agitado)	Carl Fischer, Inc., New York, 1925.
Heart Throbs	Carl Fischer, Inc., New York, 1925.
Karma (Dramatic Prelude)	Carl Fischer, Inc., New York, 1925.
Little Italy (Hurdy-Gurdy Characteristic)	Carl Fischer, Inc., New York, 1925.
Mystic Rider (Dramatic Allegro)	Carl Fischer, Inc., New York, 1925.
Punch and Judy (Humorous)	Carl Fischer, Inc., New York, 1925.
The Knight's Tournament	Carl Fischer, Inc., New York, 1925.
The Rabble	Carl Fischer, Inc., New York, 1925.

A Love Sonnet. Carl Fischer, Inc., New York, 1925.

American Fantasia. Edward Schuberth & Co., New York, 1898.
Now published by Carl Fischer, Inc., New York.

Belle of Pittsburg March. Edward Schuberth & Co., New York, 1895.

Cannibal Dance. Carl Fischer, Inc., New York.

Cosmopolitan March. Leo Feist, Inc., New York.

Danse Baroque. Carl Fischer, Inc., New York, 1925.

Festival March. Carl Fischer, Inc., New York, 1935.
Contains *Auld Lang Syne* theme.

Gate City March. Edward Schuberth & Co., New York, 1895.
Now published by Carl Fischer, Inc., New York.

Inauguration March. Edward Schuberth & Co., New York, 1897.
Now published by Carl Fischer, Inc., New York.

Indian Summer. Harms, Inc., New York, 1919.

Ocean Breezes. Edward Schuberth & Co., New York.

Persian Dance. Carl Fischer, Inc., New York.

Persian March. Carl Fischer, Inc., New York.

Souvenir (Romanze). Carl Fischer, Inc., New York, 1925.

Suite of Serenades. Harms, Inc., New York, 1924.
For Jazz Orchestra. In four movements: Spanish, Chinese, Cuban, and Oriental.

Suite Romantique. Opus 31. N. Simrock, Berlin, 1901.
In four movements: *Visions; Aubade; Triomphe d'Amour; Fête Nuptiale.*

The Jester's Serenade. Carl Fischer, Inc., New York.

Western Overture. Carl Fischer, Inc., New York, 1940.

Woodland Fancies. Opus 34. G. Schirmer, Inc., New York, 1901.
Suite in four movements: *Morning in the Mountains; Forest Sylphs; Twilight; Autumn Frolics.*

Yesterthoughts. M. Witmark & Sons, New York, 1900.
Arrangement for orchestra, from composition for piano.

COMPOSITIONS FOR SYMPHONIC ORCHESTRA

Irish Rhapsody. G. Schirmer, Inc., New York, 1910.

Hero and Leander. Opus 33. G. Schirmer, Inc., New York, 1900.
Symphonic poem.

Badinage. Edward Schuberth & Co., New York, 1895.

Columbus Suite. Opus 35. G. Schirmer, Inc., New York, 1903.

Dramatic Overture. G. Schirmer, Inc., New York, 1938.

Golden Days Overture. G. Schirmer, Inc., New York, 1939.

COMPOSITIONS FOR STRING ORCHESTRA

Air de Ballet. G. Schirmer, Inc., New York, 1912.

Serenade for String Orchestra. Opus 12, No. 4. F. Luckhardt, Berlin, 1889.

Forget-me-not. G. Schirmer, Inc., New York.

Sunset. G. Schirmer, Inc., New York, 1912.

ORCHESTRAL ARRANGEMENTS OF WORKS OF OTHER COMPOSERS

At Dawning. Carl Fischer, Inc., New York.
By Charles Wakefield Cadman.

Kamenoi Ostrow. G. Schirmer, Inc., New York.
By Anton Rubinstein.

Land of the Sky-Blue Waters. White-Smith Music Co., New York.
By Charles Wakefield Cadman.

Love's Dream (Liebestraum). G. Schirmer, Inc., New York.
By Franz Liszt.

Narcissus. The Boston Music Co., Boston.
By Ethelbert Nevin.

Scarf Dance. G. Schirmer, Inc., New York.
By Cécile Chaminade.
The Cat and the Mice. G. Schirmer, Inc., New York.
By H. Leonard.
The Donkey and the Driver. G. Schirmer, Inc., New York.
By H. Leonard.
The Flatterer. G. Schirmer, Inc., New York.
By Cécile Chaminade.
The Rosary. The Boston Music Co., Boston.
By Ethelbert Nevin.

UNPUBLISHED ORCHESTRATIONS OF THE WORKS OF OTHER COMPOSERS

Air de Ballet. By C. Chaminade.
A Music Box. By Liadow.
Chant Sans Paroles. By Tchaikovsky.
Erotik. By Grieg.
Gypsy Melody. By Dvořák.
Humoresque. By Dvořák.
Melody in F. By Rubinstein.
Organ Offertory in G. By Batiste.
Polish Mazurka. Opus 7, No. 3. By Chopin.
Poupée Valsante. By Poldini.
Sextette from "Lucia." By Donizetti.
Song Without Words. By Mendelssohn.
Spinning Song. By Mendelssohn.
Spring Song. By Mendelssohn.
Quartette from "Rigoletto." By Verdi.
To Spring. By Grieg.
Valse. Opus 64, No. 1 (D Flat). By Chopin.
Wiegenlied. By Brahms.

BAND COMPOSITIONS

American Girl March. Edward Schuberth & Co., New York.
Baltimore Centennial March. Edward Schuberth & Co., New York, 1897.
Defendam March. M. Witmark & Sons, New York.
Written for 22nd Engineers, N.Y.G.
Eldorado March. Edward Schuberth & Co., New York, 1894.
Inauguration March. Edward Schuberth & Co., New York, 1897.
President's March. (McKinley.) Edward Schuberth & Co., New York, 1898.

The Veiled Prophet March. Edward Schuberth & Co., New York.
Three Solitaries (Polka). M. Witmark & Sons, New York.
For three cornets or trumpets with military band accompaniment.
Twenty-second Regiment March. Edward Schuberth & Co., New York.

'CELLO COMPOSITIONS WITH PIANO OR ORCHESTRAL ACCOMPANIMENT

Alla Mazurka. (Unpublished.)
Piano accompaniment.
Bagatelle. (Unpublished.)
Piano accompaniment.
Berceuse. M. Witmark & Sons, New York.
Piano accompaniment. Written in Stuttgart in 1884.
Concerto, First Violoncello, Opus 8, 1882. (Unpublished.)
In D major; three movements. The composer's holograph full score, including a manuscript of the violoncello part, is in the collection of Herbert manuscripts deposited in the U. S. Library of Congress.
Concerto, Second Violoncello, Opus 30. Edward Schuberth & Co., New York, 1894.
In E minor. First performed by the New York Philharmonic Society, under Anton Seidl, with the composer as soloist.
La Cinquantaine. Edward Schuberth & Co., New York.
By Gabriel-Marie. Arrangement by Victor Herbert.
La Serenata. Boston Music Publishing Co., Boston, 1911.
Piano accompaniment.
Légende. (Unpublished.)
Pensée Amoureuse. G. Ricordi & Co., Milan, Italy, 1905. G. Schirmer Inc., New York, 1940.
Petite Valse. G. Ricordi & Co., Milan, Italy, 1905. G. Schirmer, Inc., New York, 1940.
Polonaise. (Unpublished.)
Romance. G. Ricordi & Co., Milan, Italy, 1905. G. Schirmer, Inc., New York, 1940.
Scherzino. 1885. (Unpublished.)
Serenade, from *Suite,* Opus 3. Carl Fischer, Inc., New York, 1903. M. Witmark & Sons, New York.
Piano Accompaniment.
Suite. Opus 3. Zumsteeg, Stuttgart, 1882.
In five movements: Allegro Moderato, Scherzo, Andante, Serenade (Andantino grazioso), Tarantelle.

VIOLIN COMPOSITIONS WITH PIANO ACCOMPANIMENT

À La Valse. G. Schirmer, Inc., New York, 1915.
Canzonetta. Carl Fischer, Inc., New York, 1928. G. Schirmer, Inc., New York.
An arrangement for violin and piano of a theme from *Serenade for String Orchestra*, Opus 12, No. 4.
Cavalleria Rusticana. Edward Schuberth & Co., New York.
By Pietro Mascagni. Arrangement of the Intermezzo.
Little Red Lark. M. Witmark & Sons, New York.
Arrangement of an old Irish melody.
Mirage. G. Schirmer, Inc., New York.

PIANO COMPOSITIONS

Air de Ballet. G. Schirmer, Inc., New York.
Piano arrangement of the orchestral piece.
Al Fresco. M. Witmark & Sons, New York.
American Rose Waltz. M. Witmark & Sons, New York.
Devotion. Harms, Inc., New York, 1921.
A Love Sonnet for the Piano.
Duo. Harms, Inc., New York, 1923.
Estrellita. Waltz. M. Witmark & Sons, New York.
From the score of *The Princess Pat*.
Fleurette. Waltz. M. Witmark & Sons, New York, 1903.
Get Together. Fox Trot. M. Witmark & Sons, New York.
Published by Herbert under the pseudonym *Nobel MacClure*.
La Coquette. Valse Brilliante. M. Witmark & Sons, New York, 1900.
La Ghazel. Improvisation. M. Witmark & Sons, New York, 1900.
Marion Davies March. Harms, Inc., New York, 1922.
Mountain Brook. Imitative. M. Witmark & Sons, New York, 1900.
On the Promenade. Morceau. M. Witmark & Sons, New York, 1900.
On Your Way. One Step. M. Witmark & Sons, New York.
Published by Herbert under the pseudonym *Nobel MacClure*.
Pan Americana. Morceau characteristique. M. Witmark & Sons, New York, 1901.
Later orchestrated by the composer and dedicated to John G. Milburn, Pres. of the Pan-American Exposition, Buffalo, N. Y.
President's March. Printed in the *Ladies' Home Journal*, Feb., 1898.
Now published by Carl Fischer, Inc., New York.
Punchinello. Characteristic. M. Witmark & Sons, New York, 1900.
Under the Elms, Souvenir de Saratoga. M. Witmark & Sons, New York.

Valse à la Mode. M. Witmark & Sons, New York.
Published by Herbert under the pseudonym *Nobel MacClure*.
Whispering Willows. Intermezzo. M. Witmark & Sons, New York.
World's Progress March. M. Witmark & Sons, New York, 1916.
Yesterthoughts. Meditation. M. Witmark & Sons, New York, 1900.

FLUTE AND CLARINET DUET WITH ORCHESTRA

L'Encore. M. Witmark & Sons, New York, 1910.

SONGS

NOTE: A number of songs have been published since Herbert's death which were not written as songs by the composer but are adaptations of themes of instrumental numbers for which words have been written. These are indicated in the list by (*) preceding the title.

Ah, Love Me. Opus 15, No. 3. Edward Schuberth & Co., New York, 1895.
Words by O. E. Ehlers; English version by Sophie Schneider.
A Maiden Went into the Field Alone. Opus 18. Luckhardt, Berlin.
For mezzo-soprano. German and English text.
An Easter Dawn. M. Witmark & Sons, New York, 1917.
Sacred Song. Words by Glen MacDonough.
**Badinage*. Edward Schuberth & Co., New York, 1935.
Words by Holland Robinson; vocal arrangement by Harold Sanford.
Confession. Opus 13. Luckhardt, Berlin.
German and English text. Also with orchestral accompaniment.
**Day Is Here*. G. Schirmer, Inc., New York, 1940.
Words by Lorraine Noel Finley. Adaptation of Herbert's *Liebesleben (Love's Token)*.
Dream On. Harms, Inc., New York, 1922.
Indian Lullaby. Words by B. G. DeSylva.
Equity Star. Harms, Inc., New York, 1921.
Words by Grant Stewart.
**Exile's Haven*. G. Schirmer, Inc., New York, 1940.
Adaptation of Herbert's *Heimweh (Longing for Home)*. Words by Lorraine Noel Finley.
Flower of My Heart. Opus 4. Zumsteeg, Stuttgart.
German and English text.
Fly Away, Little Bird. Opus 18. Luckhardt, Berlin.
German and English text.

Fowling. Opus 10. Luckhardt, Berlin.
From *Wanderer's Songs*. Text by Rudolph von Baumbach. German and English text.
Give Your Heart in June-time. Harms, Inc., New York, 1925.
Words by Grey & Atteridge.
God Spare the Emerald Isle. Harms, Inc., New York, 1923.
Words by William Jerome.
Heart o'Mine. Harms, Inc., New York, 1924.
Words by Lawrence Eyre.
If Love Were What the Rose Is. M. Witmark & Sons, New York, 1914.
Words by A. G. Swinbourne.
If You but Knew. Opus 15. Luckhardt, Berlin.
For mezzo-soprano. German and English text.
I Love You. Opus 14. Luckhardt, Berlin.
German and English text.
**Indian Summer*. Harms, Inc., New York, 1939.
Words by Al Dubin.
I Want to Be a Good Lamb. Famous Music Co., New York, 1940.
Words by George V. Hobart.
Jenny's Baby. Edward Schuberth & Co., New York, 1895.
Words by John Ernest McCann.
Little Old New York. Harms, Inc., New York, 1923.
Words by William LeBaron.
Longing for Home (Heimweh). Dieckmann, Leipzig. Edward Schuberth & Co., New York.
For Alto. German and English text.
Lora Lee. Harms, Inc., New York, 1922.
Words by Joseph J. C. Clarke.
Love Laid His Sleepless Head. M. Witmark & Sons, New York, 1907.
Words by A. G. Swinbourne.
Love Song. Dieckmann, Leipzig. Edward Schuberth & Co., New York.
For Alto. German and English text.
Love's Hour. G. Schirmer, Inc., New York, 1912.
Words by Rida Johnson Young. Written for, sung by, and dedicated to Signora Luiza Tetrazzini.
Love's Life. Opus. 15. Dieckmann, Leipzig. Edward Schuberth & Co., New York.
German and English text.
Love's Oracle. M. Witmark & Sons, New York.
Words by Edward Peple.

Love's Token (Liebesleben), Opus 15, No. 2. Edward Schuberth & Co., New York, 1888.
Words by Brunold; English version by Henry Burck.

Mademoiselle. 1938.
Arranged for the score of the motion picture, "Sweethearts" by Herbert Stothart from the song from "Sweethearts" (Opera score) *There Is Magic in a Smile.* Words by Bob Wright and Chet Forrest.

Mary Came Over to Me. Harms, Inc., New York, 1922.
Words by Irving Caesar.

Mary's Lamb. Edward Schuberth & Co., New York, 1898.
Words by Edward E. Kidder. Written for 1898 Lambs' Gambol.

Me and Nancy. Harms, Inc., New York, 1895.
Words by John Ernest McCann.

Molly. M. Witmark & Sons, New York, 1919.
An Irish Love Song dedicated to John McCormack. Words by Rida Johnson Young.

My Heart Is True. Opus. 21. Luckhardt, Berlin.
For mezzo-soprano. German and English text.

Old Ireland Shall Be Free. M. Witmark & Sons, New York.
Four-part song. Words by F. J. Rooney.

Only You. Opus 15. Dieckmann, Leipzig. Edward Schuberth & Co., New York.
German and English text.

Peace (Frieden). Dieckmann, Leipzig. Edward Schuberth & Co., New York.
For Alto. German and English text.

Remembrance. G. Schirmer, Inc., New York, 1915.
Words by Carl Weitbrecht. English translation by Fanny Lover Schmid.

Silent Rose. Edward Schuberth & Co., New York, 1888.
Words by Ida von Duringsfeld; English version by Max Bendix.

**Some One I Love.* Leo Feist, Inc., New York, 1935.
Words by Haven Gillespie.

Spring Song. Opus 14. Luckhardt, Berlin.
German and English text.

**Summer Serenade.* G. Schirmer, Inc., New York, 1938.
Arranged from *Badinage* by Herbert Stothart. Words by Bob Wright and Chet Forrest.

Sweet Harp of the Days. Edward Schuberth & Co., New York, 1915.
Words by Samuel Lover. Dedicated to John McCormack.

The Faded Rose. Opus 15. Dieckmann, Leipzig. Edward Schuberth & Co., New York.
German and English text.

The First Kiss. Opus 13. Luckhardt, Berlin.
German and English text.

The Friars' Song. M. Witmark & Sons, New York, 1907.
Words by Chas. Emerson Cook.

The Innkeeper's Daughter. Opus 10. Luckhardt, Berlin.
From *Wanderer's Songs*. Text by Rudolph von Baumbach.

**The River Song*. G. Schirmer, New York, 1940.
Words by Lorraine Noel Finley.

The Secret. Opus 14. Luckhardt, Berlin.
German and English text. Words by James Russell Lowell. Published in *The Music of the Modern World*, edited by Anton Seidl; Copyrighted in the U. S. in 1897.

**Thoughts of Love*. G. Schirmer, Inc., New York.
Arranged by Carl Deis from *Pensée Amoureuse*. Words by Margaret Bristol.

To Thee, My Queen of Beauty. Opus 5. Zumsteeg, Stuttgart.
For male quartet.

When Knighthood Was in Flower. Harms, Inc., New York, 1922.
Words by William LeBaron.

**Yesterthoughts*. M. Witmark & Sons, New York.
Words by Stanley Adams.

CHORAL COMPOSITIONS

Call to Freedom. Oliver Ditson Co., Boston, 1918.
Text by Victor Herbert. Patriotic Ode originally written for men's voices but now available in many arrangements. A short version called *God Shall Guide Us*, arranged by Rob Roy Perry for use in schools.

Christ Is Risen. M. Witmark & Sons, New York.
Words by Victor Herbert. Four-part anthem. A choral anthem for Easter for soprano (or tenor) solo and alto (or bass) solo and mixed voices.

Columbia Anthem. Edward Schuberth & Co., New York, 1898.
Words by Clay M. Greene. Unison chorus with piano accompaniment, later arranged by Victor Herbert for orchestra and band accompaniment.

Eventide. Opus 20. Luckhardt, Berlin.
From *Wanderer's Songs*. Text by Rudolph von Baumbach. For male chorus. With English and German text.

God Shall Guide Us. Oliver Ditson Co., Boston, 1940.
Words by Victor Herbert. *(See Call to Freedom.)*

O'Donnell Aboo! G. Schirmer, Inc., New York, 1915.
Arrangement for chorus of men's voices of the air *Roderich Vich Alpine dhu*, the Clanconnel War Song, A.D. 1597, words by M. J. McCann.

Orange, White and Blue. G. Schirmer, Inc., New York.
Words by John R. Pine. Written for ceremonies in 1916, in commemoration of the landing of the first Dutch settlers on Manhattan Island, May 4, 1626. The orange, white and blue flag of this Dutch colony was raised at Battery Park.

The Cruiskeen Lawn. G. Schirmer, Inc., New York, 1913.
Arrangement of an old Irish air. For men's voices, a cappella. Dedicated to the Mendelssohn Glee Club, N. Y.

The Hail of the Friendly Sons. G. Schirmer, Inc., New York, 1913.
Words by Joseph I. C. Clarke. For men's voices, a cappella. Dedicated to the Glee Club of the Friendly Sons of St. Patrick.

The New Ireland. G. Schirmer, Inc., New York, 1914.
Words by Joseph I. C. Clarke. For men's voices, a cappella.

The Sunken City. Opus 20, No. 1. G. Schirmer, Inc., New York, 1897.
Words by Rudolph von Baumbach; English version by Dr. Thomas Baker. For men's voices, a cappella.

Widow Machree. G. Schirmer, Inc., New York, 1915.
An a cappella arrangement for men's voices of Samuel Lover's song.

CANTATA

The Captive. Opus 25. G. Schirmer, Inc., New York, 1915.
For soprano solo, baritone solo, chorus and orchestra. Poem by Rudolph von Baumbach. English version by George Harris, Jr. Written for the Worcester, Mass., Festival, September, 1891.

Current Records of Victor Herbert's Compositions

VICTOR RECORDS

4446	Thine Alone I'm Falling in Love with Someone	Allan Jones, with Orchestra conducted by Nat. W. Finston
4447	Some Day Sweethearts	Allan Jones, with Chorus and Orchestra conducted by Nat. W. Finston
11932	Natoma Dagger Dance	Boston "Pops" Orchestra
26249	A Kiss in the Dark Gypsy Love Song	Lew White at the Organ
20558	Al Fresco	Sam Herman
22333	Gypsy Love Song	Jesse Crawford
1280	Gypsy Love Song	Reinald Werrenrath
1402	Gypsy Love Song	Renee Chenet
24896	Italian Street Song	Jeannette MacDonald
7745	Neapolitan Love Song	Richard Crooks
1343	Ah! Sweet Mystery of Life	Richard Crooks
4323	Ah! Sweet Mystery of Life	Jeannette MacDonald and Nelson Eddy
22333	Ah! Sweet Mystery of Life	Jesse Crawford
35921	Ah! Sweet Mystery of Life	Waring's Concert Orchestra
21371	Ah! Sweet Mystery of Life	Troubadours
4281	Ah! Sweet Mystery of Life	Nelson Eddy
24896	Ah! Sweet Mystery of Life	Jeannette MacDonald
1402	Kiss Me Again	Renee Chenet
20922	Kiss Me Again	Troubadours
1371	I'm Falling in Love With Someone	Richard Crooks
4280	I'm Falling in Love With Someone	Nelson Eddy
26346	March of the Toys	Tommy Dorsey and His Orchestra

4281	'Neath the Southern Moon	Nelson Eddy
4280	Tramp, Tramp, Tramp, Along the Highway	Nelson Eddy
35926	Suite of Serenades (1) Spanish (2) Chinese (3) Cuban (4) Oriental	Whiteman's Concert Orchestra
24282-A	Kiss in the Dark—Organ	Jesse Crawford
26602	Badinage Selections from "Sweethearts"	Renee Chenet
26431-A	A Kiss in the Dark—Cornet	Leonard B. Smith
26637-B	A Kiss in the Dark	Kenny Baker
26679-A	Sweethearts	Troubadours
26680-B	Kiss Me Again	Shilkret—Troubadours
27319-B	Sweethearts	Webster Booth
26745	{A Kiss in the Dark {Indian Summer	Webster Booth

VOL. I HERBERT MELODIES—VICTOR CONCERT ORCHESTRA—VICTOR SALON GROUP
(Including Anne Jamison, Jan Peerce, Thomas Thomas)

C-33 (12589—12593)
Ah! Sweet Mystery of Life
Air de Ballet and Al Fresco
Babes in Toyland, Selections
Badinage
Fortune Teller, Selections
Kiss Me Again
March of the Toys
Naughty Marietta, Selections
Red Mill
Sweethearts

VOL. II HERBERT MELODIES—VICTOR SALON ORCHESTRA

C-11 (9903—9907)
Babette, Selections
Eileen, Selections
Fleurette. 2. Under the Elms
Land of My Own Romance. 2. Serenade
Natoma, Selections
Only Girl, Selections
Pan Americana
Princess Pat, Selections

Rose of Algeria, Selections
Yesterthoughts. 2. Punchinello

THREE RED SEAL RECORDS MADE BY VICTOR HERBERT: VIOLONCELLO SOLO, WITH PIANO ACCOMPANIMENT
(Available in record shops specializing in old records.)

64239	*The Low Back'd Car* (Samuel Lover)
64298	*Scherzo* (van Goens)
677-A	*The Angel's Whisper* (Samuel Lover)
677-B	*Petite Valse* (Victor Herbert)

COLUMBIA RECORDS

7364-M in Set M-415	Ah! Sweet Mystery of Life
4107-M	Ah! Sweet Mystery of Life Naughty Marietta
7367-M in Set M-415	Czardas
7367-M in Set M-415	Dream Girl
36473 in Set C-80	Fleurette
7367-M in Set M-415	For I'm Falling in Love With Someone
7367-M in Set M-415	Gypsy Love Song
17135- D	Gypsy Love Song
7366-M in Set M-415	Habañera. (From "Natoma.")
P-17141-D	I'm Falling in Love With Someone
7365-M in Set M-415	Indian Summer
7367-M in Set M-415	Italian Street Song
7365-M in Set M-415	A Kiss in the Dark
7365-M in Set M-415	Kiss Me Again
36048 in Set C-50	Kiss Me Again
7364-M in Set M-415	March of the Toys
7367-M in Set M-415	Moonbeams
Set M-415	Music of Victor Herbert
7367-M in Set M-415	'Neath the Southern Moon
7364-M in Set M-415	Streets of New York
7366-M in Set M-415	Sunset
7364-M in Set M-415	Sweetheart Waltz
7364-M in Set M-415	Thine Alone
P-17141-D	Thine Alone
36047 in Set C-50	Thine Alone
7365-M in Set M-415	When You're Away
17135-D	When You're Away

DECCA RECORDS (in Albums)

VOL. 1 A-38 Album of Victor Herbert Melodies
(With Victor Young and His Orchestra)

2315 Ah! Sweet Mystery of Life ("Naughty Marietta")
Sweethearts (If You Ask Where Love Is Found)
From "Sweethearts" Bing Crosby

2316 I'm Falling in Love With Someone (From "Naughty Marietta")
Gypsy Love Song (From "The Fortune Teller")
Bing Crosby and Frances Langford

2317 Italian Street Song (From "Naughty Marietta")
Florence George (Soprano) with Max Terr's Choristers
Selections from "The Fortune Teller" (Opening Ensemble—The Lily and the Nightingale—Romany Life)
Victor Young and His Concert Orchestra

2318 Toyland (From "Babes in Toyland")
With Max Terr's Choristers and Rudy Vallée
March of the Toys (From "Babes in Toyland")
Victor Young and His Concert Orchestra

2319 Indian Summer (An American Idyll)
Yesterthoughts Victor Young and His Concert Orchestra

VOL. 2 A-72 Album of Victor Herbert Melodies

2680 When You're Away (From "The Only Girl")
Thine Alone (From "Eileen") Bing Crosby

2681 A Kiss in the Dark
'Neath the Southern Moon (From "Naughty Marietta")
Frances Langford

2682 Kiss Me Again (From "Mlle. Modiste") Florence George
I Want You to Marry Me (From "The Red Mill")
Victor Young and His Concert Orchestra

2683 Moonbeams (A Serenade) (From "The Red Mill")
Rudy Vallée and Max Terr's Choristers
To the Land of My Own Romance (From "The Enchantress") Victor Young and His Concert Orchestra

2684 Punchinello
Pan Americana Victor Young and His Concert Orchestra

VOL. 3 A-73 Album of Victor Herbert Melodies
Played by Harry Horlick and His Orchestra

2685 Love Is Best of All (From "Princess Pat")
Miss Dolly Dollars (Entr'acte from "Miss Dolly Dollars")

2686 Badinage—Fleurette
2687 Jeannette and Her Little Wooden Shoes (From "Sweethearts") Air De Ballet
2688 Habañera and Vaquero's Song (From the Opera "Natoma")
Al Fresco (Intermezzo from "It Happened in Nordland")
2689 Suite of Serenades—No. 1 Spanish
Suite of Serenades—No. 3 Cuban

VOL. 4 A-82 Album of Victor Herbert Melodies
Played by Harry Horlick and His Orchestra

2850 Kiss Me Again (From "Mlle. Modiste")
Sweethearts (If You Ask Where Love Is Found) (From "Sweethearts")
2851 I'm Falling in Love With Someone (From "Naughty Marietta")
When You're Away (From "The Only Girl")
2852 A Kiss in the Dark
'Neath the Southern Moon (From "Naughty Marietta")
2853 Ah! Sweet Mystery of Life (From "Naughty Marietta")
The Streets of New York
2854 Gypsy Love Song (Slumber On, My Little Gypsy Sweetheart) (From "The Fortune Teller")
Toyland (From "Babes in Toyland")

DECCA RECORDS (Single)

1232 Ah! Sweet Mystery of Life
231 Ah! Sweet Mystery of Life
2984 Ah! Sweet Mystery of Life
29071 American Fantasie (2 Parts)
23123 L'Encore
231 Gypsy Love Song
525 Gypsy Love Song—Vocal Chorus
2936 Indian Summer—Vocal
2821 Indian Summer
145 Italian Street Song—Vocal
1294 Kiss in the Dark
18199 Kiss Me Again
178 Kiss Me Again—Organ
188 Kiss Me Again—Canary Birds
1096 Kiss Me Again
2906 March of the Toys

3029	Rose of the World
1232	When You're Away
3424	Yesterthoughts—Vocal
3395	Yesterthoughts
18176	Gypsy Love Song—Violin
4235	Indian Summer
4213	March of the Toys
18176	Romany Life
4235	Yesterthoughts

Index

NOTE: Where English names of musical compositions, novels, short tales, poems, and plays begin with *The, A,* or *An,* the italicized titles have been alphabetized with reference to the first important word, the article following the comma at the end of the title. Similarly, with foreign titles, the German *Der, Die, Das,* the French *Le, La, Les,* etc., have been placed last. For example: *Serenade, The; Moldau, Die; Vie Parisienne, La.*

EVERETT SHINN
1942.